DATE DUE		

A Way of Hope

A Way of Hope

Lech Walesa

Henry Holt and Company
New York

Copyright © 1987 by Henry Holt and Company, Inc., and Librairie Arthème Fayard
Translation copyright © 1987 by Henry Holt and Company, Inc., and Collins Harvill
All rights reserved, including the right to reproduce this book or portions thereof in
any form.
Published by Henry Holt and Company, Inc., 521 Fifth Avenue, New York, New
York 10175.
Published in Canada by Fitzhenry & Whiteside Limited, 195 Allstate Parkway, Mark-
ham, Ontario L3R 4T8.
Originally published in France under the title *Un chemin d'espoir*.

Library of Congress Cataloging-in-Publication Data
Wałesa, Lech, 1943–
A way of hope.
Translation of: Un chemin d'espoir.
Includes index.
1. Wałesa, Lech, 1943–   .   2. NSZZ "Solidarność"
(Labor organization)   3. Trade-unions—Poland—
Officials and employees—Biography.   I. Title.
HD6735.7.Z55W34813   1987   322′.2′0924   [B]   87-21194
ISBN 0-8050-0668-0

First Edition

Designed by Susan Hood
Map designed by Jeffrey L. Ward
Printed in the United States of America
10 9 8 7 6 5 4 3 2 1

The publishers acknowledge the assistance of several translators and experts in contemporary Polish history who helped to prepare the English-language text from the
original Polish manuscript and French translation, especially the close collaboration
of Marek B. Zaleski.

All photographs, with the exception of the two from the Bettmann Archive, were
given to the American editor by Bogdan Pietruszk (the designer of the Gdansk monument) on a trip to Poland in 1984.

ISBN 0-8050-0668-0

Contents

BALTIC SEA

Free City of Danzig
1919 to 1939

Gdynia
Sopot
Gdansk

Elblag

GERMAN
DEMOCRATIC
REPUBLIC

Szczecin

Bydgoszcz

Popowo

Vistula River

Berlin

Poznan

Lodz

Wroclaw

Czestochowa

Jelenia Gora

SILESIA

Prague

Katowice

CZECHOSLOVAKIA

Cracow

Oswiecim
(Auschwitz)

Zako
pan

P O L A N D

- - - - · Present-day Polish border

Annexed by USSR
after WWII

Northern and Western Territories
recovered from Germany after WWII

· · · · Polish border in 1939

0   150

Scale of miles

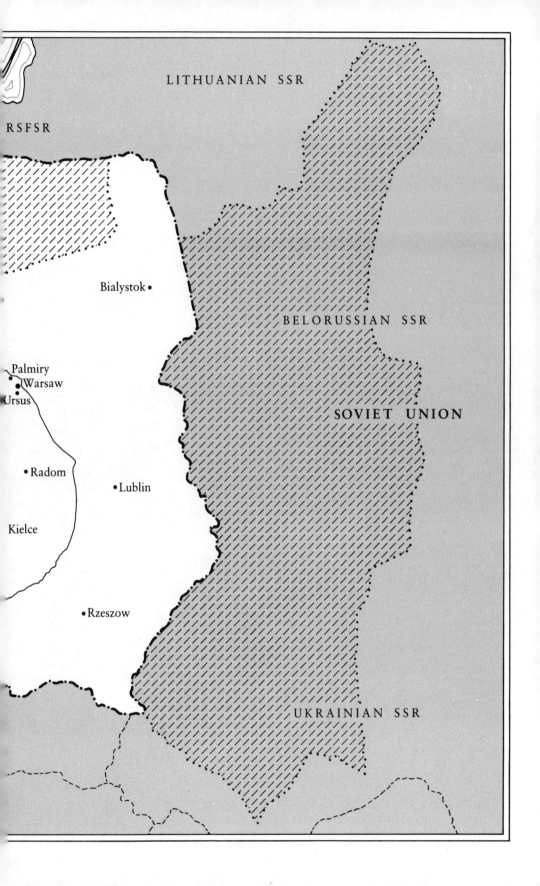

LITHUANIAN SSR

RSFSR

Bialystok •

BELORUSSIAN SSR

Palmiry
Warsaw
Ursus

SOVIET UNION

• Radom

• Lublin

Kielce

• Rzeszow

UKRAINIAN SSR

A Way of Hope

Consider Yourself Lucky, Mr. Walesa

There's a moment before I drift off to sleep when the house is quiet again. The door shuts on the last of the visitors, who have made a habit of coming to see me at all hours of the day and night. My wife has gone up to bed with the girls, and the boys, too, are falling into bed. The stage is empty. Snatches of conversation from the day's interviews start going around in my head: opinions, words of praise and criticism, the value of which only I can appreciate, warnings, encouragement to get on with things, pointed questions: could I possibly be one of those helpless prophets crying in the wilderness? Would I still be capable of playing for the highest stakes, including my own life?

It was my mother who first taught me to believe in destiny. Then, during the early years of my adult life, I began to trust in my own star instead. Later, with the benefit of experience and support from the church, I finally learned the meaning of the word *faith*. These ideas, informed by instinct, guide the choices I make in life; so far they have encouraged me to take risks, while helping me to avoid disastrous decisions.

My idea of destiny is not fatalistic or passive. On the contrary, I've been guided toward an active involvement with people and events, including life's pleasures, and recognize the individual's ability to change things—in my case, with a stubborn disregard for short-term consequences.

Someone asked me once whether Poland and the Poles were eternally in love with drama. I think that we're at the end of an era. The world, and Poland with it, is in the throes of momentous

1

change. The existence of intercontinental missiles, for example, turns the sanctity of national frontiers or borders on its head; thus the geographical position of a country like ours is no longer so significant, especially so because even the remotest parts of the world are today subject to armed intervention. Yet for us, the Soviet border is a daily reality.

There's a great deal of talk in the world about politics East and West, but, if we look closely at the situation, it's clear that each side has a mistaken idea about the other. The West is rich and well armed, but isn't seeking a confrontation; the East would doubtless like to gain more territory and resources, but doesn't have the means. Result: a clash of two impossibilities. The one side can but doesn't want to, the other side would like to but can't.

Solidarity is a further sign that a new era is beginning. The burden of the past was weighing us down and forcing us to look for new solutions; it was forcing us to confront problems of impossible complexity. We Poles are exposed to influences from all sides and life requires us to choose, to verify, to experience for ourselves, and then to assert ourselves and draw from within ourselves the necessary moral strength to effect change. Though we are caught in the vise of a fossilized system, a product of an outdated partition of our planet, in August 1980 we overthrew an all-powerful political taboo and proclaimed the dawning of a new era. The Polish nation achieved this as a force before the eyes of the world without threats, without violence or a drop of the opponent's blood being shed; no ideology was advanced, no economic or institutional theory: we were simply seeking human dignity. In both camps, free and unfree, this episode has been regarded as a revolutionary act. But we saw nothing revolutionary in what happened. We merely felt that after so many years of living upside down, we were at last beginning to walk on our feet.

If we really want to understand how destiny works, we have to give up pointless rebellion. Let us take an example: the Yalta agreement. Having been from the start a party to the struggle against Nazism, surely Poland was entitled to recover her national independence at the end of the war. Is it surprising therefore that the Yalta agreement should have aroused, and should still arouse, a deep bitterness in the Poles? But there is another way of looking at the situation. I remember a conversation I had one day with an old Polish general. He had played an active part in the events of 1918, when this country recovered its freedom and independence, and later, during the Second World War, when the Polish Government-in-Exile was formed first in Paris, then in London, while he witnessed the odyssey of the Polish army under General Anders, from the Middle East to Monte Cassino in Italy. He finally returned to Poland as it was after the Yalta agreement. A high-ranking military man, he had been in direct contact with the men responsible for redrawing the map of Europe: with Stalin and his bureaucrats, who set their seal so firmly on the new system of government, with Beria and company in the Soviet secret police, also with General Eisenhower, commander-in-chief of the Allied forces on the western front, and with a host of London officials. Until his dying day, this old soldier could never accept the way the frontiers had been modified; he felt that Poland had been betrayed, slipping its traditional ties with Western Europe and passing before his very eyes into the Soviet sphere of influence. During the course of our conversation I asked him to try to imagine what Poland might have been without Yalta. What would have become of this country worn out by war, alongside such a powerful neighbor? Even the West, for all its pragmatism, seemed fascinated by the revolutionary ideas coming out of Moscow. This, then, would probably have been Poland's fate: slowly, but unavoidably, it would have drifted toward the East, and, in the end, inevitably, it would have been absorbed. Yalta spared us this fate, which would have led to painful disillusionment, or, worse still, to the loss of our national identity. The Yalta trauma created effective immunities, it speeded up the history lesson, giving us the opportunity to involve ourselves as closely as possible in practical work, instead of looking on, mesmerized, from a distance. The lesson is over now; Poland has delivered its findings to the rest of the world. There are no new textbooks dealing with the state of the world which do not make mention of this lesson.

I do my best to look on political events in the same light as my personal problems, and to try to resolve them similarly. I never take a tragic view of life. Even if nothing in this world really depends on us, that shouldn't excuse us from putting all our efforts, in a dignified way, into finding the best possible solutions, and the most honest ones. I've met too many embittered people, politicians especially, who'd been forced out of office and were obsessed with one overriding idea—their own—beside which nothing else counted, nothing else even existed. This is why I always find it difficult when people ask me what my theory is: what theory I identify with totally. To tell the truth, I don't identify myself with a theory at all. Not because I'm a skeptic, but because I'm a man of the soil, not the academy.

A few years from now, perhaps the situation will have changed and certain decisions taken previously may turn out to have been ill advised. One, however, strikes me as exemplary: the decision to erect a monument to the Gdansk shipyard victims and others of 1970. I myself spent several days in prison for having fought to see that monument raised. Originally we thought of erecting a great pile of stones, later of putting up a simple commemorative plaque. But even that idea was banned. And it was because of this ban that the monument, when it was finally raised, became a social and Christian symbol of huge political significance, an exhortation to a whole generation to think of Poland with all its might.

Of course, fundamentally, events obey their own internal logic, and we have to take life as it comes. But one has to help it along only a little to come up with solutions which are a great deal better and richer than those resulting from fine theories, purely national ideals or test-tube ideas (how truly dangerous these can be!). In my political activities I have fortunately been guided by the instinct of a man born into a large family, and father of one in his turn. Our family has always produced swarms of children, and it's probably this simple biological fact that helps me to keep going in the face of life's uncertainties. I regard everything that I've achieved in life as merely a sort of loan. After all, from a religious point of view, nothing we receive—be it beauty, happiness, or money—is ever more than that. If we accept that we are only the temporary guardians of life's various gifts, it's easier not to lose our heads, or give way to despair.

I am aware that I have already lived the best moments of my life. From now on, every day brings me closer to the unknown. I shall have to face bigger problems, harder tasks; perhaps the worst is yet to come. This is how I see my future, and I try to prepare myself for whatever it may bring. All the same, I've never wished or prepared for a leadership role: paradoxically, it's because I never really wanted it, absorbed as I was by quite different concerns, different problems which needed solving, that I found myself out in front, leading the others—"leading the flock," I call it with a smile.

At a moment of controversy in September 1980, I said to those who were attacking me: "Please, gentlemen, take my place! I've led the first phase; the agreements with the government have been signed; now it's up to you!" They didn't want to listen. Later, a number of them attacked me again. That's the way of things: when the situation is critical, few want to put themselves on the firing line; as soon as it gets easier, the attacks and the ambitions start up again. For my part, I took everything as it came, the good and the bad, without elbowing my way forward. Now that we've set Solidarity in motion, though still beset with endless difficulties, people tend to feel they're rather lucky that I came along when I did; as some have said, if Walesa didn't exist, they'd have to invent him.

One day I received a letter that said: "You should consider yourself lucky, Mr. Walesa. You've hardly been affected by martial law and even His Holiness finds time to come and chat with you. All my life I've behaved decently and what have I got to show for it? Nothing! And when I went on pilgrimage, I only caught the tiniest glimpse of the Pope in the distance. Is that really fair, and do you deserve all you get?" You're probably right, my friend. All her life my mother wanted to go on a pilgrimage to the Black Madonna at the fourteenth-century Paulist monastery of Jasna Gora in Czestochowa. Instead of which she went to the United States, where she was killed in a traffic accident in 1975. She never did manage to make that particular dream come true. And just look how things work out: *I* was the one who stood before the shrine of the Black Madonna; *I* was the one who slept in the monastery of Jasna Gora. Without my having to lift a finger, fate granted me what had been my mother's dearest wish. Had I deserved it? I doubt it. When I think of how good my mother was, I can only say that she deserved it more than I did. But since I was invited, should I have refused to go? I even start to wonder, when I spend an hour talking with the Pope: am I taking someone else's place? Aren't there a hundred other people waiting to see him, and with better reasons?

Fate has been showering me with blessings like these for some

5

time now; but there *was* a time when it reserved only bad luck for me. Things could change again. Maybe someone will blow my head off. There's no guarantee that my final hand will be a good one. Then everyone will be able to say that plenty of people helped me, but that, in spite of it all, I achieved a little something by myself.

It's time now to provide an account of that "something." In order that it should be as complete as possible, and present diverse points of view, I have drawn here and there on my archives, already quite extensive. They contain files of my correspondence, texts of interviews, drafts of statements, a number of tape recordings, and finally my "action journal," started at the beginning of 1983, soon after I returned home from imprisonment. I have also drawn on the help of my colleagues, who, during several years of joint activity with free access to both my files and my home, have for their part been able to assemble a great deal of information and eyewitness accounts, and record the outcome of critical meetings and conversations; their contributions form an integral part of my account.

To assist readers unfamiliar with the key events of Polish history and the details of Solidarity, a brief chronology appears at the beginning of the book as a guide to the hard-to-reach background regions of my story.

An outline map of Poland is included to help readers locate places of importance in the story and to indicate Polish borders before and after the Second World War.

A Brief Chronology

(Key events of Polish history referred to in the narrative, prepared by Marek B. Zaleski, M.D., and Benjamin Fiore, S.J.)

1791

Constitution creates modern constitutional monarchy: legal protection for all citizens, religious freedom, hereditary throne, permanent army.

1794

Kosciuszko's Insurrection: In Cracow, General Kosciuszko, a hero of American Revolutionary War and Polish-Russian War (1792–1793), leads troops to regain territories lost in first two partitions. Polish troops are defeated; Kosciuszko is taken prisoner, and Third Partition, together with loss of statehood, follows. Russia and its allies, Prussia and Austria, divide Poland (1795).

1797–1815

Polish Troops in the Service of Napoleon: Polish legions in Haiti (1797), Prussia (1806–1807); creation of Duchy of Warsaw (1806); war with Austria (1809); war with Russia (1812); Congress of Vienna (1815) creates Kingdom of Poland under Russian control; old capital, Cracow, is declared free republic under Austria's protection.

1830–1863

Ill-fated Uprisings: November—Polish-Russian War (1830–1831); *Spring of Nations*—against Prussia and Austria (1848); *January*—

against Russia (1863), remove last traces of Polish independence; period of intense Russification follows.

1918–1939

Polish Independence is regained after World War I; border disputes ensue with Czechoslovakia, Ukraine, Lithuania, and old enemies— Russia (Soviet Union) and Germany. *Polish-Soviet War* (1919– 1920) results in victory under Marshal Pilsudski at Warsaw ("Miracle on the Vistula") and Polish recapture of part of historical eastern borders (Treaty of Riga, 1921). Political instability and hostile neighbors prompt Pilsudski to lead *coup* (1926): Constitution is suspended, opposition suppressed until Pilsudski oversees formation of new civilian government and new constitution (1935).

1939

Invasion of Poland: On August 23, 1939, Molotov (Soviet Union) and von Ribbentrop (Germany) sign a treaty of alliance with a secret protocol delineating the "fourth" partition of Poland. Thus, free to invade Poland, the Nazis attack; on September 17, 1939, the retreating Polish army confronts Soviet troops, who, without a declaration of war, seize and occupy the eastern half of the country. Polish army capitulates on October 5, 1939; military and civilian leaders who left Poland for France form government-in-exile to organize autonomous military units to fight Germany: in Norway, in Battle of Britain, etc.

1942–1946

Polish Armed Forces in the Middle East, North Africa (Tobruk), and *Italy* (Monte Cassino, Ancona, Bologna); second break of diplomatic relations with Soviet Union occurs when Nazis discover mass graves of Polish officers in the forest near *Katyn*. All evidence indicates that the victims (over 4,000 officers) were former internees from the Kozielsk Camp and were executed by Soviets in the spring of 1940. *The Jewish Holocaust* and the *Warsaw Ghetto Uprising:* in 1942 Nazis round up Jews in all occupied countries and transport them to the extermination camps where some 6,000,000 are murdered. Before the deportation, Jewish inhabitants of many cities (Warsaw, Lodz, Cracow, etc.) are isolated in separate ghettos; the Polish resistance (AK) through its emissaries (Jan Nowak, Jan Karski) informs the Western Allies of the ongoing mass murder, but the allies fail to react decisively. The Jewish fighting organization (ZOB) leads an uprising, but it is defeated by overwhelming German forces. The ghetto is razed and virtually all Jewish fighters perish.

1945

Yalta and Potsdam Conferences: In an attempt to keep the Soviet Union as an active member of the alliance, the Western powers make significant concessions to Soviet demands at Yalta (February) and Potsdam (July). The West recognizes the political interests of the Soviets in Central Europe, accepts *de facto* the Soviet-sponsored PKWN as the provisional government of Poland with the proviso that it hold free elections.

1949–1954

Reign of Terror: The Communist Party's control is based on two factors: censorship and the dreaded activities of the Office of Security (UB); hundreds are arrested, tortured, and executed; among the opposition leaders arrested: Stefan Wyszynski, the primate of Poland (September 1953), held for three years.

1956, June

Poznan Workers' Protest: Demonstrators seize the District Offices of the government and the Party; 74 are killed and 300 injured in three days of clashes with government troops.

1968, March

Student Protests: The media initiate a campaign to pit workers against students and intellectuals; the latter are portrayed as Zionists to stir up anti-Semitic attitudes. Intellectuals, the church, and even Diet deputies (Catholic caucus *Znak*) rally to the defense of the students; many workers believe the propaganda and refuse to aid the students.

1970, December

Gdansk Protest: Price increases of basic items bring protests (December 14) in the coastal cities of Gdansk, Gdynia, Szczecin, and Elblag. The striking shipyard workers attack; troops, brought in to quell the strikes, fire at workers.

1976, June

Radom and Ursus Protests: The authorities announce steep (an average 47 percent) increases in prices of basic food products. In response, nearly 75 percent of the large enterprises call a strike. The most violent protests occur in Radom, where strikers burn Party offices, and Ursus; protests also take place in Plock, Grudziadz, Lodz, Gdansk.

1976, September

Formation of the Committee for Defense of Workers (KOR): In July 1976, a group of intellectuals openly defends workers persecuted for their participation in the June protests; group represents a variety of political views (even members of the Party); in September 1976, it forms the Committee for Defense of Workers (KOR).

1977, November

Creation of the "Flying University": Under the inspiration of Andrzej Celinski, lectures on topics that are either ignored or tendentiously presented in official courses are offered.

1978, March

Creation of the Free Trade Unions (WZZ): First in Katowice (March) and then in Gdansk (April); in both instances militia and security forces begin harassment that results in arrests.

1979, July

Creation of the Young Poland Movement (RMP): Opposition movement created by Gdansk students under the leadership of Aleksander Hall.

1980, July/August

Strike: Strikers demand wage increases, an end to preferential treatment of police and security employees, immunity from prosecution, dissolution of official trade unions. In Gdansk, the immediate cause of the strike (August 14) is the recent dismissal of Anna Walentynowicz and the earlier dismissal of Walesa. Upon winning concessions, Walesa (chairman of the Inter-enterprise Strike Committee [MKS]) announces an end to the strike, but pressured by colleagues, reverses the decision and declares continuation of the strike in solidarity with striking workers in other enterprises.

1980, August

Gdansk, Szczecin, and Jastrzebie Agreements: Negotiations result in a series of agreements in Szczecin (August 30), Gdansk (August 31), and Jastrzebie (September 4), and the 500 Days of legalized Solidarity.

1980, November

Registration of NSZZ Solidarnosc to become the first legal independent trade union in a Soviet-controlled country. In May 1981, negotiations between Walesa and Premier Jaruzelski result in *Rural Solidarity.*

1981, September

The First Congress of NSZZ Solidarnosc: The Congress elects Walesa president and calls for broad economic and social reforms.

1981, December

Imposition of Martial Law: By December 13, internal and external communications within Poland are cut and leaders of trade unions, opposition groups, intellectuals, and some clergy are arrested.

1981–1987

Resistance: Surviving leaders of *NSZZ Solidarnosc* call for a general strike. Strikes erupt, but are crushed by ZOMO police detachments; work slowdowns; uncensored underground publishing flourishes.

1982, April

Creation of the Temporary Coordinating Committee (TKK): Underground Solidarity body is created four months after the imposition of martial law.

1982, October

Delegalization of NSZZ Solidarnosc: Property confiscated (December 1982); TKK calls for a boycott of the new government unions and a general strike.

1982, November

Walesa Released from Internment but is kept under constant surveillance; eludes guards and meets secretly with the TKK, April 1983.

1983, July

Martial Law Lifted but restrictions of the original decree are incorporated into law.

1983, December

Nobel Peace Prize: Announcement of the award lifts spirits of Polish society. Walesa, fearing that he may not be permitted to return to Poland and in solidarity with those imprisoned, declines to travel personally to Oslo.

1985, November

Dismissal of University Presidents: 33 presidents of various universities are removed by the authorities; others resign in solidarity.

1986, July

Amnesty: The authorities announce a general amnesty and release 20,000 individuals (out of 114,000) including 225 political prisoners, among them Michnik, Lis, Frasyniuk, Bujak, Modzelewski.

1986, November

New Repressive Legislation Against Uncensored Publications: Long prison terms and high fines, as well as confiscation of motor vehicles, for possession of uncensored materials; penalties may be imposed in summary proceedings.

1987, June

The Third Polish Pilgrimage of John Paul II: Pope confronts government by repeatedly bringing up "eternal significance" of Solidarity and 1980 accords, underlining his support for human rights.

Roots

I will begin with our family history. I have my sister Izabela to thank for jogging my memory and more. The records and memoirs that she has collected reflect the experiences of a simple Polish family; they people that house and those fields I know so well with men and women bearing the same name as mine.

It's the wild mallows my sister—my only sister—still sees when she looks through her bedroom window. During those summers, they were the first thing you caught sight of on waking: nature's way of salvaging a hint of poetry from the surrounding grayness. These mallows continued to play their part in my reminiscences. They flowered for a long time, up against the walls of the house, creating in our young eyes an illusion of abundance and profusion, of vigorous life. The seasonal, almost theatrical decor they provided masked the miserable architecture of the house. From the outside, this house aroused a nostalgic feeling of permanence and solidity, the feeling evoked by one of those much-loved places that are a reminder of a lost childhood.

But the land on which the house stood utterly deprived it of anything approaching nostalgia. Our neighbors had avoided it, deeming it too dreadful to live on. The edge of a little pond, in the heart of a marshland overgrown with tall grasses, seemed a perfectly foolish place to build, unless purely as a temporary step, while waiting to embark on some new stage in one's life. It must have been a tradition in our family to do just that: in my grandfather Jan's lifetime, when the lands were divided up and the marshland was allotted to my father Boleslaw, there was immediately talk of moving.

The landscape changes abruptly as soon as you leave the marsh, skirting the pond to join the local road. The path becomes dry and dusty. Seen from this angle, the pond and our old shanty look almost picturesque. A simple, unadorned wooden cross stands where the road curves at the edge of a birch wood. In summer you don't even need shoes to walk along this path. The fine, soft sand is pleasantly refreshing on the soles of the feet. Every now and again, the path crosses a thicket until, finally, it intersects the road leading left to the village of Chalin.

Popowo, my native village, was no more than a scattered hamlet, then there was Sobowo with its parish church, and Chalin with its school and shop—the Walesas' universe was contained within the points of this triangle. From Gdansk, you travel south, along the banks of the Vistula as far as Grudziadz, where you cross the river, then, via Torun, you push on as far as Lipno and head for Dobrzyn. From Dobrzyn, Popowo is only a stone's throw.

Perched up on the steep banks of the Vistula, Dobrzyn was the center of a region that has been politically unstable since the Middle Ages. Traders from the East used to cross it and then follow the course of the Vistula in order to reach Gdansk on the Baltic Coast. Over the centuries, the town was ravaged by numerous wars: first by pagan tribes, Teutonic Knights, and Swedes, then by the Prussians, Russians, and finally the Germans. Historians have emphasized how these events, over time, have molded the specific character of the town's inhabitants: the people of Dobrzyn are courageous, stubborn, but also receptive to change—characteristics peculiar to border peoples, who played such a decisive role in Poland's history.

During the Royal Republic, the convocation of a regional assembly—the Dietine at Lipno—brought Dobrzyn a degree of autonomy. But at the end of the eighteenth century, when the partitions began, the Polish state ceased to exist for over a hundred years.

Mateusz

It was sometime at the end of the eighteenth and the beginning of the nineteenth centuries that our ancestor Mateusz settled on the lands at Popowo. My sister Izabela remembers an old hardback book, yellow with age, which she used to read at our Grandfather Jan's house, and which told the story of Great-Grandfather Mateusz and of his brothers. Apparently, he came over to Poland in possession of a considerable fortune which his father had amassed somewhere in Western Europe, in France or perhaps in Italy. Most probably in France, where descendants of his cousins, or perhaps even of his brothers, are still living today. One story has it that he was briefly an economic emigrant in America, returning to Europe with a sizable fortune. No one knows the reason why Mateusz came looking for refuge in faraway Poland. It must have been a fairly serious one: people say, in fact, that he decided to change his name (but which one?) and to settle well outside the trade routes and populated towns, in the midst of Dobrzyn's unspoiled forests and lakes. He had had enough of "roaming the world," maintains the family chronicle, even though Walesa, literally translated, means "he who roams."

Mateusz—still according to the family tradition—then bought 315 *morgi* of land—about four hundred acres—in other words, virtually all of Popowo at that time. He was a good cultivator, marvelously adept at getting the most out of the soil. He also earned himself a reputation as a clever and effective manager by letting out small sections of forest in the neighborhood of Rumunka in exchange for the tenants clearing them, and entrusting the management of the inn at the crossroads to the local Jew. At that time, the inn combined the functions of small shop, public house, and bank: it was a place to borrow money or to find out what was going on among the local people. The inn served as a means of communication between manor and hamlet, landlord and peasants, fulfilling a crucial role at the heart of this rather closed rural community.

Mateusz was generally respected. He knew how to talk to people, give out advice and settle affairs without being overbearing. Despite his relatively recent arrival, there was something about him, moreover, that made people treat him as the heir to these lands. The family remembers him as a prudent and God-fearing man, picturing him harnessing his horse to his rig, or walking around inspecting his fields with a rosary in his hand. He had the little wooden manor house built and decorated it with a portico, symbol of opulence, and his wife had servants to help with the house and the children. Toward the end of his life, Mateusz suffered a tragic setback when this house he loved so dearly was destroyed by fire. After his death, the estate was divided up between his children, his sons receiving the land and his daughters the crop harvest and the remaining household furniture.

Among Mateusz's sons, those mentioned most frequently are the eldest, Jan (a very common Christian name in the family), Konstanty and Wincenty, each of whom led very different lives. Following the national uprising of 1863 against the Russian occupation, Konstanty and Wincenty were sent to Siberia and were unable to return to Poland for many years; in order to escape the reprisals, Jan went off to stay with some remote cousin in France, where he enjoyed himself immensely. He only returned to Rumunka, which he had received as his share of the inheritance, to get more money, and, bit by bit, on each visit, he sold off the forest and fields, leaving his wife, and a yearly increasing number of offspring, to look after the house.

Jan

Jan's eldest son, also christened Jan, and who is none other than my grandfather, followed in his father's footsteps, living more in France—frequenting the casinos and frittering away his fortune—than at home in Poland: he scarcely knew his own children. At the beginning, there was still one servant at the house, a local village woman who helped with the housework, but soon, with an increasing family to feed, Jan no longer had the means to pay her—a sign of the family's rapid impoverishment. On his return from one of his numerous trips to France, he sold all the cultivated land he had left and his large family was then plunged into complete poverty. In 1916 the family's problems were compounded by the death of Jan's wife during her confinement with Stanislaw, later to become my stepfather. After a few years, Jan, now getting on in age, remarried and produced five more children. The decline of his branch of the family was thus complete by the onset of the First World War. Of the original fifty acres of land, only a fragment remained, to be divided up among a whole swarm of children.

The Great War, regaining of independence, the rebirth of the Polish state in 1918, and the Polish-Soviet War of 1919–1920 form a chain of events which directly affected our family; my uncles, my father Boleslaw's older brothers, played an active part in them.

This was a strange period in the contemporary history of Poland, then reemerging as a state on the European map. The frontiers of the second republic were still the object of endless barterings. The then head of state, Marshal Jozef Pilsudski, eager as he was to demonstrate the Polish presence in the East—within the ancient historical boundaries preceding partitions—before any definitive decisions could be taken, and deeming that the *fait accompli* spoke louder than international guarantees, ordered his armies to advance as far as Kiev, where the Red army drove them back, forcing them to retire as far as the Vistula. The Russian threat produced a spontaneous mobilization of the whole country, leading to the decisive victory that Polish history and the Polish consciousness commemorate as the "Miracle on the Vistula." It was without doubt a crucial moment in the making of the country and preserving its existence as a nation. Only once did the Red army "propose," with bayonets, that Poland should join the revolution; despite all the political divisions which had opened up during the first years of Polish independence, our reply was a unanimous "no." This *no* determined both our victory and the shape of institutions to come—but only for two decades.

The family chronicle reflects all these historical events, but the account is dominated by the personal experiences of my grandfather and of my uncles. Grandfather Jan had the reputation of being a "political man" and was said to be a member of the Polish Military Organization (POW), which prepared servicemen to fight against the occupying forces. He himself boasted of his relations with Marshal Jozef Pilsudski, the future head of state, whom he claimed to have snatched from the clutches of the Russians during the battle of the Vistula, when the Polish troops were retreating in disarray toward Warsaw. Pilsudski was among them, pursued by a party of cossacks; Jan, who was in his service at the time, disguised him in women's clothing and sent his pursuers off on a false trail. The episode is viewed with grave reservations by historians, who do in fact mention a similar incident in Pilsudski's career, which they think entirely authentic but to have occurred elsewhere. His biography also notes a visit made by the marshal to this region, but situates it two years later, after the Polish-Soviet war had ended. How much of the family account is truth, and how much fiction? Hard to say. The fact remains that in Grandfather Jan's house Pilsudski was a cult figure. For a long time, the Walesas kept an old, rather faded photo of the marshal in military boots and greatcoat, in company with Grandfather Jan. During his own lifetime he used to show it proudly to the grandchildren, his most assiduous listeners in his old age, hungry for stories where imagination filled in the gaps left by reality.

His two eldest sons had both been present at the battle of the Vistula in August 1920. One had been taken prisoner by the Russians. At home, the family remembered his two letters describing the prison camps, the poverty and ignorance of the population, and the inhuman fashion in which they were treated by the new Soviet authorities in Russia.The other son, the fighter of the family, famous in the region for his exceptional strength, fell in combat to a detachment of cossacks near the village where he had been born. People say that his assailants slaughtered his horse just as he was crossing the river; that he would probably have gotten away scot-free if he hadn't gone back to look for the gold he'd hidden under his horse's saddle. He met his death in an ambush. Such, at least, is the version of events still current today among the inhabitants of Popowo.

My sister Izabela still has a good memory of Jan: an old fellow with a huge mustache, full of life, always visiting one or other of his sons. He was received by them with something of an ill grace: once he got going, comfortably installed at the corner of the stove or on the little bench in front of the house, no one could halt the flow of his reminiscences about his escapades in the towns of Western Europe, his binges in the casinos, his bancos, his pranks, his romantic conquests. The women, especially my mother, lost no time then in pushing him out of doors. At the end of his days, he ran out of money and became frugal; he stopped buying himself cigarettes and rolled his tobacco in little strips torn from newspapers, though always after reading the newspaper line for line first.

One of the oldest inhabitants of Popowo, Kazimierz Pawlowski, today aged eighty-four, has a clear recollection of the great Walesa tribe:

> They lived a bit farther down, among the alders, not very far from our house. The Walesas were poor. They lost the lands they'd inherited from Mateusz, and other people bought them up. In 1917 I knew Jan well; he was a strong-minded fellow. He took an interest in politics, and read a great deal. But the episode with Jozef Pilsudski was pure fancy; he was just trying to brag. . . . To my knowledge, nothing of the sort ever happened. He was educated, and knew how to divide up the land as well as any surveyor. At Chalin we often used to see him at the grocer's bar dipping into a box of goodies, drinking his alcohol neat and always trying to sell something in order to make some money. It went through his fingers like water, and his own children lacked the basic essentials. His sons didn't take after their father. First Zygmunt, then Boleslaw, worked on the neighboring estates building houses, and sheds for the animals. Boleslaw settled on a neighboring farm, took over his part of the inheritance and began to make good use of it. He was a good boy, not in the least proud; well, he was a son of Poland, wasn't he? . . .

Father

The brothers divided up between them the little that was left of Jan's property. My own father, Boleslaw, born in 1908, received seven acres of rather mediocre land, from which my future stepfather, Stanislaw, was to deduct his portion a few years later.

These plots of land were too tiny to enable any kind of self-sufficiency. The three eldest brothers, Zygmunt, Boleslaw, and Izydor, soon made a name for themselves in the region as excellent carpenters. They built houses at Brudzyn, Sobowo, Chalin, and Dobrzyn, erected village churches, cattle sheds, and barns. An old photo shows them in front of a small house in mid-construction, dressed in short jackets buttoned up to the neck and military-style trousers tucked into their boots—looking more like soldiers than country carpenters—Boleslaw standing in the middle, arm in arm with the woman whose house they were working on, and holding a long joiner in his hand. He was the one who was in charge of the family team, and he had little sympathy for either of his brothers if they botched up a job. Tall and powerful, he had remarkable eyes: their gaze was firm and resolute, imperious even. This is especially noticeable in a photo which he gave "Miss Fela," his future wife and my mother, and which he signed "Walesa," in a hand not dissimilar from my own. Tastefully dressed—straight, dark jacket, white shirt, and brightly colored tie—he is sitting with his left hand on his knee, his right propped on his hip, looking straight ahead, without the shadow of a smile on his face. It's a distinctive face: broad and virile, with prominent cheekbones, hair pulled back to reveal a broad forehead, a pronounced chin, straight nose, wide, thin mouth, small ears, thin mustache, and piercing eyes under bushy brows. "When I look at that photo," says Izabela, "I see my father as if it were yesterday. I was the eldest of the children, so I'm the one who remembers the house, our mother and our father best. Father was a rather calm, thoughtful man, always attending to the needs of his family. But he was also unbending and ambitious, often pigheaded in his relations with other people and extremely fastidious in his work." My sister thinks I look like my father, except that he was taller and slighter and, though I've got his nose and his mouth, my eyes are more like my mother's.

"Miss Fela" Kaminska, from the neighboring village of Pokrzywnica, must have been terribly keen on Boleslaw for her, only a young girl of seventeen, to have succeeded in overcoming her parents' reservations and persuading them to consent to the marriage. Her mother knew a lot about the world and life in general: twice married and twice widowed in the United States, married a third time in Poland, she had read a great deal and owned a library which contained the major works of nineteenth-century and early-twentieth-century Polish literature, including in particular Henryk Sienkiewicz, Ignacy Kraszewski, and Boleslaw Prus. This woman clearly had a different future in mind for her adored youngest daughter. In his curiosity about the world, if not in character, Fela's father was the equal of her mother: he had read a lot, he was up-to-date with all that was going on and reacted passionately to the events marking Poland's renaissance. His family were local people in the bargain, natives of Dobrzyn, with son succeeding father, each of them flourishing the same huge mustaches. In their family, each generation boasted at least a teacher or a priest, a monk or a nun.

The Walesas, on the other hand, were constantly reminded that they weren't local people, that they'd squandered their fortune and, worse still, their lands—selling off what a Polish peasant holds most sacred. The family still talks about the hostility which these differences provoked, but, shortly after the marriage, Boleslaw proved himself by venturing, along with his brothers, into an increasingly successful building construction business.

The young couple had found it hard at first, not having a home of their own or even the basic necessities for bringing up their first child, Izabela. For three years, little "Iza" had had to stay with her grandparents at Pokrzywnica. It was during this period that they built a makeshift home typical of those that had been built in the region for generations: a wood-and-daub hut adjacent to a little cowshed, both of them housed under the same thatch roof. The shed was soon tenanted by a cow, some pigs, and chickens. The interior of the house comprised two minute rooms, one of which was the kitchen, which had a huge hooded fireplace where the sausages were hung, a range of saucepans suspended along the wall, and a big rustic table with a wooden bench on either side: it was here that the family sat for meals. This shanty stood at the edge of the pond, not far from the forest, surrounded by plum and cherry trees planted by my father. There was also a kitchen garden, a fairly rare commodity in the region at that time. This garden was the children's favorite playground.

An old, yellowed photograph, rather faded and cracked, taken on the occasion of a grand family reunion in 1938, shows Grandmother and Grandfather Kaminski, my mother with "Iza" and Edward, sitting on a bench placed in front of a backdrop of tall reeds. My father, Boleslaw, is missing: they had been waiting for him, but he hadn't been able to get back in time from Rokita, where he was finishing off a convent (the building is still standing today). The Jewish photographer who had been brought specially from Dobrzyn was in a hurry and couldn't wait for him to return. He extricated from their case a tripod and a camera with bellows, shoved his head under the black cloth and asked each of the group

22

to look straight at the camera. He captured a moment in the life of our family, whose center of gravity resided in our Pokrzywnica grandmother rather than in the Walesas: the women in pretty, fashionable dresses and dainty shoes, Grandfather in a dark suit and waistcoat, white shirt, and dark tie, the children all in white; Mother, graceful and slender, with her shining eyes, in a spotless dress set off with red carnations around the slightly décolleté neckline, looking more like a city lady than a peasant.

This photo is also a reflection of the universe in which Grandmother Kaminska lived. She divided her life between the grown-up children from her first two marriages, who lived for the most part in the States, her youngest daughter, at Popowo, and her well-kept farm at Pokrzywnica. Her inexhaustible energy and lively curiosity were known well beyond the immediate circle of her relatives, and she had earned herself the nickname "the American tourist." She crossed the ocean in order to meet up with her children, but also to see her cousins, and friends and acquaintances she had made while she lived in the United States. As a young girl, like many other Poles at the end of the nineteenth century, she had gone over to the States to make her living, but after the death of her second husband, just before the First World War, she had returned to Poland accompanied by her youngest children. Slim and graceful, rather proud in her bearing, she liked to dress tastefully, as can be seen from a number of other snapshots of her. Ambitious, determined, eminently hard-working, and kind to those around her, she had passed on all these qualities to her youngest daughter, Feliksa, who resembled her both physically—she was just a little slighter—and in her nature and her attitude to life.

This photo taken in front of the house reflects certain changes that were occurring in Poland during this period. If it was easy to find a Jewish photographer in the small neighboring town of Dobrzyn—which numbered several thousand inhabitants at the time—this was no coincidence. The Jewish population, formerly concentrated in the eastern sector of Poland, annexed during the "partitions," partially to the Russian empire, partially to the Austro-Hungarian one, was now gradually spreading into other provinces. Conditions were propitious for the development of a number of small businesses which ensured employment for the poorest of those flocking into Polish territory from the East. From the economic point of view, the Jewish community was highly diversified and comprised representatives of all the social classes: from the bankers and big industrialists of Lodz, admirably captured in the renowned director Andrzej Wajda's film *Ziemia obiecana (The Promised Land)*, to the masses of exiles seeking to establish themselves in the small towns, which they sometimes virtually took over, forming up to eighty percent of the population.

Dobrzyn clearly reflected the thrust of economic progress which, on the national level, saw the construction of the Central Industrial Region (*Centralny Okreg Przemyslowy*—COP), straddling two rivers, the San and the Vistula; farther southwest, the rise of an important center of mining and metallurgy; and, finally, the construction of the town of Gdynia, built on the sandy coastline twelve miles from Gdansk, according to plans by the architect Tadeusz Wende, with a port, developed entirely by the new Polish state, that was to be the most modern in the whole of the Baltic. In less than twenty years were thus laid the foundations of a modern industry which, in certain branches, enabled the Polish nation to match the best Western achievements. Poland was "spreading its wings"; a modern aeronautic industry was born and began to manufacture models that were one hundred percent Polish. The new state gave further proof of its creative energy when, in the space of eight months, it constructed, from base to summit, a cable car line which goes to the top of the Tatra Mountains (some six thousand feet) on the Polish side of the Czech border. A thousand similar activities combined to create a situation which had, henceforth, all the characteristics of an "economic miracle," though such achievements were never again to be paralleled in any area.

But let's get back to the end of the thirties. . . . During this period my father was earning a decent living; there was even talk of building a new house and extending our land. Everyone had a high opinion of his carpentry work, but they also valued him for his good sense and sound judgment. Frequent quarrels used to break out in the family, and they could last for years, however trivial the causes: brothers and sisters would bicker about their share of the paternal inheritance, about boundary lines and rights-of-way across fields. Boleslaw and Jan used to arbitrate in these fights, and when Jan left to visit his cousins in the United States, Boleslaw took over as head of the family.

Toward the end of August 1939, the brothers were called up to serve under the Polish flag and were soon engaged in the furious fighting which took place in the vicinity of Mlawa. Boleslaw and Stanislaw were taken prisoner by the Germans but were released and returned home after a few months. Jan, then in the United States, volunteered to join the American assault forces in the Far East. On his return home, he was awarded a disability pension for life by the United States government. No one really knows what happened to the other brother.

It was during this period that the "new order" began to hold sway in Popowo: the German colonists settled on the best lands while their rightful owners became farmhands on their own property. The Walesas suffered the common fate. Young and old alike were forced to go and work like slaves on the military fortifications along the rivers, the Vistula, Drweca, and Skrwa. The villages emptied out; women and children, left to fend for themselves, had no means of saving the farms from ruin. Sobowo's parish priest died in a concentration camp and after that the doors of the church were kept locked. During the winter of 1943, the German offensive in the East was broken, and the men of Popowo and its environs were rounded up and taken away.

My sister Izabela recounts that at the time she didn't really understand what was going on. Father often went off in the direction of Plock, taking something with him each time, and our house was full of comings and goings: pigs were slaughtered and vodka was distilled; people came at odd times of the night, gathering in the little cowshed, and probably sleeping there too since, on several occasions, Izabela was asked to take them blankets. She was nine at the time, the eldest of the children. (Edward, three years her junior, had been born in 1937, Stanislaw in 1939, while I was born [in Popowo like the rest] on September 29, 1943, at three-thirty in the morning.) The local children brought food to the men who were hiding out in the woods. It had to be taken to Brudzyn or Lagiewniki and it was easier for the children to get by without being noticed and to avoid the German patrols. Not far from the house, the undergrowth was almost impenetrable and there were several hideouts there. It was shortly after the great raid launched by the Germans that our father was arrested and taken away. Mother was pregnant with me at the time. Armed men on horseback had come looking for him earlier; a search had been under way and apparently they'd found something incriminating. The family was thunderstruck, and Izabela had run off to hide in the woods with Edward; on their return, our father was no longer there and Uncle Stanislaw had been picked up with him.

All the men arrested during the great roundup of the winter of 1943 were imprisoned at Chalin, on the site of the future school. Many were beaten to death there; long afterward the bloodstains could still be seen on the walls. The majority of prisoners were men who had defaulted from work on the fortifications. They were kept at Chalin for only a few days, and it was there that my father and uncle became separated. Stanislaw succeeded in escaping just when his convoy was about to enter a concentration camp, probably Dachau. No one knows exactly how he managed to get away, but one day he told Izabela's son some details of which she herself was ignorant. He had hidden in the loft of a German house; a young German woman, no doubt employed by the owners, had discovered him and had taken care of him. She was pretty and sweet-natured, and, according to our uncle, they soon fell in love. He returned from Germany dressed like a member of the Gestapo, and at the sight of him Izabela nearly died of fright! People immediately suspected him of collaborating with the Nazis, but these suspicions were allayed when he was arrested for the second time, though after the war a number of people still continued to wonder about him.

After his arrest, our father was compelled to do forced labor near Lipno, then was imprisoned at the work camp at Mlyniec. The prisoners, crowded in camps that were unheated in winter, suffered terribly from the cold. When they went to sleep with their heads against the partition wall, their hair would freeze and stick to the wood. Father, weak and racked with coughing, began to develop problems with his lungs and his condition deteriorated rapidly due to lack of medical treatment. When he at last came home for good, he was utterly exhausted, suffered frequent hemorrhages, and was already full of regrets for a life he felt was drawing to a close. He was to remain with us barely two months.

In May 1945, Uncle Stanislaw also returned from the camp. He began working again straightaway, living at Uncle Izydor's house and eating at ours. Father's condition was so serious that the priest was called to administer the last rites. On the very brink of death, he had waited for Uncle Stanislaw's return so that he could die in peace, repeating that he couldn't give up his soul before entrusting us to his safekeeping. He made Stanislaw swear solemnly that he would take care of us and he entreated my mother to look after Edward and me, stressing that one day she would be proud of me. He was lucid right up until the end. At about four in the morning, while we children were asleep, with Grandmother Kaminska watching over us, he calmly asked my mother to wake us and send us out. And so he died. He was buried at Sobowo. I couldn't go to the funeral, which was attended by the rest of the family along with numerous people from the neighborhood: I was eighteen months old at the time.

A year later Mother decided to marry Stanislaw. Izabela was mortified; she still had the most vivid memories of our father, of how kind, mild, and even-tempered he'd been, and our family Christmases together, brimming over with happiness. This second marriage broke that spell and she couldn't forgive our mother: she felt that she should have just stayed with us, and that we should have managed on our own. It was no more than childish jealousy, but she infected us all with it, inciting us against our stepfather: for a time we ran off into the woods and refused even to see him. We never did really accept him. Today, my sister recognizes that her behavior was misguided and that, in his own way, Stanislaw did take care of us. But the punishments he doled out felt different from those our father had inflicted: they hurt twice as much. My mother didn't seem particularly happy in her second marriage either. Our stepfather was capricious: good-natured one moment, he would explode with anger the next, though his behavior toward us was no doubt modeled to some extent on our own toward him. Mother had three more sons by Stanislaw: Tadeusz (1946), Zygmunt (1947), and Wojciech (1951).

My sister recalls that it was at about this time that I developed certain mannerisms which I exhibit to this day whenever I'm feeling annoyed: I would lock my hands behind my back, put on a thoughtful expression, and keep my mouth tightly shut. Edward, Stanislaw, and she nicknamed me the "village mayor." I was fairly even-tempered and rarely got upset, except that I couldn't bear to be treated as a child. At home, anger and resentment were, in any case, formally forbidden. If we ever glowered at each other at the meal table, my mother would notice it at once and we had to excuse ourselves immediately. Similarly, before going to church, we all had to make our peace with each other. I loved my mother dearly and I was fiercely defensive of her. Although I was the youngest, I often used to stand up to our stepfather and play the protector. I think that, probably because of Izabela's influence, I never really managed to accept Stanislaw and our second family, even though, of all Boleslaw's children, I was the one who stayed at home the longest.

As soon as I left home, all that once bound me to my family and to the village of Popowo, where my ancestors had settled and lived, and where I myself was born, withered away, and I've never really tried to preserve any ties with the past. I'm more interested in facing a new day than in looking backwards. It's not in my nature to be nostalgic. Not that I mock people who become attached to their birthplace and cultivate an image of their "little homeland." Yet there are those who seem to assimilate the notion of Homeland with a capital *H*. Personally, I don't feel this sort of attachment. Perhaps that's a flaw in my makeup, or the result of having had an unsettled life. I've always felt that I made myself, without having to rely too heavily on my family. I've never bothered to make a collection of family mementos. The album put together for me recently isn't very thick: portrait photos of our maternal grand-parents, our parents and stepfather, a few snapshots of us children, me during my military service, Danuta, our wedding photo, and then Danuta and me with our children at the seaside. A dispro-portionate part of the album is devoted to the Solidarity period.

I didn't know my paternal grandfather or my maternal grand-mother very well. Even when they were old, they hardly ever came to see us, to take us out for walks, educate us, or bring us treats. Grandfather had his own farm to look after, he had to make himself useful, and the same went for Grandmother, who was to end her days living under our roof: for her, life in the country meant mending, washing, sewing, and knitting. So, at home, it was our mother who was responsible for educating us children, whom she loved enormously. She is the only person from my childhood I still have a really clear recollection of. She was a cultured woman, although her education had been restricted to four years of school. She took an interest in history and current affairs, and read a great deal. At the end of the day, when work in the fields had slacked off, neighbors used to come and ask her advice about things, and her sisters-in-law and the village women would pay her visits. In the evening, she would sometimes read to us. She had an attractive voice, gentle and soothing, and we took great pleasure in these moments. She read us *The Sibylline Oracles*, a book which was going the rounds of the villages, Sienkiewicz's *The Teutonic Knights* and his historical trilogy, and *The Ancient Tale* of Kraszewski. All the stories our mother told us had a moral in them: they taught one to be honest, to strive always to better oneself, to be just, and to call white white and black black. Mother was very religious. She led the hymns and prayers at the foot of the open-air statue of the Virgin and, in winter, our neighbors came to our house to say their rosaries. My faith can be said almost to have flowed into me with my mother's milk.

After Father's death, our stepfather was always thought of as "the other man." He made every effort to bring us up properly, probably more than a real father would have done. He also tried to behave equitably toward the four of us—three brothers and a sister born of his wife's first marriage—and not to show any preference for his own three children. He kept us on a tight rein, however. Living conditions in the country were extremely tough at that time: because of disputes about land, brothers wouldn't speak to each other for twenty years at a stretch, and would only make up at the funeral of one or the other parent. (Our uncles' lives were like that, and at times took on tragic dimensions.) Children were brought up differently in the country from those in town. Even the youngest had his or her own jobs to do: there were too many mouths to feed to allow for idlers. At the age of five we tended the geese, at seven we took the cows out to pasture, at ten we took care of the other animals and did a variety of manual jobs—all that on top of school. The craftiest children pretended to be unusually interested in learning some subject or other if they wanted to avoid a particularly difficult or unpleasant task.

We owned a small farm of four acres. The house was simple and lacked electricity, which wouldn't come to Popowo until the late 1950s. As the children grew up, each went to school in turn (we used to walk the four miles, barefoot as often as not), leaving younger brothers to complete the chores. For at least two hours in the afternoon, I chopped up straw into small bits for the livestock, as my younger brothers played at hanging on to the chaffcutter. After years of trampling the straw on the barn floor, my feet became covered with corns and calluses which still cause me pain today: a vivid reminder of just what farm work entailed.

My full brothers and I used to do additional hours on our neighbors' farms, and during vacations all four of us would work from daybreak till nightfall at Mr. Michalski's private brickworks. During the autumn, we saved every penny we could in order to buy what we needed for the winter. The parcels sent from the States by Aunt Janina Brolewicz, my mother's sister-in-law, were a tremendous help to us. The bigger the packages the greater was our excitement—especially my sister Izabela's. My mother, on the other hand, seemed humiliated by this situation. She was a woman who would rather not have owed anyone anything, and her pride was hurt as a result. Given the conditions prevailing in the countryside at the time, we children were nevertheless remarkably well looked after. My mother was cleanliness itself, and she dressed us as well she was able, but always immaculately. Clothes were carefully mended and ironed. The same held true for the house: it was frequently repainted, or at least whitewashed, floorboards were kept swept, and everything smelled pleasantly of soap. The care our mother bestowed on us set us apart from the other village kids.

Today I scarcely know how to tell my children what my own childhood was like, and it is hard for them to understand. Who would have thought that when harvest time came around, we were actually short of bread? Sometimes two months could go by without our seeing so much as a crumb. Yet today I'd love to have another taste of that loaf baked over a woodfire in Dobrzyn. I was sent to fetch bread for the first time at the age of eight. Six miles of little lanes separated Popowo from Dobrzyn. I walked along, dawdling right and left off the path, attracted by the flowers and the birds, and wandering across fields; and when I reached Dobrzyn, there was no bread left and I had to return home empty-handed. . . . Slices of bread with butter or lard were a real treat. Each year, before the harvest, we ate meat only on Sundays, and then in small quantities. For lunch in winter we were allowed potatoes and boiled noodles served with lardons. The menu improved in summer. We were brought up on milk: we didn't sell it, our one and only cow having to feed us all. There were delicious mushrooms—which we used to pick to garnish omelettes—and the fish which I caught with a net in the neighboring pond.

Our mother didn't much like the country. Discouraged by the deterioration of our family circumstances, she was getting us ready to leave. Our stepfather wasn't hugely interested in the country either; he set his sights elsewhere, to become a "peasant-laborer." He got a job as foreman of a team of masons and learned how to plan and draft on paper what he and his team were going to construct in solid materials. They erected churches, and farm and other buildings, most of them in wood. Work was scarce after the war and our stepfather found it hard to meet the family's needs. He made frequent trips to town, where he took up selling food products from door to door, as people had done during the German occupation. He didn't have much luck with the land: the sugar beets which grew well in the region never flourished at all with him, but he harvested the beet crops owned by others during the sugar campaign and did piecework whenever he could.

He wasn't particularly interested in politics, but he did like listening to the battery-powered shortwave radio. In the evening, we listened to foreign stations and that's how I became an enthusiastic listener myself, eagerly absorbing information transmitted from various parts of the world. Since then, I've learned just how important this access to information from a number of different sources is, of not being limited to a single one, so-called "official truth." Later, during the strikes and riots, and when all communications, internal and external, were cut following the declaration of martial law in December of 1981, western shortwave radio (with its long-distance signals) provided the single source of information about events in Poland.

At our house there were long discussions about the pros and cons of every plan and every decision that was made, however insignificant. I've lost this habit, either through lack of time or perhaps because I don't wish to burden Danuta unnecessarily. I used to listen to my parents while I was working away on my job of the moment. Whenever my stepfather had to go to some office or other to settle an administrative formality, he and my mother discussed every step, every sentence, anticipating and arranging everything in advance: "I knock at the door, I go in and I say: 'Good morning, I've got such and such a matter to settle with you. . . .' " My mother would niggle: "No, wait, you mustn't start like that. . . ." They carried on endless conversations of this sort, often making me laugh. I thought to myself: "Dear Father, you'll have forgotten the whole lot before you've even got through the door! If one of the secretaries bumps into you, spills her cup of coffee and then accuses you of being clumsy, all your fine preparations will have been useless. You can't foresee and program everything." Most of the time, matters followed a different course from the one my parents had anticipated. They submitted themselves to the outcome, too helpless to intervene and too meek to assert themselves. And that included occasions such as when an unscrupulous postman failed to deliver the mail on time; to my parents he represented the outside world, the "administration," against which they were quite incapable of defending themselves. In such cases, they prepared themselves as if they were about to engage in a pitched battle and then, as soon as the door opened and the postman came in, they became utterly paralyzed.

As children, we rarely argued at home and never swore, though there were sometimes quite sharp verbal exchanges, especially between my parents. When the discussion livened up, they would both speak at once. I kept out of it, perfectly aware that neither was listening to the other, that they didn't even hear one another. Once, I tried to join in and was put firmly in my place by both of them, suddenly in agreement again. But when I was seventeen I said to them one day: "Now, just listen to me! Whichever way you look at it, if both of you talk at once, you might as well both be deaf. Sit down, think carefully, and each of you explain your arguments without getting worked up." I still laugh today when I remember the look on their faces! Later, during the night, I heard them talking things over again: "He's right, you know, that's exactly the way it is. . . ."

Growing up in this atmosphere, I played the part of a lucid spectator. I've never wanted to reach a compromise with a world which imposes ready-made solutions while swearing that things can't be otherwise. Whenever anyone tries to persuade me that a deep-seated logic governs all human actions, a picture comes into my mind of travelers going in different, often diametrically opposed, directions. The trains move toward their destinations and their movement acts as a confirmation of these destinations. And yet, if you look more closely, putting yourself in the place of such and such a passenger, you'll see that, for years, he has been doing the Gdynia-Gdansk journey, for example, in order to reach his place of work at the Gdansk shipyard and then return to Gdynia, where he lives right bang next door to another shipyard, in every way similar to the first. And that, for another passenger, exactly the same thing applies, except in reverse. Throughout their lives, they nevertheless continue to do the same journey. From early on, my practical mind has been attuned to such absurdities. My childhood memories clearly illustrate the truth of this. The motives and reasons that guided our parents in their daily lives were like an open book for us. I still have a mental picture of the things they did over and over again, of their sense and their absurdity, and I can see just what each contributed to our parents' lives. The real sadness was their indecision. They didn't even eat enough to have the energy and spirit necessary to leave that old shack of theirs one day and build a proper house. And they talked of leaving the country life for America. But when they finally went in 1973, they didn't go there out of a sense of adventure. The decision to go was dictated by common sense and tradition: in our family there had always been someone on the other side of the ocean. It was in our blood: one or another went over there so that the rest of the family could count on some security and a chance of financial help. Simple people calculate things in a simple way.

Beyond the immediate family life, I had my cousins and my schoolfriends. The school we all went to in Chalin was situated in a little manor house surrounded by magnificent gardens, which had formerly belonged to a family of the nobility, since disinherited. I was a sort of "decathlonian," pretty good at a number of subjects, but never outstanding in any one. I didn't excel in Polish, or music, or drawing; on the other hand, right up until the fifth grade—when I was still keen to do well—I was excellent at all the exercises that demand speed with numbers, not memory—arithmetic and logic—and could even keep up with our teacher. It was he, too, who got me interested in sports. He was passionate about archery. Under his guidance, I decided to try my hand at it and gained third place in a regional competition, winning a real leather ball. For all that, I didn't stand out much from the other pupils and didn't really spring into life until the last bell rang. Our games were scarcely original. In summer we used to rush to the edge of the lake, fling ourselves into the water and swim out as far as possible, until we ran out of breath; or we played soccer with a ball made of rags or stuffed with horsehair. In winter, when the ice on the ponds began to crack, we would jump from one little ice floe to another, with five yards of freezing cold water under our feet. It was a test of courage: the one who went out the farthest from the edge of the lake was the winner. In this kind of competition I frequently outdid my schoolfellows, but not in much else.

The first time I left Popowo properly goes back to our end-of-term trip. The class photo, dated June 2, 1958, was taken on the beach at Gdansk, where I was to return the second time nine years later, to settle permanently.

The following year I had left home for good. On my mother's advice, I had enrolled in a training program at Lipno, in the "agricultural mechanization" section at a vocational school.

Lipno, capital of the district, was a conglomeration of fifteen thousand inhabitants, a town with a long and exciting history, marked by periods of great splendor. When I lived there, a few vestiges of that former splendor still remained: commemorative plaques informing the reader that, at the time of the Royal Republic, the Dietine of the Dobrzyn district used to meet there; and an old church, perched on top of the hill, around which the wagons going to market used to make their way through narrow streets. The more energetic local farmers, including my neighbors from Popowo, came to do their shopping there. Our school was outside the town, on the edge of a vast and magnificent park, at the entrance to which, on a piece of rising ground, stood a statue of Saint Anthony, towering over its surroundings. This Saint Anthony was probably meant to protect the inhabitants of Lipno, and especially the young girls, from the veritable plague of fellow students whose reputation in town wasn't the best.

The school was designed to prepare, in three years, a young good-for-nothing like me for work at the POM (*Panstwowy Osrodek Maszynowy*, State Agricultural Depot) or else in industry, which was recruiting young people for jobs in towns or in the industrialized cities along the Baltic. The main thrust of the teaching was directed at the sort of professional training which would later be put into practice, while the general teaching—Polish, math, history, geography—was limited to instilling a rudimentary knowledge that wouldn't tax even the least able of the students. Some of the teachers, however, wanted to change the mediocre reputation of the training courses, and teach us more. I personally took a particular interest in the workshop sessions, where we had a variety of equipment at our disposal and where I could say that I learned my trade. In the other subjects I was considered "satisfactory." I got "good" twice on my end-of-term report: one for business management studies, and one for gymnastics, and even one "very good": for conduct, surprisingly enough.

It was a conduct which nevertheless caused me a number of headaches, the teachers' board finding fault with it on more than one occasion. For this special training we were boarded away from home at a school where we frequently skipped class or went to look for excitement in the town. We were caught there on several occasions with cigarettes in our mouths or wandering around without our caps on, which was forbidden. During my turns as assistant supervisor, I used to try and salvage my reputation, compromised by the label "smokes and is a troublemaker." Mr. Rybacki, our supervisor and future director of the school, had it in for me. He kept giving me different jobs to do, which I nevertheless accomplished successfully, earning myself a reputation as a good organizer. I never had any problems with my peers. When it was my turn, I woke everyone up half an hour earlier than usual and we spent the time till breakfast good-humoredly scrubbing the corridor. Once we'd finished the job we'd been assigned, everyone was happy.

History, it has to be said, was my weak point. One year I really landed myself in trouble when I received three failures at the end of the term. I didn't appreciate the value of history until much later. As a subject, it seemed to me remote from real life, an abstraction, describing people and facts devoid of the slightest link with reality as I knew it. The fifties were not, in any case, an ideal period for trying to understand world history from the Polish national viewpoint. It was an era dominated by tendentious or conjectural analyses, elaborated from a foreign point of view, using the classic jargon of communism, and presenting the facts from the angle of the eternal class struggle. I was all the more inclined to reject this picture of the world because it differed substantially from what I heard at home and at church. My own conception of the world was in any case quite different, inspired as it was by my own experience and my relations with fellow students, teachers, and all those people I had generally encountered in life.

A dozen or so amateur photos, unfortunately of rather poor quality, offer a testimony to my technical school era. They are undated, but I think I was already in my last year then: on the very brink of adulthood. The series of photos portrays four boys and two girls of the same age, all dressed according to what they believed to be the canons of current fashion. I'm wearing a pair of trousers which are quite narrow at the bottom, a light-colored shirt, and a silk scarf knotted at my throat. The poses captured by the photographer—probably one of our friends—show me playing at being a bit of a dandy. In almost all the shots I'm pulling one or another of the girls toward me, while my fellow students are relegated to the role of mere extras. There's a deliberate nonchalance in my poses. The girls meanwhile are visibly trying to disengage themselves from my possessive grasp, coy and consenting at the same time. What strikes one most is how self-confident I was then, how assured my look and gestures were. And that, too, was a pose.

The ball organized for the end of the school year in 1961 also marked the end of a life free from worries. Now I was going to have to work. I soon managed to land myself a job as an electrician with the POM at Lochocino. The work involved repairing electrical apparatuses and machines, and I settled into it quickly. It was at this time that I was first referred to as a mechanic with "the golden hand." At the end of two years I was called up for military service. I returned home in 1965, taking up my work again at the POM, but this time in the Lenie branch, even closer to Popowo. Home was emptying at the time: Izabela had got married after passing her technical exams and had left for Sochaczew, where she had been taken on in a workers' cafeteria; she lives there today as a housewife. Edward soon became independent too: he attended the technical school of construction work, was then employed on various building sites before finally settling in the vicinity of Lodz, where he still runs his own farm. Once he had left vocational school and done his military service, Stanislaw established himself in Bydgoszcz, where he continued to work while taking courses at the technical school. And so now I was the eldest at home.

In the social climate of the Polish countryside then, the POM was synonymous with change; it was the expression of a new agricultural policy that involved instituting farm cooperatives, while at the same time dismantling private holdings, and offering a Polish countryside bereft of cottage industries new agricultural machinery. A new type of peasant-laborer had made his appearance, who belonged neither to the town nor to the country. He worked for the POM in order to earn his living, but even more important, to have access to spare parts, machinery, and other materials he could use to farm his own small plot of land. Country people reacted to the "new" in their own way—traditionally—and the POM employees devoted a good part of the timetable reserved for the upkeep of the tractors and state farm machinery to working on their own projects. A black market of sorts had thus established itself and was tolerated by the supervisors, who were well aware that the private farms still constituted the region's principal agricultural resource, and that these farms required mechanized equipment—however rudimentary. This constituted a tacit form of opposition to the collectivization of the countryside: theoretical plans were adjusted to fit the reality.

How should one describe a POM employee at this time? He wore work dungarees that were sharply creased, the inevitable beret cocked at a fanciful angle, and always kept in his pockets his tools, which otherwise were liable to disappear into thin air. The village paid "in kind," more often than not in alcohol, for all the small services we rendered. The more skillful and versatile a man was, the more he was appreciated (especially by the girls) for his "golden touch" and ability to help out anyone.

Within the POM I had earned the reputation as one of the best technicians in the district, that's to say within a twenty-mile radius. I learned to repair everything, from a harrow to a television set, from WFM and Jawa motor bikes to Frania washing machines. I felt important and when I made an entrance at a dance, there was a wild celebration: Walesa's here! The orchestra livened up and a bottle of vodka landed on the table. I had money, and everyone knew me because I had rendered each of them a service. I often did quick little jobs which no one else could be bothered with. People either came to me or else I went to their homes. I was somebody, it seemed I had found my place in life.

But one afternoon I had to break off from it all—I had suddenly felt a profound disgust for my work. The POM seemed to me a dead end, suffocating, eventually unbearable. And, suddenly, my reputation as the best mechanic at the POM and in the whole area struck me as derisory, utterly unimportant, ridiculous. I can't bear ridicule—real ridicule, the sort you're aware of yourself; I have too great a need for my actions and efforts to be taken seriously and to be accorded a certain weight. Simple pride, I guess. Added to all that, an affair I was having with a young woman was unraveling. It wasn't really love, but just a relationship I persevered in without any real conviction. The girl, sensibly, took the decision for both of us and broke it off. I wasn't really sad, but I felt lonely and empty. People had thought that we would stay together, and in the end she was the one who dropped me: it was a hard blow to my pride. Hence, my decision to leave and get far away from home. I also felt ashamed because my mother seemed to expect the world of me, and I had to do something. I was now twenty-four and I hadn't achieved anything of any significance and felt I'd wasted too much time already.

So, on that afternoon, I quickly made my arrangements to leave the POM, without feeling the slightest regret. As I was still unsure of myself, I went back home, reluctant to tell anyone that I was making a big decision. I simply said that I was going off, that I needed a change of air. I took some money and a coat, and left for the Dobrzyn station.

Why the Baltic Coast? At the time it seemed that it was simply that the first train to leave was heading in that direction: Gdynia, via Gdansk. But I understand better today; important decisions are never made like that, at least not for me. There was the sea; and the school trip had left me with the memory of something vast, stretching out endlessly—possibly freedom. A big town, a port, adventure, and not unlike the eel, instinctively submitting to the will of the current, I let myself drift toward the Baltic region, by the sea where I would find—or lose myself—at last.

The Gdansk Shipyard

The Gdansk shipyard has played a crucial role in my life for many years, but there were four special occasions that I will always remember. The first was on May 30, 1967, immediately after my arrival in Gdansk. Just as I was leaving the railroad station, before I'd even had time to look around, I ran into Tadeusz, my old acquaintance from the technical school in Lipno. He told me he'd been working at the shipyard for the past few years and suggested I do the same. I went straightaway to the employment office, filled out the necessary forms, and within a few days became employee 61 878. I began work as a naval electrician in shop 4, in the Mosinski crew. That was where the events of December 1970, the second noteworthy occasion—described later—would find me three and a half years later.

The third occurred when I went to the shipyard on the morning of August 14, 1980, four years after I had been fired for organizing activities. The members of the Free Trade Union had been informed of the workers' strike in Lublin, earlier in August, and because of my seniority (I'd been at the shipyard—off and on—for almost ten years) had chosen me to lead the shipyard workers. I wasn't sure I'd even get to work that day since I was being shadowed by agents of the SB (security police), who kept me under as strict surveillance in those days as they do now. They were dogging my every footstep, making me stick out like a sore thumb. I had taken the streetcar, and they had ample opportunity to observe that I was heading for the yard. My theory at the time was that the authorities were determined to effect certain political changes unrelated to free trade union activities, a speculation that was eventually to be proved correct. They intended to turn both the strikes and the strength of our movement to their own advantage on a nationwide scale, but they underestimated our determination.

The entire shipyard had been in a ferment from the moment the gates opened that summer morning because of an editorial in *Robotnik (The Worker)* listing our demands, among which were the reinstatement of Anna Walentynowicz, a key leader of our movement who had been fired, and a wage increase. I remember that I got off the streetcar at the stop in front of the shipyard, but I didn't head straight for the front gate because I didn't have a valid worker's pass. Instead, I walked past a school situated between two entrances to the yard, and there, at the end of an alley, got into the yard by jumping over the gate.

On August 16, Gniech, then the director of the shipyard, agreed in principle to my reinstatement as an electrician as I, too, had been sacked. It was a Saturday morning, the day we began the second phase of our strike in support of the workers in other enterprises and factories in Lublin and elsewhere.

The fourth occasion was when I presented myself at the offices of the Gdansk Shipyard in March 1983, after martial law had been lifted. This time, as a precaution, everything I had said was recorded to permit verification later on.

Although I had been a valued employee at the POM, I felt completely lost when I first started work at the shipyard in 1967. After spending several years surrounded by the carcasses of rusting farm vehicles, which I used to take apart, down to the last rivet, out of simple curiosity, I'd turned into a pretty good technician. When I climbed up into my first ship on the stocks in the yard, I got lost almost immediately among all the levels of scaffolding, and I had to face the fact that I was just one of thousands of other workers there. A painful truth, but there was no going back. At the shipyard, because of the specialized nature of the work, I realized that I couldn't use many of the skills I knew by heart from earlier jobs. To be a specialist worker, with one small task, never appealed to me.

The workers in the shipyard didn't form a homogeneous group or community similar to those I had been a part of in the countryside, where workers quickly learn everything there is to know about one another. Each individual's interests and motives, along with the entire community's, become crystal clear in no time at all. The shipyard houses a hierarchy of castes and each functions according to its own self-restrictive laws. The engineers and professional men, for example, make up one caste, as do the technicians. A wide range of specialized professions are hierarchically organized and each is accorded varying degrees of importance. Within each specialized field, the hierarchy is based on differing levels of responsibility: managers, supervisors, foremen, and simple workmen. Finally, a distinction is made between those who have held the same job for years and are thus the permanent members of a work crew, and the "temps" who move from one job to another as though playing hopscotch.

I started out in the Mosinski brigade, a gang of electricians whose job it was to lay cables on large factory fishing boats. It's not easy to lay dozens of yards of cable as thick as your forearm from the generator to the main control panel. The length of the cable, with all its bends, undulations, and branches, had to come out exactly right. In order to measure the cable correctly, we unrolled it from the spool along the ground, taking the necessary curves and contortions into account. If mistakes were made and the cable turned out to be too short or too long when work on the ship was completed, we were simply out of luck because the cable could be neither shortened nor lengthened.

My first job was to "do the ends," dividing the cable into sections, separating and stripping all the wires. Then someone else would splice the wires so that I could pull the cable, acting as a hauler.

The highest ranking workers, the elite, in our yard were those in machine shop M-5, who handled the final assembling of the engines. Shop M-4, one step down, dealt with general engineering, and there you'd find some skilled workers such as good lathe or milling machine operators. The pariahs of the shipyard labored in the hull. But the worst job, in my view, was boiler making, where thirty-five-pound hammers were used on sheet metal heated with blowtorches. It was not until the mid-1970s that they began to surface the sheet metal by heating it uniformly, which allows it to straighten out on its own. The painters in shop 1 were also regarded as pariahs. They worked in a real hell: seventy percent of them were "temps," and few lasted long. They had to scrape and smooth every square inch of a ten-thousand-ton hull by hand with a file. The sheets of metal were assembled without having first been cleaned or primed. It wasn't until several years after I arrived that they perfected the technique of priming the metal beforehand. Now it seems that everyone wants to be a painter, but in earlier days it was slave labor.

Of all the assembly shops, A-4 was the one that required the most specialized skills. There were a few jobs for beginners, like pulling cables, but the rest involved closely coordinated assembly work to integrate fittings and instrumentation. Because everything had to be in place already when we laid the cables, we first had to calculate the position of each opening through which the cables would pass. This work was handled by experts, while less experienced workers took care of the other cable work. The crew of shop 4 was followed by shop 5, the joiners. A-4 came directly after A-3, which did the metal work, and A-2, which installed all the pipes and ducts, from five to six hundred yards of them on each ship. The electricians moved to do their jobs once the fabric of the ship had been installed. We obtained equipment and supplies from the shop store, or, if they didn't have what we needed, from the central warehouse on Holm, a small island off Gdansk. With the exception of the engineering crews of M-4 and M-5, the electricians had the best working conditions.

Created in 1946 or 1947 from the merger of three separate companies, Gdansk shipyard had become a large-scale enterprise by 1960. Yet it lacked the most elementary accommodations for workers, such as proper lockers, changing rooms, or lavatories, not to mention drying machines for workers' clothing. More than forty percent of the men worked out in the open air, rain or shine, and when autumn came, with its wet weather, workers left for home soaked to the skin. The lucky ones would stuff their pea jackets or oilskins into metal cupboards, where they had no chance of drying out overnight, only to put them on wet again the next morning. That's when you'd really feel the cold! Dryers were installed in other workplaces but not in the shipyard for decades. As for even thinking of washing. . . . The authorities invested no money in improving working conditions until after 1970, and almost at once severe budget cuts brought these projects to a halt. There wasn't even a workers' cafeteria until the mid-1970s.

By the early 1960s, most of the shipyard workers suffered from stomach ailments, a situation that was more or less inevitable, although at first I couldn't understand why. Everyone began work at six A.M. After getting up early, without time for breakfast, the men worked hard until nine A.M. with nothing but an occasional cigarette to keep them going. There was only one meal break for the entire shipyard, between nine and nine-fifteen. The workers would get something to eat at stalls set up on site. Women would slice and butter bread, preparing sandwiches, pickles, and cheese spreads for the men waiting in line. Yet the vendors could serve only about ten customers in fifteen minutes, which left dozens of others waiting for up to three-quarters of an hour for their turn, time that came right out of the pockets of men doing piecework. The soup and snack shops that began serving workers in the 1970s were just a dream a decade earlier. When I arrived our shipyard looked like a factory filled with men in filthy rags, unable to wash themselves or urinate in toilets. To get down to the ground floor where toilets were located took at least half an hour, so we just went anywhere. You can't imagine how humiliating these working conditions were.

The first two years at the shipyard were a probationary period. Everyone who made it through those two years had a chance of staying on permanently. When a man had had two years to get used to things and make the grade, he understood that he had to take good care of himself, just as he took care of his tools. Sometimes the doctor would refuse to pass someone at one of the periodic medical examinations, and then the man would have to abandon his profession or take a lesser job at the yard. This was a real setback, especially if a man went from piecework to work by day and a loss of half his salary. Yes, we all realized how important it was to stay in good health. The foremen knew who they could count on for overtime: not single men, but guys who were married and needed the extra pay. They'd grab any overtime, and they drove themselves hard. But the unmarried ones knew their limits, and wouldn't trade their free time for more money.

Production at the shipyard is based primarily on piecework, which is a great way for management to evade its own responsibilities. Every individual strives to earn as much as he can, but because there's no one around to deliver the necessary materials to the proper work stations, the yard is in perpetual motion—a chaos of comings and goings, with people running around in search of necessary pieces of equipment, even though supply departments have supposedly been established to eliminate this problem.

The big draw was that working in the yard offered the opportunity to learn a profession. Some young men thought they might someday get to sign on on one of the ships they helped build, as though the shipyard also represented a way to ship out as a sailor. This wasn't exactly wrong, because the simple fact of having worked in the yard meant that a man had a good chance of at least doing his military service in the navy. For nine out of ten of the lower-level workers who came from all over Poland, the yard represented the first step toward going to sea.

The one thing the shipyard did offer was job training to all personnel. Every year, eight to nine thousand of the fifteen thousand workers attended professional training courses, with the result that although the shipyard itself employed only six hundred welders, for example, more than forty thousand Polish workers obtained their welder's licenses at the yard. I think I can safely say that half the welders in Poland were trained in the yard, and Gdansk is considered to be the best yard in the country. At the Paris Commune shipyard in Gdynia, the Northern shipyard, and other yards handling repairs only, the most demanding jobs are filled by men trained in Gdansk. Relations between the workers and management were paternalistic at best, and still are today. The managerial staff was made up of old hands, many of them natives of Gdansk, some of whom had worked in the Schichau shipyard, which had been erected by German industrialists before the Second World War when Gdansk was known to them as the Free City of Danzig. In the 1960s these men shared responsibility with workers who had begun their training in the shipyard itself toward the end of the 1940s. After three or four years, anyone who showed a touch of initiative was allowed to join a training program.

The job assignments are handled by foremen, who therefore have power over workers' wages. In former days, one could pay for a copious meal, with plenty of vodka, for several people at

Chez Kubicki, an excellent Gdansk restaurant, with work vouchers that were accepted as general currency. The waiter would then resell them to another worker, like a hawker crying his wares: "I've got work vouchers for 2,500 zlotys,[1] who wants some?" If someone needed to round out his salary, he'd buy these vouchers. The same thing went on in other restaurants, at Under the Chestnut Tree or at the Buccaneer. This barter and financial fiddling was common in the shipyard, too, and it's not hard to see why.

The same patriarchal system controlled the wage scale. If one of the old guard got married, he made more money than usual for a few months, and nobody complained. He'd be the one selected to get the highest-paying jobs in his crew, and he'd be offered work vouchers at attractive prices. The atmosphere within a work gang was affected by these tacit arrangements, which could strengthen or disrupt ties among the workers. The distribution of bonuses, job assignments, and the schedule of paid vacations were also sources of conflict.

The 1960s brought a decade of smooth sailing and modest prosperity for the higher-ranked workers. Some would flatter themselves that they'd taken a step up the social ladder. They were able to obtain housing in the Tri-City, the urban center formed by Gdansk, Gdynia, and Sopot, after barely four or five years, or sometimes only two, if there was a demand for their particular skill. These living conditions permitted a more settled existence: the opportunity to start a family, to socialize with friends, to live and die in peace—in short, the prospect of a fairly decent life. And that was something, after all. Eighteen hundred workers lived in cheap dormitories owned by the yard, two thousand others camped out in rooms rented from the local Gdansk population.

The rooms rented from hostels or the locals were not all of equal quality. The better hostels offered the advantages of the socialist life-style: various clubs and social activities open to all, at least in principle. There was even a yacht club, although it was restricted to workers with considerable seniority, and besides, it didn't seem to square with the image appropriate for the average worker.

---

1. A Polish zloty, in 1987, was—at the official exchange rate—worth about half of one American penny or 200 zlotys to the dollar. On the black market, the dollar is worth five times more—that is, 1,000 zlotys.

The workers' hostel on Tuwim Street was the most attractive, and the lodgers knew how to dress up the rooms with a picture, maybe only a calendar, or perhaps a decoration of plaited straw.

By far the worst was the hostel on Klonowicza Street. It was a tenement block four floors high, inhabited by six hundred people. Later on when one of the buildings was reserved for married couples, I lived there myself after my marriage to Danuta. At the entrance there was a wicket gate and a sentry box, a bit like in an army camp. A vacant lot stretched between the buildings, a wasteland of scorched grass and empty bottles.

Every payday ended with fights and a dozen bashed-in doors. You had to see it to believe it: a guy drunk enough to kick down doors, and break in on his buddy and girlfriend! There were other scenes I prefer not to describe. The hostel naturally had a bad reputation in the neighborhood and caused trouble for the management at the shipyard. The caretaker, usually a woman, had to get used to all the drinking and fighting, and when she did, she'd wind up supplying the lodgers with vodka herself. If she was a timid soul, she wouldn't last two months. The hostel had three buildings, one each for men, women, and families. At the end of the corridor on each floor there was a kitchen and shower. In the family building, the rooms had two or three beds, four at the most. The hostel provided a metal bedframe with a lumpy mattress, a floor and four gray walls, all in a filthy state and reeking of mildew, a rickety table, and two chairs, each missing at least one leg. A man could drink and sleep at the hostel, but he couldn't really live there. Between the living conditions at the hostel and the working conditions at the factory, the men were caught in a vicious circle. These living conditions improved somewhat by the early 1970s, when new furniture was purchased and the floors and walls were repaired.

A worker who survived the stress and dangers of the yard and hostel life would eventually arrange to share a room in the city with a few friends. The shipyard paid the rent, but the lodgers usually gave the landlord something extra out of their own pockets. Sharing was cheaper than living alone, and, most important, it was more civilized, although the hostel on Klonowicza Street suited a great many workers perfectly.

Only single men could rent rooms from the locals, however,

which was why I had to take lodgings on Klonowicza Street after I was married.

When I was single, I'd first rented a small room from a couple named Krol at 28 Kartuska Street, a room I shared with three other chaps for two years. The lodgings were on the ground floor of an old building not far from the shipyard, near the center of town. Our room had one table surrounded by four beds, and the windows looked out onto a very noisy road on a streetcar route. Our quarters were hardly luxurious, but we liked them because of the family atmosphere we shared with our landlords. We helped them with the housework, mopping the floor on Saturdays, brushing a coat of white paint on the walls or repairing the light fixtures when we had time. We acted as chaperons for the family's eldest daughter whenever she went to a dance. Mr. Krol had been an agricultural engineer before the war. Sometimes we spent the afternoon talking politics together. He listened regularly to Radio Free Europe and reminded me of my stepfather. I always addressed Mr. Krol as "Chief," and he would call me "Mr. Chairman," a convention we honored until his death.

Close by the house was a building that enjoyed a sinister reputation throughout Gdansk: it housed the offices of the SB, security police.[2] Their agents lived in the neighborhood, and one occupied a room right over the one I shared with my friends. Years later, this man turned up in the team of agents assigned to keep tabs on me at the end of my internment. He followed me everywhere, close on my heels, going to work with me in the morning, coming home with me in the evening, even keeping me company on weekend fishing trips or "solitary" walks in the woods. Today I ask him to give my regards to the family of my former landlords; he never fails to do so.

When a man signed on at the yard, the first thing he had to do was find his footing in the city. A kid on his own, far from his

2. Though the term "police" is not used in Poland, there are four types of law-enforcement bodies to be aware of: MO *citizens' militia,* Western-style police who handle road and city traffic and ordinary crime; ORMO *Voluntary Reserve of Citizens' militia,* a paramilitary organization hiding behind the designation of a "social organization" assisting the MO—members are nonuniformed and unarmed; ZOMO *mobile units of citizens' militia,* who are specially trained riot police; and SB (formerly UB), who are nonuniformed undercover or secret police.

family and the traditions of peasant life—the parish priest, relatives, members of the entire village who always knew everything about everyone—suddenly found himself in a big city. Now he could do what he liked with his spare time, his Sundays, even his own money (and, in spite of everything, the salaries were much higher in the shipyard than in other sectors of the economy), but he had to be self-reliant to survive.

Work at the yard was demanding, which didn't leave us much time for getting to know the city and its ways. Shortly after my arrival in Gdansk, while I was out with some fellow workers, I met a young woman who had what seemed to me a very exotic name: Lala. In the course of that evening, through various hints, she gave me to understand that her father was a person of some importance in Gdansk, so highly placed, in fact, that it would be better for me if I didn't know exactly what his job was. Gdansk is showing me its best side right away, I thought, and I spent more and more money on our dates, racking my brains to come up with ways to impress Lala. I didn't think it proper that she should be involved with a mere electrician just starting out at the shipyard, so to spare her any embarrassment on that score, I invented a story to the effect that I'd recently been appointed to head a small business concern. One morning, the charm was broken when I ran into Lala, all muffled up in a shawl, delivering milk on a street in my neighborhood. I immediately confessed to her that I worked at the yard. The magic was gone, however, leaving in its place a slight feeling of uneasiness between us, and we avoided each other from then on. I realized that the glamour of a big city can disguise the most ordinary little schemes and pretensions.

The next young woman I went out with was attractive, level-headed, sensible in every respect, and I didn't feel at all self-conscious about exposing my peasant background. She worked as a nurse in a hospital near the shipyard. And yet, our friendly, direct, no-nonsense relationship wasn't really what I was looking for. One day I passed by a flower stand and caught sight of a pair of mischievous brown eyes in a sweet face framed by long dark hair: it was a vision I couldn't get out of my mind. A few days later I went back to ask her what time she got off work. She told me she lived with her aunt in the suburbs, in Brzezno, and like me, had recently arrived in Gdansk from a country village. Her name was Mirka, but I preferred her middle name, Danuta, or Danka, as I soon began calling her.

I had known other girls who seemed to suit me better, and yet Danuta was someone special, I found myself thinking to my surprise, as I listened to the first strains of the wedding march—our wedding march, no less (the marriage came about quite naturally only months after we met). We started married life poor as church-mice. There was no question of going back to my bachelor's quarters, so, with virtually no money, we began our years of wandering, from one inhospitable rented room to the next, leaving a bit of ourselves behind each time we moved on. We finally found a place to our liking on Beethoven Street, an attic over a hairdresser's salon run by a woman who had been repatriated from the Polish territories annexed by the Soviet Union in 1939. As compensation for possessions abandoned in the Soviet Union, she had received a small, rather uncomfortable detached house, where she had opened up her hairdressing business, and where she lived with her young son. But her troubles didn't end there. Her lover, we soon discovered, was mentally unbalanced, and he used to disrupt the whole neighborhood by his behavior. I had to rescue this poor woman many times when he'd get angry over some imagined slight; more than once he went after her with an axe. We tried to do what we could for her, knowing that, like us, she didn't have any family in Gdansk. I became sponsor at her son's confirmation. Danuta used to give her a hand in the garden, and in the spring, when it was time to turn the earth over, I'd take the spade to her little patch of ground, glad of the chance to get close to the soil. Despite its inconveniences, we felt at home in that small attic.

I gradually came to understand the essential difference between working in the structured shipyard and working for an enterprise as loosely organized as the POM. The prevailing atmosphere at the POM was cheerful and easygoing. If there were bonds of solidarity among the workmen, it was because these people knew each other well and were on good terms. It seemed that nothing was easier than lending a helping hand or paying off a debt of gratitude, even at a moment's notice. At the yard, things were radically different: there, each one of us was just a tiny cog in a vast machine. Although we did represent a certain collective strength that had to be taken into account when things weren't going well—and they rarely did—we worked in an atmosphere of unrelieved tension and gloom. The men were dressed alike, in shabby attire, and we seemed to behave in a vaguely military fashion, almost by reflex. We identified ourselves instinctively by social class, following the lead of shipyard slogans that seemed to surround us at every turn. Even though most of us realized we were being manipulated and this knowledge gave us a certain superiority over the directors of the shipyard, the fact was we were shuffled about in a way which left us with little control over our destinies.

Mindful of their mistakes in Poznan in 1956, the authorities were careful by the late 1960s to go after their objective in a roundabout way; instead of simply reducing the hourly wage, they sent their "brains" into action: political economists, engineers, and accountants. Their aim was to push us in order to cut costs. In the new system the worker wasn't simply assigned the job of making a table, for example, but was also required to finish it within a specified period of time. He was no longer being paid for making a table, but for devoting a certain number of work hours to this task. That allowed them to set up an arrangement whereby the twenty hours initially allotted to the manufacture of a table, for which the worker earned 1,000 zlotys, could be successively reduced to fifteen, and then to ten hours, which cut the wages proportionately. So now the worker who wanted to earn the same 1,000 zlotys as before had to build two tables in the same amount of time.

This wage-saving policy imposed on us resulted in an overall loss (to the workers) of about a million work hours a year. In order not to exceed the production costs on a ship (calculated in hours), the engineer was thus obliged to shorten the time allotted to each task. The money saved, at our expense, and which didn't benefit the engineer in any way, served to aggravate the mutual distrust between labor and management. Management washed its hands of the whole responsibility for the plan by hiding behind obscure economic laws.

While I was beginning to understand how this type of management planning worked to our disadvantage, the climate of oppression at the shipyard was reinforced by an accident that claimed the lives of twenty-two workers. In order to step up productivity, arrangements had been made to mobilize almost two thousand men to install the final fittings and equipment on a ship, two hundred of whom were working overtime in the hold. Some had been working for thirty-six hours at a stretch on this vessel, which had already been filled with fuel, again to save time in order to meet an overly exacting schedule. The last stages in constructing a ship are always nerve-wracking: you'll see foremen under considerable stress, not to mention the workmen. It seems that someone must have slipped up that day while cutting or welding a fuel pipe. Inevitably, fuel leaked out, causing an explosion, and because the hatchways in the hull were sealed off, the firefighting equipment was unavailable. Though workers attempted to cut through the sheet metal with acetylene torches, supplies of acetylene were inadequate for the task. Thus, twenty-two men were burned alive in the hold of the *Konopnicka*. Later on, at the shipyard trial, management admitted that "given the need to reduce delays affecting delivery on the ship, the technological process had been disrupted."

A few hours after the explosion, in the locker rooms, the men were complaining about inadequate safeguards and other problems. At break time, I usually joined one particular group of workers—the vocal ones—as I had done at school, in the army, and at the POM. Each day following the accident, I had a few more people around me to listen to what I had to say and to fill me in on what I didn't yet know about conditions in the yard. I became good friends with a man in my own crew named Henryk Lenarciak, who was originally from a little village near Bialystok. It was to prove a lasting friendship, and Lenarciak was by my side in August 1980 as head of the committee for the construction of a monument to the shipyard victims of 1970.

The abortive student revolt of March 1968 was still fresh in the minds of the men at the yard at the end of 1970. At the time, many workmen had let themselves be influenced by the deceitful insinuations of official propaganda aimed at turning the worker against the student, the intellectual, and even the yard's engineers and the professional men—who, it was suggested, were responsible for the poor wages the men were receiving and the unpaid overtime they were forced to endure under the new system. Clearly, the officials were leading both sides around by their noses. When some striking students from the engineering school drove a van on to the grounds of the shipyard and attempted to explain the ideas behind the student movement—which were, essentially, freedom of expression and the fight against censorship—they didn't spark much interest. Piasecki, then the director of the shipyard, received the student delegation in his office, and after a round of coffee, soon got the upper hand. It's true that he did spare them a beating at the hands of the ORMO, who were waiting for them at the shipyard gates (the bonus for student-bashing earned the militiamen up to 2,000 zlotys at the time). So the students left as they'd come: empty-handed and disillusioned. For our part, several of us tried to make our fellow workers understand that if the students and intellectuals were targets for repression, then that was sufficient reason for us to support them—a faint flicker of solidarity.

There were about twenty student trainees from the engineering school working in the shipyard. The morning after one confrontation between authorities and the students, somebody in the locker room noticed a trainee whose back had been clubbed black and blue. We paraded him, shirtless, through the shipyard, chanting: "Are we going to let them beat up our children, the children of workers and peasants?" That same day, the forces of law and order were routed in Wrzeszcz, a suburb of Gdansk. Apparently, some protestors had armed themselves with coiled steel springs, which when pulled back and released, served as projectiles. When the militia charged, without shields or other protection, they met unexpected resistance, running head-on into the released steel springs. Totally defeated, they suddenly realized that the riot hadn't been stirred up by intellectuals, but by workers who had taken the side of the students. One militiaman, covered with blood, shouted: "Sweet Jesus, what kind of shit have we got ourselves into!"

The authorities in Gdansk weren't able to snuff out the revolt at its source, and Kociolek, the first secretary of the Party in Gdansk, was roundly booed when he appeared at the engineering school. This prominent figure was the perfect caricature of a Party politician; always motivated by an obtuse dogmatism, Kociolek was frequently shoved out of the picture by his superiors, only to reappear on the political scene when the "hard-liners" needed a scapegoat when they mounted their counteroffensive against the social changes of the early 1980s.

A wave of meetings had swept over the entire country in March of 1968 to signal official disapproval of the student protestors. In like manner, a few years later, we would be "invited" to beat up the workers of Radom and Ursus, whom the authorities were denouncing as "idlers." For the moment, however, the shipyard scheduled a meeting intended to make up for the poor reception Kociolek had met with at the engineering school. The organizers meant to play it safe, so the Shipyard Party Committee printed up and distributed diagrams showing where everyone would be sitting in the auditorium: the front seats were reserved, as usual, for guests from Okopowa Street,[3] who had no real connection with the shipyard. There followed, in the prescribed order, a Party secretary, a worker, a foreman, and so on for each workshop. We were perfectly aware of what was going on, so I urged our crew to boycott the meeting. But events took their own course. Kociolek had hardly begun his speech when a great many workers burst into the hall through two doors that had been left open for ventilation. Driven by curiosity, the men had been gathering outside for a few minutes, but when they heard "Comrades, our Party—," they broke into jeers and catcalls. Kociolek couldn't control the situation and, once again, he proved to be a total failure.

You could say that March 1968 marked my initiation into politics. I saw the same base behavior at the shipyard as I had seen at Lenie or Popowo, the same deceptions, the same scramble to look good in the eyes of the powers-that-be, but whereas before everything had been on a reduced scale, involving little more than the reputations of a few people on the make, at the shipyard the stakes were much higher, and the contemptible behavior of the authorities automatically took on a political dimension.

Here's another example: the Gdansk shipyard, renowned throughout the world for its ships, which are highly rated in *Lloyd's Register*, was suddenly renamed "Lenin shipyard." Since this certainly wasn't a good business move, one might suppose that there had to be some important reason behind it, perhaps political pressure from the East. The truth is a lot simpler. Piasecki, the director of the shipyard at that time, had given an ill-advised interview to the newspaper *Polityka*, which specialized, under the editorial lead-

3. The security police have their headquarters on this street.

ership of Mieczyslaw Rakowski, in promoting western-style Polish "managers." Piasecki had rashly boasted about his income, his passion for pleasure boats, and his luxurious tastes, thereby making an enemy of First Secretary Gomulka, who had no use for people who deviated from the life-style he himself favored. Piasecki fell into such disgrace that when a new ship was launched at the yard one day, not a single important dignitary showed up. Piasecki had simply ceased to exist. That's when he decided to counterattack by sticking Lenin's name onto the shipyard. The yard became the Lenin shipyard, and since the higher-ups couldn't very well ignore the rechristening ceremony, Piasecki made it back into favor.

Management style would vary according to circumstances: they put the screws on, then they'd ease up a bit. They were constantly trying to gauge the mood among the workers, and they rarely overstepped the limits of what people would put up with. For example, after the accident in the holds of the *Konopnicka*, funds were released to placate the work crews, who refused to return to their jobs on the damaged ship. Almost every crew had lost a man in the fire. Hourly wages were increased and certain jobs were pegged at a higher rate. These raises were supposed to make us forget the twenty-two victims.

At other times, management introduced incentive programs to increase productivity, but always without necessary technical improvements and new equipment. The workers were not deceived and reacted defensively: production fell during regular work hours, and the men spent the day milling around looking for tools or materials, getting ready to work overtime. The result was long afternoons and evenings of senseless labor that, if better organized, might easily have been taken care of during the normal working day. Poor management finally wore out even the best men. Drinking on the job picked up again, and since we were checked at the gates to prevent us from sneaking in alcohol from outside, the men started making it right in the shipyard. There's no limit to human ingenuity in these situations. While the workshops were being searched for hidden stills, alcohol was being produced in the most unlikely places: on the top of construction cranes, for example!

When top management heard about this state of affairs, they decided to "shake up" the shop foremen instead of dealing with the root of the problem. So one fine day, all the foremen were replaced. They weren't fired, simply switched from one position to another. This game cost one foreman his job: as in musical chairs, you have to grab a seat quickly or be left out. He didn't move fast enough, I thought, even though he was a well-qualified specialist. I later learned he was laid off, not because of slow reaction, but because of his Jewish background. An "anti-Zionist" purge had begun in March by order of the authorities.

The atmosphere at work then went from bad to worse. Nobody felt safe. There was a climate of uncertainty everywhere. The workers wanted real bosses, men they could trust and respect, for whom they might sometimes be willing to make an extra effort, on a man-to-man basis, something they wouldn't do for distant higher-ups. One no longer heard statements like: "Chief, I wouldn't have done this for anyone but you." Bonds were being broken, and at a very bad time. December 1970 wasn't far off.

In the last months of 1969, my personal life claimed an unusual amount of my time and energy. There was my marriage to Danuta, an attempt to renew ties with my family, and the search for a new place to live, since we were about to outgrow our old place. Danuta had decided right from the start that we'd have a large family. As you know, there had always been lots of children on my side of the family, and I saw no reason to break with that tradition. We were ready to accept as many kids as God saw fit to send us, at least as many as we could feed. What with all the cares of daily life, I couldn't help feeling more and more out of touch with my relatives in Popowo. We didn't have enough money to visit our respective families very often, and our home in the city was much too small to invite them to come and stay with us. So life seemed to be putting more and more distance between them and us, and we were growing apart.

In the final months of 1969 and the early part of 1970, all we heard about was that the production quotas hadn't been met. We didn't pay much attention at first, presuming that this was all propaganda to get us to work faster. Those slogans had lost their meaning and effect. Christening ships with names like *Soldek*, *Makowski Brigade*,[4] *Unity*, and *Workers* which aroused some enthusiasm at one time, was now old hat. Especially since the idea of Stachanovism[5] had never gone down too well in the shipyard, where the prevailing attitude was hardly supportive of the Party system. The yard's club for young people, the ZMS (Association of Socialist Youth), was another symbol that made the workers' blood boil. It was pure fiction, since the youth group couldn't sign up more than five percent of the shipyard personnel, but when there was a launching ceremony, the ZMS got all the attention. There they'd be, sitting in the front row, showered with medals! As if that wasn't enough, membership in that organization gave its members priority in obtaining housing, or even land to build on, and then the ZMS co-op would help them finance a small house at a good price. So a few workers were rewarded for keeping a puppet organization going. The rest of them were fed up with this kind of special privilege and political hogwash: they knew they were paying for it with their own blood. Men like my coworkers in the Mosinski brigade had to travel long distances to and from work, year after year, and had little to show for their hard labor, with little possibility of finding lodgings in Gdansk, or of being able to raise a family. Human dignity and the chance to be fully responsible for one's own life were not available options. We were constantly treated like simple day laborers, and force-fed slogans we couldn't relate to.

It was no secret to anyone that our production schedule was inflated at year's end. We always slipped in a vessel that wasn't completely finished so that we could claim one hundred percent fulfillment of our planned objective. This ship might still lack some equipment that hadn't been delivered on time, for example, because the railway was having problems with ice on the rails somewhere in Silesia. Deals were made, management would work things out with the client: if they'd agree to confirm delivery of the ship on December 31, we'd give them a color television or something

4. The names of workers honored as "Heroes of Labor."
5. A movement begun in 1935 by Aleksy Grigorievich Stachanov in the Soviet Union, which aimed at increasing productivity without proportional compensation for the workers.

similar. And that's what was done with the Russians, our biggest clients. The ship would be finished five or six days later, and everything would be back on track. These "adjustments" weren't usually any more serious than that, even if it did mean running a little late on the next job and creating the same situation at the end of the following year. But by February 1970, things were different. We were ten to twenty percent short on our production plan. Besides which, vessels still under construction hadn't been closed up before winter, which was absolutely essential if finishing work was to continue through the cold weather. To everyone's surprise, this time the production plan was completely compromised.

Even today, it's completely unclear whether the "shake-up" of shop foremen and the ensuing deterioration of morale, plus the hiring of two hundred new men hastily divided up among the work brigades in late 1970, was done out of stupidity or after deliberate decisions. Perhaps, just perhaps, the workers were being used as a political cat's-paw, to facilitate the replacement of Gomulka's men with Gierek's team. Later on, reflecting back on that period, some people remembered that most of the two hundred men hired in November turned up at the forefront of the movement that led the workers into the streets during the strike in December 1970. Was I aware of this at the time? I have to admit that I didn't see the connection then. Poland's crises seem to be characterized by the simultaneous realization, on the part of both society and government, that things have got to change. The problem is that each side wants different changes, and they don't share the same aspirations for long: just long enough, in fact, to complete the usual power shuffle. No one has time to articulate aspirations anyway; things happen too fast, there's just panic. Lots of problems are more or less left to chance, and end up falling by the wayside. You never know when you start something how things will turn out. Arguments fly thick and fast, everyone hopes to get what he wants before it's too late, because he knows that the opportunity for change is short-lived, and that soon we'll all be back in the stranglehold that has held us in thrall for forty years now, effectively stifling all meaningful discussion and real political action. That explains why in 1980, ten years after the explosive events of December 1970, workers weren't interested in finding out which flunky was coming out on top higher up, concentrating instead on the question of their own union, a union that would defend them against whoever was in power in the future. During the sixteen months following August 1980, for the first time in the history of working-class Poland, we were able to take charge of our own problems instead of being helpless dupes, mere pawns in the power struggles of others. Despite the need for profound reforms in Poland, the authorities continue to waste three-quarters of their efforts on the usual shuffling around of officials in top jobs and the other quarter on buttering up Moscow. But I am getting ahead of myself.

In Poland, the events of December 1970 represented the last phase of social revolution on a national scale to have been inspired by old models we were taught to revere. In fact, we sang the *Internationale* because there weren't any other songs capable of expressing the anger of a workers' insurrection in contemporary Europe. All our models came from the East; in speaking of December 1970, people would say: "It was a Kronstadt,"[6] with scenes "like in a film by Eisenstein." And yet, it seemed that no one wanted the events in Poland to be a rehash of someone else's history. On the contrary, we wanted to make our own way, the Polish way, and we tried desperately to find someone in the power structure who would understand our needs. Yet, what we ran into was a wall of fear, rage, and impotence, a complete absence of will at the top, and a government's total inability to understand or discuss our demands. In the end, we were obliged to take to the streets to make ourselves heard.

6. The 1921 uprising in the Soviet naval base on the Baltic Sea, in which the sailors' demands—for elections by secret ballot, freedom of speech, press, and assembly, and the release of political prisoners—were rejected by the central authorities. The sailors were massacred.

December 1970

We went on strike when, just before Christmas, the government announced a rise in the price of basic commodities, including food. It was a time when people were already struggling to make ends meet and the price rises hit hard, though it was the young, less well paid, who were the most affected. The government's move provoked unanimous protest.

On Saturday, December 12, Party officials turned up in different teams to read out the memo issued by the Politburo, and addressed to Party members, on the subject of the price rises, which was then supposed to be followed by a so-called debate. No such thing took place: a woman stood up (she worked as an engine driver) and said that times had been less hard under Hitler, that she didn't know how she was going to manage, since she had three children and a fixed salary. (Piecework allowed people to swallow each price rise more easily; the management would say "Okay, men, let's take on a bit more work and you'll make it up again.") But an engine driver got his 1,859 zlotys a month (in 1970, about $18.00), and not a penny more. Nobody added anything. The woman was crying now.

The strike at the shipyard broke out on Monday. It started in the engineering workshops and the hulls. The people working there had trained at the Zülzer works in Switzerland and at the Baumeister works in Denmark. They were the elite of the shipyard, highly skilled and experienced men, who formed a perfectly organized team. The engine drivers (there were about thirty of them) earned a pittance and were among the prime movers of the strike.

One of their jobs was to distribute the coffee around the workshops during the morning break: a perfect opportunity to distribute the password for the strike at the same time.

After the break, the entire workforce went over to the management's offices, where they began negotiating through the window. Clearly, the director could only speak to the few rows of workers, but once loudspeakers had been connected, the rest of the crowd joined in, shouting out questions about what was going to happen next, and how everyone was going to manage. The workers demanded to speak to a representative of the local authorities, but none of them was willing to come over. So they went themselves to the office of the Party District Committee, singing on the way the national anthem, "Poland has not perished," the "Internationale," and "God protect Poland." This crowd, by now several thousand strong, was greeted by one of the deputy secretaries of the Party committee, since the first secretary was away from Gdansk at a Party plenary meeting in Warsaw. A few preliminaries were exchanged and then a wave of shouts ending with, "Give us bread!," rose up. The crowd demanded the dismissal of those responsible for the economic policy, and called also for changes in the organization of the trade unions. Then a loudspeaker car approached, summoned by the District Committee. The deputy secretary took over the speaker, vainly exhorting the demonstrators to go back to work. They overwhelmed the loudspeaker car and took it over, turning it into a free rostrum. They drove it first to the shipyard, and then to the engineering school, where the workers apologized to the students for having failed to support their protest in March 1968, calling on them now to join their strike. The first clashes with the militia followed: there were arrests and a number of people were injured.

That Monday, December 14, our brigade had the day off as we had just finished work on one hull and were about to be transferred to another one. I was in the city shopping for a baby carriage for Bogdan, our first son. On Tuesday I turned up for work at 6:30 A.M. with everyone else. Lesniewski, our workshop leader, was doing his best, with the help of the foremen, to get us back to our posts. But just at that moment, the men from other shops went past, urging us to follow them to the management offices. At that point Lesniewski gave up trying to cajole his men back on to the ship and, with a mere "If that's what you want . . . do what you like!," he withdrew into his office, slamming the door behind him. We immediately joined up with the men working on the hulls and set off together toward the management offices. We were about four thousand strong, maybe more. It all started in a fairly light-hearted manner: Zaczek, the shipyard director, opened his office window and said in a jovial tone, "Good day to you, glad to see you again . . . ," and everyone laughed, relieving the tension. It's true that the reasons for the strike were not linked directly to the situation in the shipyard. Nonetheless, the crowd gathered there soon began to chant their demands, answered by the director, who was standing at his window with Jerzy Pienkowski, first secretary of the Shipyard Party Committee. It was freezing outside and there was snow on the ground. The crowd began demanding the release of those arrested by the militia: it turned out that one group that had visited the Party District Committee the day before hadn't returned, and rumors were circulating.

It was later that morning, if I remember correctly, that Pienkowski released a devastating piece of news. According to him, a German flag had been raised at Holm, the island near Gdansk where the Germans had built submarines during the war, and where we now had our supply depot. He said, "The Germans have landed and the German flag has been raised," providing a glimpse of a phony management scenario to be reproduced later. I leaped forward: "Listen, it's a trick. A smokescreen. What landing? What Germans? What are these daydreams?" It was clear that Pienkowski was plotting something while he distracted us, and with the rest of the Shipyard Party Committee, he had thrown on a brand new set of work overalls. It was terribly funny: the members of the committee disguised in overalls in order to pass as workers! They were easily recognized: their overalls were spic and span whereas ours were worn and dirty. They were up to their old tricks again.

At last a few of us decided to go and find the yard's director. We went up to his window so that we could be seen and heard from the courtyard below. The director asked us what it was we wanted exactly. I asked if he was able to secure the release of the workers arrested on the previous day, and get the rise in food prices rescinded. He replied that he could do neither. I asked him again if he intended to satisfy our demands; his answer was "No."

There was a loudspeaker in his office. I grabbed it to relay what I had just heard to the crowd. And I asked, "What do we do now?" The men below shouted, "Let's go there now!," and the whole crowd slowly began to move off. I was still in the director's office (there were between five and eight of us) and was just about to leave when the director closed the door with his foot, saying, "I see that the crowd listens to you more than to me. . . . Let's come to an agreement, we'll give you money. . . . Try and hold them back, and if they still insist on going on strike, try to restrain them."

"Give all those outside some money, and if there's any left over, you can settle up with me and my colleagues here as well," I answered. His reply to this was: "We can pay you something, but not them down there."

I opened the door, ran out and caught up with the crowd, eventually pushing to the front of the marchers.

Behind the shipyard lay the garages of the intercity transports. I was marching about five yards in front of the procession when, suddenly, I saw the militia bursting out on us. There were about thirty of them, brandishing their night sticks. I thought I'd had it now: I had nothing to defend myself with, and there was no way of retreating. I was sure that the men behind me had seen me hesitate. I breathed deeply. Suddenly, I felt something like a great gasp of exhaled breath blowing from the crowd at my back; incredible as it may seem, I felt that breath physically and it was as if I was carried forward by it. Two or three minutes later, the militia had been overwhelmed. Only three or four of them managed to turn around and get away from the charging crowd by jumping over a barrier.

We kept on advancing. On reaching the Party District Committee building, we saw four men rush out and jump into cars, Volgas I think, which roared off at top speed. Once at the building, we found the committee door closed, slammed shut by the last fugitive. I glanced through a window and saw some soldiers inside standing stock-still, armed with machine guns but not aiming them at us. Barred doors and nobody to negotiate with: there was no point in our hanging around here. The crowd then split into two:

one group moved toward the militia's headquarters in Swierczew-skiego Street, the other turned back to the place where the militia-men had been routed. When I arrived at the headquarters I realized that the militia, while making a pretense of fighting, were actually hesitating, awaiting instructions. So I then addressed them from the crowd, encouraging them to withdraw if they wanted to avoid getting thrashed by the crowd. They listened quietly, then slowly beat a retreat.

A few minutes later the first group of workers, which had taken a shortcut, had reached the railway bridge. The militia were fol-lowing them but things were looking okay and no serious incidents had occurred as yet. I ran up to the group of militiamen and advised them to move off: there'd been about as many of them in front of the shipyard earlier—about forty men—and we'd got the upper hand there, so why offer resistance? I asked them. All we wanted was to free our fellow workers, we wanted no violence. While I was yelling at them, I ended up in front of their headquarters. I thought that since I was there, I would go and find out who was in charge. I was told that the commandant's office was on the third floor. I ran up the stairs and burst in to find it full of mili-tiamen; they also had a radio transmitter there. I announced that we'd come to fetch our men; if they were released then and there, we wouldn't cause any trouble. It was clear that they agreed.

In the meantime the crowd was massing in front of the building. They began throwing stones and shattered the windowpanes. I was handed a loudspeaker by one of the militiamen and, moving toward the window, I threw out my helmet and my time card so that those below would see that I was a worker. A worker below recognized me and shouted encouragement. I urged them to stop and told them that the militia had agreed to release our men without a fight but, since I didn't know who the detained men were, I asked for someone who did to come up and help me.

As a number of militiamen joined me at the window, events down below took an ugly turn. The commandant probably hadn't had time to give the order to retreat and militiamen from other floors poured into the courtyard below me, surrounding the work-ers. I heard men yelling, "Traitor, dirty bastard!" at me, convinced that I'd tricked them. Within seconds, hundreds of stones were thrown at the windows, taking by surprise the militiamen standing close to me. A number were injured and blood began to flow. I wasn't hit, but I realized then that I'd just lost the battle, and I had to get out of there fast. It was a terrible scramble, the floor covered with broken glass, stones, and injured militiamen.

People were still yelling that I'd tricked them, that I was a double agent, a spy. The militia then began throwing smoke bombs, which the crowd caught in mid-flight and threw back through the broken windows. There was smoke everywhere and it was becoming impossible to breathe. I had to get out, but the door behind had been barred by departing militiamen. Then I remembered that I had a universal wrench on me, which I first used to loosen windowframes on the other side, enabling me to breathe more easily. Then, still carrying the loudspeaker, I slipped out of the room, using my wrench, and went downstairs. The door at the bottom was locked, but its pane was smashed and, since it opened onto the back of the building, I was able to climb out through it. A few steps later, just as I was passing a vendor's kiosk, someone shouted, "You see, the man—the worker up there? He's failed us." I realized he was speaking of me.

While I was escaping, one of the militiamen lost his nerve and on his way toward the town hall, he drew his pistol to threaten a young shipyard worker who was barring his route and shot him. The crowd quickly lynched and killed the militiaman, creating another victim. There were many more to come.

Battered and utterly exhausted, I set off for Suchanin Street, where I lived. On the way, I stopped a van, and begged the driver to drop me off near my home. The man, who was trembling like a leaf, told me he'd just been threatened with a pistol. He asked me if I too was armed and I answered no, that I was on my last legs. He didn't appear to believe me, but, still shaking, he drove me home.

In the meantime, confrontations with the militia continued. A few hours after the assault on the seat of the Party Committee, both army and militia units surrendered. The soldiers were allowed to leave, but the militia were loaded onto trucks and escorted to the shipyard by workers waving the red and white flag of Poland. The militiamen were made prisoners of war, and their belts and caps, the emblems of their power, were removed from them. Then they were made to gather in front of the management building, nobody quite knowing what to do with them. At that point, I was later told, the Party Secretary appeared and, taking advantage of the chaos, he quietly led the militiamen into the shelter of the building. Even in the eyes of any who might still have been in doubt, it was now abundantly clear which side the management was on. At the same time, news kept arriving about the increasing numbers of workers being arrested and beaten up. This time, the management had lined up squarely with the opposing camp, a fact which hadn't been so obvious at the start of the riots.

By the early afternoon, two army tanks drove through the ship-yard's perimeter; one of them had run down a man in front of Gdansk station. Capturing them, the workers said later, was a bit like taking part in a film. The men stuck mud onto the slits of the tanks, which then advanced blindly some distance before coming to a standstill. The drivers were then forced to open their turrets, which was what the demonstrators had been waiting for, and they grabbed them. There were other ways of immobilizing a tank. In the town center, enormous garbage pails were anchored to heavy metal pipes; by sliding them quickly under the tank's tracks, then raising the pipes, the tanks were made to scrabble helplessly in thin air. Some of the men who had done their military service showed great aptitude in this and other acts of sabotage. Those who had served in armored car outfits took over the two captured tanks, driving them into positions in front of the second entrance to the shipyard.

I wasn't able to stay put at home for long. By 1:30 P.M., I had returned to the militia's headquarters. Either the militia had managed to disperse the crowd, or people had scattered on their own accord. The building was on fire. I noticed a food shop with its door smashed in, and as I passed by, I saw that it was crowded with people stuffing themselves with food and drink. The situation was getting dangerous: if people were starting to drink heavily, the first rabble-rouser to appear would have no trouble inciting the crowd to violence. Something had to be done quickly. I went back to the militia's headquarters on Swierczewskiego Street and spoke to one of the chief officers. I asked him what the authorities meant to do. He didn't know, but referred me to someone else who, he said, would be able to give me an answer. This man was a civilian. I asked the same question, again pointing out that people were starting to drink, some just waiting to make trouble. "We're dealing with it," he answered, pointing to the ammunition he was in process of distributing: cardboard boxes containing twenty-four rounds apiece. I was horrified: Poles preparing to fire on Poles? He wanted to know how else they could cope with the situation, what other solution I foresaw. I had to think of a speedy answer and said that what we needed was to organize ourselves. A group of workers from the yard, members of the old guard, would have to go around the town, on foot or in a car, with a loudspeaker, telling other workers to assemble at their place of work prepared to choose delegates who could open negotiations with the authorities. After listening to me, the civilian agreed to suspend preparations for his operation.

On the way back to the shipyard, I bumped into a friend who promptly ran off. That made it two people who had scampered away at the sight of me. I'd met the first one near the hospital, and when I asked him what was up I learned that there was a rumor going around that I'd been killed while at the militia's headquarters. I asked him to help me, to go around the town getting together the men from our team. He refused, telling me that I was out of my mind and that, as likely as not, I'd get a bottle rammed down my throat for my suggestion. I went to the shipyard alone. Nobody agreed to join me. In the meantime, the idea was circulating among the militia and they were announcing through loudspeakers that we were going to have to elect delegates. Meetings were swiftly organized in all the workshops. When I got back to my own, my coworkers chose me as their delegate. All the delegates then met up in the management office to choose a strike committee. I was proposed as a candidate for the overall committee, which was to consist of only three members. I don't remember who the other two were. We each had to talk about our experience at the yard, our ideas and suggestions for the future, so that one of us could be elected president of the committee. I felt I could speak the minds of the workers, and some hours later they had in fact elected me president. When I rose to thank the delegates for their vote of confidence, the director, who was sitting on my left, held me back by my jacket and whispered in my ear:

"You're young and inexperienced, and you'll make mistakes. Don't let them elect you alone. Share the responsibility between the three of you. On your own, you'll only mess things up." It seemed the room was full of people muttering that I wouldn't be able to cope. When I finally managed to disengage myself, I thanked them for their trust but said we'd share the responsibility between the three of us, adding what the director had whispered to me: that I was too young, that I ran the risk of making mistakes. That was my first false step. I was only twenty-seven at the time and I dreaded taking on the responsibility. The old fox had felt me hesitate and had held me back for just a second, but it had been enough. I had refused to take over the leadership of the strike on my own and it was led instead by a team which was forever changing its mind, which had no coherent strategy, and which proved too soft during the negotiations. We were, in short, a failure.

After the elections, we agreed to meet the next morning in the director's office. Some of the shipyard employees stayed put and the rest went home. Late that Tuesday evening, I was walking to my workshop when someone grabbed my hand and drew me into a little side room, saying, "Don't turn up at the strike committee tomorrow. If you do, you know what you'll get . . . if you're determined to turn up in spite of everything, be sure not to intervene, except to say what we want you to say. But it would be best if you didn't go at all." I answered that I would be there as arranged and that—guessing that they were SB infiltrators—I would repeat in front of everyone what I had just heard, word for word.

Because we were worried about the possibility of provocation, the strike committee and the management of the different workshops had set up night watches. As the committee representative, I was on guard at our workshop (shop 4), with Marian Firmant representing the management. Everything was quiet by midnight. We got out some old sheepskin coats and work jackets and were lying down. Sometime after 2:00 A.M., the foreman called out to us, "Workshop leaders and delegates are to go to the Health and Safety Office at 3:00 A.M." We rushed off a few minutes later. Zaczek, the director, was there, together with the entire shipyard management team, the leaders of the various workshops and, of course, the members of the strike committee. We were handed copies of the *Glos Wybrzeza* (the *Voice of the Coast*) fresh from the presses and dated Wednesday, which gave the authorities' account of the riots. The meeting lasted only fifteen minutes. "The shipyard is surrounded by the army," Zaczek told us. "The authorities have decided to fire on sight. You are free to strike if you want, but only within the shipyard perimeter. You are forbidden to go outside. Otherwise the army will open fire and your blood will flow!"

I was sure that he just wanted to frighten us. On the way back to the workshop, Firmant and I went up to the main gate. They were there. I could scarcely believe my eyes. There was no question of sleeping anymore. We sat up and waited for the dawn.

At about 5:30 A.M. Wednesday morning, I went to the management office, as agreed, but the two other members elected by the strike committee didn't turn up. They'd probably been scared off. Finding myself on my own there, I went back to the workshop. I hadn't the slightest notion of how to manage a strike; I was out of my depth.

The workers began arriving. They confirmed that the army was all around us at the first, second, and third entrances; the yard was cut off. Troops were also occupying all the nearby streets. Roads in the vicinity of the district and railway hospitals, and leading to the offices of the Ministry of Internal Affairs, were blocked with tanks. People reacted in different ways, but most of them began whistling at the soldiers outside. A woman, I later was told, went up to them yelling, "You kids going to shoot us all down, then?" By this time something in us had just snapped. It's hard to describe how people felt: it was a mixture of despair, desire for revenge, and a confused sense of impunity. Most people didn't believe that the army or security forces were really getting ready to attack the workers, or that the decision to fire would be made. In our workshop, we were doing everything in our power to stop the workers from leaving the yard. Elsewhere things were different. A number of groups were already gathering near one exit with the intention of bursting through the gates into the street, which was, of course, impossible. Lesniewski, our workshop leader, Lenarciak, Suszko, and I all went to see Zaczek. We wanted to negotiate with the district officers of the militia and the security forces to prevent their troops from opening fire, but he was unable to get through to them by telephone. The management, in any case, was reluctant to take any initiative, preferring to wash its hands of the whole business.

On returning to the workshop, I heard a burst of gunfire. The crowd froze. Seen from above, it looked like an amoeba whose incessant flow is suddenly petrified.

I thought at first that they'd only fired blanks, and I went on back to the management office. But crossing the path to the second entrance, I saw through a cloud of dust what looked like a flock of sheep fleeing; bent over like lambs in the fog, workers were crawling on all fours to avoid the bullets; others were pinned to the ground. Eyewitness accounts of what had happened were garbled and frightening. A stormy meeting had been held on the walkway in front of the management building. A number of workers had apparently been curious to learn what was going on and had squeezed against the front ranks, who were pushed closer and closer to the army cordon. One worker then stepped out of the crowd and spoke to the soldiers. The people behind him couldn't hear what he was saying and pushed closer; it must have looked as if the front rows were advancing. The workers strained to get a better look to make sure the men in uniform were Poles, not Russians in disguise. An officer gave the order to charge; people began to panic; inevitably, a burst of machine gun fire answered the shouts of panicked workers.

My worst fears had been realized: Poles *had* fired against Poles. Three people had been killed (one from our workshop) and a fourth died on his way to the hospital. Only minutes later, we raised a flag with black ribbons attached, a sign of mourning, and over the entrance gate we hung flags at half-mast, along with the murdered workers' helmets draped in black crepe. We then sang the national anthem, laying particular stress on the words: "We'll recover with the sword what the enemy forces have taken from us." Loudspeakers had been set up on the gate so that the government pawns could hear what we had to say, and we began the chant, "Murderers! Murderers! . . ."

Slowly, we began trying to organize ourselves, electing committee after committee in chaotic fashion. Workers didn't know one another, having been separated from their work teams, and were suspicious. We drew up a list of scores of grievances, before realizing that the management was only getting us to do this in order to keep us busy and distract us while they organized their assault force. Zaczek kept on repeating that if we hadn't vacated the shipyard by ten or eleven o'clock that morning, the tanks would burst in to begin shelling the yard's interior.

We learned that armored cars, tanks, and army cordons had also taken up positions around the other shipyards in the Tri-City region. Their guns were pointing at our workshops, spurring workers to take up their defense. The men in the welding workshop even went so far as to devise a method for blowing up a tank with the help of an acetylene bomb, while others constructed missile-launchers out of blocked pipes. One of these homemade mortars landed in the middle of the nearby Northern shipyard.

There were very few of us who really wanted to battle the troops, despite the foolhardy taunts of excited workers. We had a radio transmitter by this time, and were thinking of making an appeal to the West. We even envisaged appealing to the USSR, calling on them to come to help the persecuted workers. We did neither.

The militia had cordoned us off from the town, but anxious families had begun to collect close by the shipyard gates. It was an impossible situation. The workers' morale was low—we were disorganized—facts that didn't escape the director's notice during his latest tour around the workshops. We were finally shouted down when we asked for a strike vote, and the decision was made to abandon the yard. "All grievances will be taken into account, but everyone must leave," the militia commandant announced. In the hall where the voting had taken place, workers were weeping. Most saw the decision as a betrayal, though they also understood that it would probably prevent the loss of more lives. Twenty thousand of us—not six, which was the official figure—left the yard through lines of soldiers and militiamen. It seemed to take hours for the immense regiment of workers to walk away from the yard.

I went home, my "shadow" already close on my heels.

The people of nearby Gdynia had greater cause than most to remember the events of December, not surprisingly, since they suffered the largest number of casualties during the riots and were victims of a particularly insidious deception on the part of the authorities. People tend to overlook the fact that it was at Gdynia that the first agreement was signed between a strike committee and the authorities in the entire history of Poland. On Tuesday, December 15, a crowd of striking workers gathered in front of the local Party office in Gdynia. Having waited in vain for the grievances to be heard, they then regrouped in front of the Presidium of the Municipal National Council (PMRN) for the city of Gdynia. Jan Marianski, then president of PMRN, contacted Tadeusz Bejm, president of the District National Council, who agreed to pass on the entire list of grievances, drawn up at the start of the strike, to Stanislaw Kociolek, the deputy premier. He then signed a protocol of the agreement with the worker delegates. At midnight, that same day, the members of the Inter-enterprise Strike Committee of Gdynia (as it was henceforth known) were arrested.

A succession of dramatic events followed, which have imprinted themselves in the memory of the people of Gdynia. Workers were killed by machine gunfire on their way to work; the body of a murdered youth was carried around the town on a doorframe—the inspiration for an image in a Wajda film made later; people were arrested and imprisoned in the cellars of the PMRN building; the militia buried their victims in secret, by night.

Since then, every year on December 17, Father Hilary Jastak says mass in the Church of the Sacred Heart, probably the only place in Poland where this date is commemorated so faithfully.

At Szczecin, on December 17, the workers at the Warski yard, having heard of the bloody riots in Gdansk, walked out and, about an hour later, their neighbors at the Gryfia yard followed suit. Walasek, the first secretary for the district, had ample warning of the strike and he and his colleagues had packed up their things and left the Party's district offices by the time the workers had arrived. The workers sacked the empty building and set it on fire. Then they laid siege to the militia's district headquarters and the building of the District Council of Trade Unions, setting fire to both buildings. Shops were looted and clashes with army and militia continued well into the night, at which point tanks were stationed at the nerve centers of the town, with heavy reinforcements standing by in front of the Warski yard.

On December 18, a strike and sit-in was announced in the two shipyards, and strike committees were elected. The list of twenty-one demands which they drew up included the following:

1. the dissolution of the Central Council of Trade Unions;
2. the creation of independent trade unions;
3. the reduction of prices to their previous level;
4. a thirty percent pay raise.

The whole city then went on strike, the Warski shipyard acting as a focal point for strikers and supporters of the movement. On December 19 and 20, negotiations with the district authorities took place, delegates from two of the shipyards representing all the other yards. The talks took place outside the shipyards, at the headquarters of the District National Council. On December 20, agreements were drawn up in the hope of putting an end to the strike, but in such a watered-down form that they were rejected by the majority of the strikers, and the strike erupted again: at the Warski yard the workers split into two camps and around a thousand of them went home. (That night, the strike committee co-opted five new members, one of whom was Edmunt Baluka.)

But the Warski strike ended on the 22nd, at ten in the morning: the strikers were exhausted and Christmas was drawing near; from the workers' point of view, this strike, too, had been a total failure.

Two more strike attempts on January 11 and 18 failed. On the 20th, a delegation set off for the Tri-City in an effort to make contact with the strikers there, but was stopped by the Gdansk authorities. On January 22, the strike broke out again at the Warski yard, under the leadership of Edmund Baluka, and received the immediate support of the citizens of Szczecin. The district authorities were determined to stamp out the trouble and sent in the army to surround the shipyard, still considered the major point of opposition. Leaflets were dropped on the town by helicopter, stating that a small group of terrorists was holding the workers by force. On the 23rd, the strike committee sent the new first secretary, Edward Gierek, a letter explaining the movement's aims and asking him to come to the shipyard. Gierek arrived on the 24th, accompanied by Minister of Internal Affairs Szlachcic, Premier Jaroszewicz, and Defense Minister Jaruzelski. The meeting lasted nine hours and the discussions were relayed by speaker throughout the whole yard. By oral agreement, later confirmed in writing, the strike committee was turned into a workers' commission with the task of supervising new elections to the trade unions and the Shipyard Party Committee. The commission was to cease its activities on February 14. Though Gierek had rescinded some of the December price increases, he had managed to convince the Warski workers that it was impossible to lower prices further. But a February strike by women workers at the Lodz spinning mills finally turned the tables: on the fourth day of their strike, the authorities gave in and agreed to reinstate the prices as they were before December 12, 1970.

Danuta

The days of December 1970 are linked in my memory with our baby, our first son, then only a few weeks old. That Monday, Lech went to buy him a carriage. On Tuesday, he came home at lunchtime. We were then living in Suchanin Street, with Mrs. Pujszowa. He was wearing his helmet, his overalls, and his work jacket. He told me that all kinds of dramatic things were happening in Gdansk, and that the streets were running with blood. The next day he came home rather later, after four o'clock, and said he was being followed. I remember that we wanted to go and watch a film on our neighbor's television. Just before we left, two men came to our apartment to take Lech away. He took off his wedding ring and his watch, telling me to sell them if I ran out of money. He also told me not to worry, that it would all be all right, that people would help me.

That Saturday, one of Lech's colleagues came to the house and spoke of the changes which were about to take place in the government. He added that Lech would certainly be released when this happened. That Sunday, he was at home with us again. He didn't say anything about what they'd wanted from him or where he'd been locked up. Nothing at all. I think he didn't want to worry me.

I told my wife nothing. I didn't say a word to anyone. It's true they did interrogate me and that I declared—and this was recorded in black and white—that if they didn't agree to the creation of genuine worker organizations, capable of interpreting and controlling what was really happening, they'd soon be seeing quite a different scenario. It's also true that I didn't leave with my hands entirely clean: they said, "Sign!" and I signed the document they shoved in front of me. It was a so-called "Certificate of Loyalty" (*Lojalka*) to the state, and eleven years later (February 1981), during martial law, every internee had to sign it before being freed.

December 1970 was a disaster for us. It had been above all a conflict decided by force. And yet for the workers at the Gdansk, Gdynia, and Szczecin yards, myself included, it provided an incomparable experience, enabling us to understand what makes them behave the way they do in a crisis. And it convinced us that we would have to find other solutions.

A number of questions remained unanswered. We didn't know what had happened to those who'd been interned, we didn't know who was responsible for "pacifying" Gdansk, Gdynia, Elblag, and Szczecin, or where exactly the massacres had taken place. According to the official statement by the public prosecutor, forty-five people had been killed in these four cities. But a rumor was circulating that the number of dead was much higher, in the hundreds, and the newspapers also hinted that several hundred more lay wounded in the hospitals.

From the beginning of the December tragedy, the Polish church had been doing all it could to support the workers. Priests everywhere read from their pulpits a letter from the General Council of Polish Bishops addressed "To all our compatriots," and a month later, the bishops summoned the whole nation to a "prayer for their country." In parishes and provinces with large worker populations, the priests proceeded to gather information about people who had disappeared or been assassinated, persecuted, or imprisoned, and started a fund for the victims and their families. They drew up a file about mysterious burials at night, carried out in secret by the security forces and where priests had been admitted only on the express request of the families of the dead.

Even before the "changes at the top" had taken place, the managements of the Gdansk and Gdynia yards were ordered to dismiss all those who had gone on strike. At the Paris Commune shipyard in Gdynia, as many as eight hundred people were given the sack, while in Gdansk only eighteen, who were found to be in possession of looted goods, were dismissed (one of them had two bottles of brandy, another a fur cap, stowed away in their tool lockers). The atmosphere at the shipyards was explosive. In January 1971, it was announced that we were to choose delegates for a meeting with Gierek due to take place in Warsaw. Each workshop, led by the foreman and assistant foreman, organized its own elections, free from pressure from the management, which limited itself to issuing news bulletins. In our workshop three delegates were elected: Lenarciak, Mosinski, and myself.

We were collected from the yard by bus and driven to the buildings of the Presidium of the District National Council. The hall was already full of people, starting with top management and staff, and Party members: the various workshops were represented by delegates, workers for the most part. The intelligentsia—engineers and technicians—were in a minority. The date was January 25. Proceedings started with the entrance of Gierek and Szlachcic, together with Tadeusz Fiszbach, first secretary for Gdansk, and Tadeusz Bejm, president of the District National Council.

The session opened with an address by the minister of internal affairs. He began sniveling like a little boy, in essence saying the son of a worker should not have had to witness such events. He said that never again under his ministry would a Pole shoot at another Pole. Noble but unlikely thoughts. He explained how that Wednesday, the day of the shooting at the second entrance to the shipyard, he had been standing behind a cordon of soldiers and militiamen, unable to intervene. He also told us how a delegation of twelve workers had turned up somewhere in Gdansk for a meeting with the authorities, and if he, Szlachcic, hadn't personally intervened, they would quite simply have been beaten to death. More self-justification followed.

A list had been drawn up so that we each could speak in turn. Henryk Lenarciak then rose and cut short all the political bluff with a concrete request: The shipyard workers wanted permission, he said, to build a church at Przymorze, the part of town where most of the employees lived. Gierek was caught short and immediately promised permission. It would be the first large church to be built in Gdansk for many years, in opposition to the official—though unspoken—veto against building churches in the new "socialist" part of the city. The authorities failed to keep many of their promises, but they did keep this one: the church at Przymorze was built and Lenarciak was appointed president of the construction committee.

I remembered this some ten years later, in August 1980, when we were dealing with the construction of the monument in memory of the workers killed in December of 1970. Today I can see things much more clearly: some history does tend to repeat itself! The monument, a great cross and anchor, with metal figures of suffering men at its base, was built, and, once again, Lenarciak was the president of the construction committee. There is a good deal of truth in what someone said on the day we celebrated the first anniversary of the events of August 1980: "This monument is like a harpoon buried in the body of a whale. However much the whale thrashes at it and fights it, she will never be able to tear it out."

After Lenarciak, other Gdansk workers stood up to speak, but when it came to my turn, I was interrupted by workers from Gdynia, who rose to attack the government head-on. One of them shouted that his fiancée had been killed and that her name didn't even figure on the list of dead. The presidium was in turmoil, explanations were demanded, and someone was sent to check—they seemed concerned above all with winning time. While we were watching the scene, another young man got up suddenly and said: "Comrade Gierek, you're seeing plenty of death certificates thrown on the table, I don't want to add any more; there's ample proof here how many victims there've been. But let me say I can understand what our colleagues in Gdansk are saying: that street fighting always produces victims, but in Gdynia, we were dealing with people who were in revolt but disciplined, and on the other side, I don't know what to call them . . . maybe they weren't even Poles!" Once again the presidium was in turmoil. The young man recounted the following incident: he'd been near the railway tracks when he'd seen a group of people marching with red and white flags. They were chased and fired on from above. But instead of throwing their flags to the ground, they held them up proudly as they ran. Their pursuers meanwhile threw themselves on the flags, ripped them and shredded the cloth. "I want to ask a question, Comrade First Secretary," he continued, "who were those men who treated the red and white flag in that way? Who educated them? I'm not asking where they went to school, but who trained them?" Everyone in the hall froze with horror. Then Gierek stood up hurriedly and launched into some patriotic drivel.

There was a characteristic moment when Gierek, delivering his critical judgment on Gomulka, declared: "In spite of appearances, Comrade Gomulka did not enjoy good relations with the Soviet Union. From now on, with Comrade Piotr [Jaroszewicz] we're going to improve those relations with the Soviet Union, aren't we, Piotr?" We looked at one another, and it was clear to us that our "great" premier was nothing but a Russian pawn.

After Gierek had finished summing up, at least one of us should have gotten up and said, "That's all very well, Comrade, you're asking us to help you, but tell us now: who are we supposed to be helping?" But nobody did; we all sang the national anthem instead. Anyway, the men didn't have an easy retort to the rhetorical question "Will you help us?" So they answered, "We will help you." And the fact is, we did believe in it; we were bubbling over with enthusiasm, ready for positive action. I still have a photo showing Gierek at the shipyard, with the delegates all grouped around him. We were in the midst of discussions and some journalists had come to interview us. They wanted to present us as the new leaders of the workers but it soon became plain that that was precisely what the authorities wished to avoid: there was to be no celebrity for those who had played such a crucial part in the events of December 1970.

In January we founded a workers' commission, one of whose jobs it was to investigate what the workers considered illegal or unjust dismissals. The three meetings we managed to organize at the shipyards developed into a protest against the economic situation. Gathered in front of the management offices, a bunch of rough workers in dirty coveralls, and painters in overalls spotted with red lead, we seemed to make a bigger impression on the management then than had the events of December.

In town, fighting and looting continued sporadically for weeks, the most dramatic incidents occurring right in front of the shipyard. It is interesting to note, however, that productivity didn't fall and that it might even have increased. In workshop K-3, for instance, the old workers would appoint the young ones as delegates and send them off saying, "Go and brawl with them, you lot, we'll do your work for you." In our workshop, it was always Lenarciak and I who went along; not in answer to any particular summons: we simply turned up in front of the director's office in the morning break. There would just be two or three of us to start with, but within minutes hundreds of others would appear and we would eventually total between fifteen hundred and three thousand. Our meetings always caught the director and management off guard. What we wanted from them were concrete economic proposals. The first two work interruptions were short-lived: they started during the morning break and ended around ten o'clock; the third was the longest, ending around midday. On this occasion the whole shipyard put down their tools; the mood was hostile and led to a number of cars being destroyed and three workers being taken hostage. Those three had apparently sought to provoke a confrontation and drag the men into it, inciting a general row that would allow the government to finish the whole business off once and for all by picking us off, one after the other.

During this period plans for modernizing the shipyard were put into effect. The yard was on its last legs; seventy percent of the equipment and machinery was ready for the scrap heap, and work methods were antiquated. Within the space of a few days there was an abrupt turnabout: the order to modernize the yard was given, plans were drawn up for a recreation center and a holiday house for the workers. We all knew that this was no more than a gesture of reparation designed to "dry our tears." The men were saying, "First they kill our people and then they offer us a playground!" "Better and better!" was the slogan of the day; workers were in for "good times." On our arrival at the site, we were greeted by music from the local radio station; in the locker rooms, the weather forecast informed us whether to put on our padded work clothes or our oilskins. During the next one and a half hours we were treated to a radio program, which had been drawn up according to sociological prescriptions for "humanizing" work at the yard. It reported interesting anecdotes, commented on developments within the yard, announced cultural events and even the results of first and second division soccer matches. Despite these cosmetic changes, things didn't change at all for the workers.

In 1971, just before May Day, there were a number of anti-establishment protests. The carpenters had made black coffins to accompany the May Day parade; the authorities reacted strongly and the workers were arrested. Nevertheless, slogans demanding punishment for those responsible for the massacre of December 1970 still appeared in the parade, and afterwards wreaths were hung on the shipyard wall near to the second entrance, where the workers had been killed. It was the first and last time during the seventies that the authorities refrained from intervening. It has subsequently become an established practice for the shipyard director, the president of the trade union, and the Party secretary to mark the anniversary by buying flowers and walking to the cemetery to lay them on the graves of the victims. The local radio obviously reported that the flowers were an offering from all the employees at the yard. However, every anniversary, a black Volga is parked in front of the second entrance waiting for any worker with the temerity to express his sympathy directly. Official homage, as with most everything else, didn't include the workers' participation. The first to be caught was a foreman in 1973, who had placed a bunch of cyclamen at the foot of the wall; he was immediately whisked off by the men in the Volga and was subsequently given the sack. But the majority of the workers seemed to have forgotten the victims of December 1970; they were more interested in earning money. It was only in 1977 that the RMP (the Young Poland Movement) began commemorating the massacre again.

Nevertheless, members of the various workshops continued to raise money for the families of the victims of December 1970, for the victims of the fire on the ship *Konopnicka*, and for those who'd been beaten up by the militia. There was one particularly brutal incident. A technician named Kopacz had been doing overtime; exhausted, he fell down on the station platform, suffering a concussion. When he was picked up he was taken to the "sobering up room," instead of the hospital. There he was beaten to death. The militia particularly liked raiding the bar Under the Chestnut Tree, where the men tended to meet after work for a glass of beer. Again, the men would be taken to the "sobering up room" and beaten up, sometimes disabled for life: for many years to come the militia continued to take its revenge in this way for the riots of December 1970. Conversely, any of them who ventured into the part of the city where traditionally most of the workers lived, was taking his life in his hands, especially after dusk.

80

For all their drama, those days in December 1970 were an experience which bore no comparison with what happened in August 1980. They were in all respects a solitary drama, cut off from the rest of society and from the international scene. It was my impression that there was a complete lack of solidarity between the different sections of the population, in Gdansk itself and even in many workers' homes. There was a crushing sense of loneliness, fear, and uncertainty about the prospects of our movement, and, in spite of everything, only the forlorn hope that our revolt had been a necessary one. Nor was there any sign of international solidarity. I have often been asked what it was like at the time, whether we felt that trade unionists in other countries were taking an interest in our affairs. No, for us December 1970 was dark and lonely; ours was the type of cause that is lost in advance, where one can count on nothing and nobody. As far as I remember, no one in Poland was aware of any manifestation of international opinion. You might say that we were simply outside the sphere of western interest. Thirty-two million, seven hundred thousand people were in a sense crossed off the map of Europe, although this same Europe had not forgotten armed intervention in 1956 in Hungary, nor the more recent one, 1968, in Czechoslovakia.

Still, the curtain was momentarily raised on the national political scene in a manner both symbolic and involuntary, even grotesque. On Wednesday, December 16, the day of the Gdansk shipyard massacre, Deputy Premier Stanislaw Kociolek called on everybody to go back to work in an address transmitted by radio and television from a Gdansk-Wrzeszcz studio. His speech was suddenly interrupted by a loud crash when a small screen, hastily set up in the studio to serve as a backdrop for the speaker, collapsed. The screen fell down to reveal a soldier standing there in full combat dress, machine gun in hand.

Kociolek's appeal was addressed above all to the workers at the Gdansk and Gdynia shipyards. But it was out of sync with the intentions and instructions of the other decision-making bodies, in particular the army and the militia. On the morning of December 17, thousands of people went to work by train, but at the Gdynia shipyard stop and at the nearby Paris Commune shipyard, gigantic crowds were gathering because access to the shipyards had been barred by tanks. With more and more people arriving, there was no way the crowd could retreat. The tanks fired a warning volley which was immediately followed by a burst of machine gun fire. The massacre had begun.

The coastal newspapers began by publishing political communiqués, including one instituting the curfew—it was forbidden to leave one's home between early evening and dawn—but then, giving way to pressure for real news, they printed accounts that were supposed to give a "true picture of events," a sort of composite chronology reflecting the workers' experiences during the riots and the "official" picture the new team of political leaders wanted presented. A month later, the public prosecutor issued a communiqué publishing the list of dead. The central press then spoke about the hard work that had gone into surmounting the "political crisis," and about the "need to establish firm links with the working class. . . ." The authorities' new team had to be given some leeway, allowed a chance, trusted.

Wages did indeed rise, but only because the number of supplementary work hours increased. In 1972, *each* worker in the shipyard was already working an average of two hundred supplementary hours per year; in 1973 it was three hundred. During the following years, this figure grew steadily, resulting in some cases in six and seven hundred extra hours per worker per year. What this meant in real terms was that people had to get up at four or five in the morning and travel to work on a train packed to the roof, that they slaved away until six or eight in the evening and then went home only to fall asleep in their chairs, in front of a bowl of soup or the television. They worked from dawn till dusk every God-given day and in frightful conditions: in rain, wind, and freezing temperatures, or else in suffocating heat, breathing the fumes given off by lead paints and toxic concentrations of welding gases, deafened by the ceaseless din of the hammers and vibrations of the polishing machines. Anyone who doesn't know what is meant by the expression "rat-men" should come to the shipyard and see how the men crawl on their stomachs with their rust scrubbers inside long pipes just wide enough for a man's body, covered in rust and sweat, or how they creep, armed with their acetylene blowtorches, to work under the tankers' petroleum tanks. Then they'll see what's meant by exhausting, inhuman labor that ruins a man's health. Every year in the Gdansk shipyard alone, the doctors diagnose hundreds and hundreds of temporary or permanent disabilities. The Polish shipyards have certainly been modernized, but with the aim of increasing their production capacity, not of improving working conditions or the health of the workers.

It was in 1975 that a new crisis erupted. This time it wasn't a case of a shortage of ships but of an international fuel shortage. Brazil stopped paying in dollars and offered us coffee in exchange for our ships. The age of "the goose with the golden egg" had come to an end in our country: all foreign payments were blocked! All we had left was trade with our immediate neighbors. We had to sell cheaper and the government began looking for ways to economize at the expense of the workers. After a period in which the shipyards had been allowed a free hand—and even tacit encouragement—in raising wages slightly, matters took a nasty turn and the workers saw all that they'd been granted with one hand taken back with the other. People calculated that if their wages went on diminishing at the same pace, by the year 2016 a shipyard employee would be working for nothing. The men started wandering around the various workshops asking for more work. Signs of animosity and bitterness began to appear: anyone who managed to pick up work for himself and was earning more than the others would become the butt of those frequently forced to be idle or deprived of their overtime. One didn't need to be an economist to be able to draw comparisons, and for a worker a single year was enough: from one Christmas to the next, it became glaringly obvious to him that there was less food on his table than in the previous year. As far as I was concerned, the only tangible advantage I gained from the events of December 1970 and the ensuing changes lay in my duties as a representative at the Health and Safety Office, to which I was elected by the union members in my workshop. We tried our hardest to do something for our men. I argued with the management about the distribution of protective clothing, about soap, towels, any sort of small personal improvement. It was a Sisyphean task, and by the end of the first year I'd grasped the dilemma: it was impossible to achieve anything from down below, while "up there" the same rackets were going on as before. The union, such as it was, merely served as a driving belt: the shortest route for communicating Party directives to the workers, the vast majority of whom weren't even members. That's all its role was, and had been for years: to put pressure on this army of several million workers to work harder, to work and keep quiet and, when necessary, to vote for the Party's candidates.

To understand how the unions worked, one only has to look at the careers of the successive chairmen of the Central Council of the Trade Unions (CRZZ), an organ created at the end of the forties and which served to limit any tendencies to autonomy on the part of the workers. Edward Ochab, a prewar communist, who took over the chairmanship of the CRZZ in 1949, offers a perfect example. He had moved from heading one Party organization to another, eventually becoming president of the State Council.

The official trade unions had thus become the instrument employed to eliminate every possible influence of the world of workers on public affairs, and that in a country supposedly run by the proletariat! The trade unions were expected to participate in the life of the country, but, while the chairman of the CRZZ had to be a member of the highest echelons of the Party, he did not represent the workers there in the slightest.

I was forever getting worked up about the situation, and that notorious "We'll help you" made me foam at the mouth! Lenarciak, on the other hand, was as steady as a rock. He looked after the food supply for his team, solved all manner of problems as they arose: he organized the use of a crane to help us lift a cable that was too heavy, devised methods for drilling holes in the required time, and for carrying out any modifications that our work demanded. We used to collect work vouchers for him to make up for the time he'd lost in sorting all these matters out. He was conciliatory but never obsequious. He knew how to play on the consciences of foremen and management alike; in any event, none of them ever dared to undervalue him, as they did most other workers.

But even Lenarciak couldn't do anything about the lack of work. We electricians had greater opportunity to discuss the situation than those who were working above deck, under constant supervision. We simply had to go down into a cabin, blocking the doorway with a plank, and nobody could find us in that labyrinth. Our discussions focused on the need to create an organization capable of defending us. Unfortunately, we sometimes pursued these discussions in the office of the existing union—it didn't occur to us at the time that these premises might be bugged. In 1976, for example, when the secret police arrested me and repeated, word for word, what I'd just been saying to Lenarciak, I immediately suspected Lenarciak of having sold me out, but then he was picked up too and suspected me of the same thing. That was how they managed to split us up: our determination to create a new union faltered; I told myself that the time hadn't yet come, that we needed to consolidate power first.

I remember the mid and late 1970s as a time of defeat and failure, on every level: social, professional, and moral. We felt we were getting no support whatsoever from the management. December 1970 had been an essentially working-class protest which had resulted in no more than a minor intimidation of the white-collar workers: now they were going to make us pay. Gradually the management got rid of those who had been most active in the strike. I was always being given the worst work, and I was never allowed any kind of promotion. In 1976, seeing that matters were going from bad to worse, and that new uprisings were inevitable, I decided to speak my mind during the campaign for the trade union elections. But I did it very badly, allowing my anger to get the better of me. During the election meeting in my workshop, I called the trade union a union of puppets and denounced the speeded-up launchings of ships as part of our "unpaid work": launching a ship two weeks ahead of the set date merely meant three months spent repairing the damage done by floating the ship prematurely—and all that just so someone could collect crosses and medals. I stressed the lack of firm economic planning and, speaking about the situation in the country as a whole, I pointed out that the changes promised after December 1970 had never come about, that the murderers were still not punished or even known. How was I to know what sort of person I was working alongside? Maybe he was a criminal. I have said Gierek did not keep his promises, he lied to the people. My speech up to that point had been greeted by applause, but then I got carried away and began to shout. My aim had been to speak to this audience in a measured fashion, in order to win their support and gain the opportunity of being elected as delegate at the general elections; but I'd gone over the top—out of control.

Officially, I continued to be my workshop's delegate for the general elections, with my mandate in my pocket. But my trade union career then came to an abrupt halt. I was summoned to the director's office, where the secret police were already waiting for me. They told me to give up my way of talking. Supposing I were elected, would I be prepared to say what they wanted, they asked. No, I replied, I would change every word at the last minute, and speak what was on my mind. Then they threatened me with "falling sick," having to "take a holiday" so that I couldn't turn up at the conference. "Even if I had a fever," I said, "I'd be there." That was the end then. They made a quick phone call, and the guard grabbed my elbows and dragged me to the gate of the shipyard.

I tried another tack, addressing myself to the authorities at the district trade unions office in Kalinowskiego Street. The district representative for the shipyards told me he would intervene in my favor: what more could I ask? But when I went back there to look for my cigarettes, I heard him talking to Lubienski, the president of my shipyard's trade union. He was saying: "Listen, there's a man called Walesa who has been to see me . . . he let slip all kinds of things. What do you think we should do about him?" I knew I'd had it then. I was not dismissed on the spot, I was simply given notice. They went on paying me until April, when I received a letter of dismissal. At the same time, they gave me quite a large sum of money in compensation.

Officially, my dismissal was signed by one of the managers named Piecko, who had succeeded Lesniewski, but the decision had been taken by someone important, probably a member of the Party Executive Committee. Before it was typed out, the text of the minutes of any trade union meeting would be read by the Party secretary, the workshop foreman, and the secretary of the yard's trade union council. Normally, if there was a passage which any of them took objection to, it was quite simply crossed out of the minutes. This time, all three were in agreement and they decided to cite my speech in its entirety and see me punished. Lenarciak, who was still at the yard, wanted to start proceedings, but it wasn't worth the trouble. I'd left the shipyard now; a new chapter in my life was just beginning.

These events in my own life coincided with the announcement in June 1976 of the rise in the prices of basic food products. The atmosphere in the shipyards was stormy. This time, however, it wasn't Gdansk but Radom and Ursus that influenced the course of events in Poland. Things happened there along the same lines as at Gdansk in 1970, but on a smaller scale, and luckily, without the troops opening fire on the crowd, although a number of workers were beaten up by the militia. On the evening of these events, Premier Jaroszewicz appeared on television to withdraw, with bowed head, all the price rises planned for the coming years—each a flagrant breach of contract, which, according to the official version, "followed consultation" with the working class. The only real advisers—the workers of Radom and Ursus—were treated as "troublemakers" and "hooligans"! And the order went out to plants throughout Poland to identify and denounce similar troublemakers.

Danuta and Family:
A New Home

We had been living in the Stogi quarter for four years now. It was a working-class district, on the eastern side of Gdansk, separated from the center by an industrial area and by the Motlawa canal. It was in fact a real town within a town. The tenement buildings on Wrzosy Street, where we lived, were full of people like us, just waiting for things to improve. Adjoining these tenements were tiny plots of land, in whose poor, sandy soil, it was a struggle to get anything to grow. They had sheds on them too, where pigs and chickens were kept. A few yards of woodland separated this district from the beach, the Gdansk *Klondike*, where teams of secret prospectors looked for pockets of amber with the help of water pumps. They conducted an interminable guerrilla warfare with the militia, whose officers were often their accomplices. This business with the amber was exploded when an oil refinery was built on the site, as part of one of Gierek's investment projects. The refinery, which was to transform the crude oil brought here by tankers from the Persian Gulf, was part of a bigger plan to build a new port: the Northern Port. With one wharf designed for coal, another for fuel, this new port was supposed to make us independent of Russia and to guarantee Poland an autonomous role as both importer and exporter. This fine program never got off the ground. When the Arab countries stopped selling us oil, the tankers were laid up, and the fuel wharf lay idle. In Silesia, meanwhile, the gigantic Katowice steelworks were being built at top speed and this project, involving, as it did, a heavy investment program, was to put Poland in Russia's debt for many years to come. The wave of investment which had been unleashed the length of the coast was making a wasteland of whole sections of Gdansk. Take the Siarkopol sulphur factory, for example. It chucked out great clouds of lethal yellow smoke and the surrounding region was gradually turned into a yellow desert. The old Hanseatic city of Gdansk was being eaten away by acid rain and phosphorus deposits. Stogi beach, until then the finest of all the Tri-City beaches, was closed to swimmers. Economic statistics kept referring to the fall in the Poles' life expectancy, though it had already been at the bottom of the European scale to begin with. All this happened almost imperceptibly, masked by a "propaganda of success" which left no room for any suggestions or arguments other than those the Party and the state wanted us to hear.

It was in such a climate that, shortly after the protests at Radom and Ursus, the Committee for Defense of Workers (KOR) was founded by a group of intellectuals. They were trying to achieve what we had failed to achieve at the shipyards: an effective organization to protect workers and to avert an otherwise inevitable catastrophe. It was not simply that everything in the country was rigidly controlled by a small elite of self-perpetuating Party members. Those who had acceded to power during the decade from 1970 to 1980 were perfectly aware that their era of prosperity would be short-lived; thus they threw themselves into it with reckless abandon. The life-style of the ruling class was determined accordingly, the tone being set by individuals such as the son of Premier Jaroszewicz, who paraded around with celebrated singers and starlets and drove around in luxurious cars (he was known in the West as the "Red Prince"), and by Maciej Szczepanski, the high-living head of radio and television, and a protégé of the first secretary of the Party. Villas, yachts, hunting parties, weekend trips by helicopter were the order of the day; Poland was heading for bankruptcy and these people were living in a dream world. I never dreamed at that time that I would one day be a "guest" at one of these discreet governmental residences, enjoying a splendid cuisine together with exceptionally vigilant bodyguards!

The years in Wrzosy Street were happy ones for Danuta and me and for our family, although we lived on a very tight budget. For many years now I have found in Danuta a source of unfailing strength and support. When we first married, she was easily dispirited, defensive, or pessimistic, but over the years her courage and determination have grown, and now they form a sort of protective screen around me. There have been times when I've even had to defend members of the secret police from her fiery reaction when they broke into our home. That's Danuta seen from the outside. But she's also a woman of surprising gentleness and delicacy. There's a kindliness about her, which a single word or tiny movement can betray; it's like an invitation to another sort of life, one that isn't all struggle, but the fulfillment of our nature as human beings: a life of affection and contentment. Keenly observant, Danuta is one of those people who doesn't need explanations, but who can penetrate intuitively to the heart of things and suggest, in a word, the right tone to adopt, or the correct solution to most problems. I owe many of my most important decisions to her. Not that she ever told me what to do exactly; she simply talked to me in a way that helped me to see things from a new angle, to modify my point of view. I never tried to make a comrade in arms of Danuta. But she soon demonstrated astonishing insight into the problems I was addressing, and during my year's internment at Arlamowo, she took over virtually all my public speaking assignments. And she probably did it better than I myself would have done at the time.

We were a family of four when we moved to Stogi: we two and our two sons, Bogdan and Slawek, who was then two months old. We seemed to produce a new child with unfailing regularity every two years. Important political events are marked for us by events in our family calendar: Bogdan was born in December 1970; Przemek's birth came with my dismissal from the yard; Magda was locked up with me at the militia's headquarters when she was still in her stroller; Ania's birth coincided with the great strike and the birth of Solidarity; Maria-Wiktoria was born during my internment, and I saw her for the first time when Danuta brought her, already several months old, to Arlamow. The last of the family is little Brygida, born after martial law was lifted.

I watch them grow and I often wonder what will become of them. Each of them is bounding with energy, and they have had to struggle, from the earliest months, to make places for themselves in the family and in life. Each one does it in his or her own way.

My youngest son is, I think, most like me. Magda stands out from the other girls on account of her obvious acting talent; at seven she is already quite a little lady, and very beautiful too. I feel a mixture of pleasure and apprehension when I think about Przemek's extraordinary tenacity, Slawek's perspicacity, and Bogdan's quiet reserve (possibly due to the fact that he was being nursed during the events of December 1970, when the streets were running with blood); each offers us pride and worry.

I have never made much of my role as father of the family. With Danuta, I've washed the babies' diapers, bathed and fed the children: there was simply too much to do to think of specifying what was a wife's and what was a husband's job. This physical contact with my children, from the earliest moments, has brought us close forever; during those times when I wasn't able to devote enough attention to them, the bonds between us held strong.

We were young and happy. We often went for walks with our five children, through the little wood to the beach, where I would swim after work in the summer, or in the opposite direction toward Motlawa in the center of town to visit Danuta's aunt, or to Weterplatte, in front of the monument. The problems began in the evening when we had to wash and feed the five little ones, and put them to bed. We had to unfold their beds every night and when the children got bigger their mattresses and pillows would take up almost the entire apartment, which consisted of two tiny rooms, the smallest being only five feet wide. In the larger room, our lives were concentrated around a sofa, a cot, and a table. There was a sewing machine in one corner, which also served later on as a stand for an ancient Roneo (stencil) machine used for printing leaflets.

But at that time, our organization and our trade union activities were the farthest thing from my mind. After my dismissal from the yard, we were inundated with financial worries and I speedily signed on at an enterprise for mechanical repairs, ZREMB, not far from where we lived. I worked at a section for overhauling vehicles in Stogi. It wasn't a bad job there. I was one of the few electricians working on cars and I was often sent to the management offices in the Orunia area of Gdansk, where I had the opportunity of meeting new people.

Two months had elapsed since I'd left the yard and the secret police had at last stopped following me; they simply watched me from a distance. In any case, at the time I didn't have any contacts likely to interest them. I got to work in a car assembled for my own use from old parts. There was a scrap iron depot right next door to the ZREMB, where old Warszawas were dumped when they were withdrawn from circulation, and I got hold of one for 4,500 zlotys and patched it up. We went off on holiday to visit Danuta's old home in the dilapidated Warszawa. My financial circumstances had improved: I was getting extra money from doing odd jobs and repairing cars belonging to friends, who would then recommend me to other people, with the result that I was never short of work.

During the first quarter of 1978, the first issues of a bimonthly newspaper for the independent unions, *Robotnik* (*The Worker*), began to appear. It was written by a small group of people who were not afraid to stand up and be counted (the newspaper printed the names and addresses of all the editorial staff), and it was through the paper that I got to know the Wyszkowski brothers: Blazej and Krzysztof. I also met up with another group of young graduates and members of what was later known as the Young Poland Movement (RMP), who dedicated part of their activities at that time to commemorating the events of December 1970, together with other historical events linked to the struggle for Polish independence. These encounters added to the experience I'd gained at the yard. The first reference I heard to the independent movement was in 1977, on the May Day celebration of the December 1970 tragic events; then, I'd heard about it again in December. The movement wasn't prospering yet; the members had formed themselves into small isolated groups, few people knew about them, and worker participation was in reality almost nil. In a meeting with Wyszkowski, and later with Andrzej and Joanna Gwiazda, I told them that they'd have to do things differently.

Our hour was approaching. Each of us was moving toward the same end by his own path. The moment was drawing near when all these paths would converge to become one.

The Birth of the Free Trade Unions

It's difficult to say precisely where a river begins. It seldom springs from a single source. More often than not, it starts as a number of small mountain streams, which join together to flow downstream around natural obstacles, occasionally disappearing underground before it finally finds the right direction and rushes off with one accord. Upstream, you can't be sure that this flow is really a river, whereas someone miles downstream, who can see it fill its banks while cutting a well-defined course, is in no doubt about its character.

During the seventies, Gdansk was like that network of streams, whose ideas would later merge to form a powerful current.

We were in the second half of the "Gierek decade," December 1970 to September 1980. The order to build the "Second Poland," which had gone out in 1972, was still in force, but three-quarters of the loans from the West were hanging fire, invested in industrial projects that failed to bring the expected returns, and it had become obvious that this "Second Poland" wasn't going to be for everybody. A question mark hung over the program of mass consumption, characterized by such slogans as "a little Fiat for everyone," along with "decent housing for every family." We kept going, for better or worse, but with no recognizable goal to head for on the horizon. Our rigidly centralized economic system, inefficient and unworkable as it was, couldn't be saved by loans, technology, or occasional contracts with the West.

It was in reaction to this impasse that "a number of amendments to the Constitution" were announced. These turned out to be no more than legal modifications designed to bring Poland into line with constitutional amendments already enacted in the other Eastern bloc countries. We were paying the price for our economic "open door" policy toward the West and the price was high. Henceforth our Constitution was to embody the principles of Party supremacy and a closer alliance with the USSR, together with constraints on citizens' rights. These changes left no one in any doubt about the Party's future intentions.

In June 1976 price increases were announced across the board; thus Gomulka's economic failures had finally rebounded to undermine the Gierek government. Workers at Radom and Ursus immediately protested against the announcement, destroying whatever credibility Gierek still retained, especially in the West where his team was considered by many to have inaugurated the most "liberal" and economically progressive regime in Eastern Europe. In the eyes of the Soviets and Eastern bloc leadership the situation was taken as evidence of the failure of his adventures with Western bankers.

The protests led to reprisals, and once again the church felt called upon to speak out. The Polish primate and bishops were opposed to the plan to revise the Constitution and succeeded in limiting the amendments that were introduced. The troubles at Radom and Ursus were followed in November 1976 by another episcopal letter which stated:

> Since last June, during which month the country was disrupted by incidents in many places of work, the episcopate has been pleading with the authorities to grant an amnesty to the workers, who merely demand decent living conditions and to restore to them legitimate social rights. The primate and bishops of Poland have on several occasions referred in their pastoral letters to the right of workers to defend their individual and collective rights. None of our interventions has elicited a response. This is why the Conference of the Episcopate considers it its duty once more to call on the Polish authorities to do what is necessary to maintain that peace in society which is essential to the well-being of the country. In order to surmount the present crisis, the government's program of action must take into account the best traditions of our national

culture and the popular involvement in the public affairs of the country. We are dealing here with the rights of all citizens, whatever their philosophy, their professional status, or their attitude toward the Party. There is no doubt whatsoever that the solution to all our difficulties, including the economic ones, can be found by extending and guaranteeing the liberties of our citizens.

The letter was written in a language that everyone could understand, whatever their position in society. Similar language was used again with a few changes in emphasis, by KOR in September 1976. Some of those in KOR were motivated by purely moral reasons, for others these reasons were allied with their own ideology. It was mainly because of various differences in religious and political beliefs that KOR quickly ran into problems. KOR's influence and philosophy developed in response to past events: in March 1968 it was largely an intellectual movement; in December 1970 its strategy was primarily concerned with labor relations; and now KOR had to combine the two strands into an effective movement able to exploit the potential trap of official newsspeak, without falling into it, and by deliberately phrasing its announcements in the language of Marxist ideology. It was a jargon which contained the old formulas of magic significance for the Party: the "working class," the "dictatorship of the proletariat," "socialism." Like crooked poker players the authorities had marked the cards, but KOR was the one who insisted on using a clean deck. They spoke of "the workers," so a "workers' defense committee" was created; while they revered socialism, KOR's demands centered on appropriate working conditions for all workers. Instead of simple slogans, KOR could employ their meaningless words to advocate real participation in public affairs, not the usual mediation by Party functionaries, together with a demand for democratic elections to all the top government jobs in the country. After all, *we* were the proletariat: the government leaders were caught in a trap of their own making.

KOR decided to confront the authorities head-on, and its leading members willingly revealed their identities—names and addresses—in their uncensored publications. They had failed as yet to gain the support of the masses, but it was now only a question of time. Because KOR was primarily an association of intellectuals *in support* of the workers, not workers themselves, many of us looked upon the organization with suspicion in their earliest days. It didn't take their leadership long to earn our respect.

The church, meanwhile, continued to preach about human rights and moral law. Its recommendations, initially strictly evangelical in tone, were soon drawn up into a practical moral program, embracing all aspects of human life, by the new Pope during his first pilgrimage to his native country. The invocation of a moral order was the most revolutionary response that could be made to the increasingly dogmatic socialism practiced in Poland, and people were caught up in this wave of moral reawakening—each expressing it in his or her own way, at work or in the home, in professional and in personal relationships.

The river which was to produce the flood of August 1980 had been swollen by other runoffs: more and more people were finding that there was no room for them in Gierek's Poland. The Wyszkowski brothers from Gdansk were among them. Krzysztof was a carpenter's joiner by day, and at night the underground publisher of the works of Witold Gombrowicz. A few years later, he became editorial secretary of the weekly *Solidarnosc*. His brother Blazej went to an engineering university in Gdansk, won a title of junior world champion sailor, before devoting himself to our cause. The two brothers worked together with a French firm building a chain of hotels in Poland; it was a chance to earn big money, but that wasn't what they really wanted. They were brimming with energy and ideas, more competent by far than their contemporaries in the Association of Socialist Youth. But for all that, it was the members of the state-sanctioned organization, not the likes of the Wyszkowski brothers, who were promoted to important positions and who exercised political power. There's no slot in official Poland for people like the Wyszkowskis, just as there's no room for Andrzej Gwiazda and his wife Joanna, human rights activists who tackle needed social reforms head-on.

These were people interested in politics not as a game of calculated moves played out in a system as ossified and limiting as that which existed in postwar Poland, but as a lively endeavor with common goals, demanding knowledge and culture, personal experience and ability, not to forget enthusiasm. Politics in that sense hadn't existed in Gierek's Poland. Historian Aleksander Hall and the lawyer Leszek Kaczynski typified this spirit of commitment. For these two and their younger friends, most then high school students, the experience of March 1968 had been especially telling. They didn't feel the fear which paralyzed university students and recent graduates at the time: fear which had been instilled by reprisals, expulsions from the university, and the threat of being blacklisted for jobs. The young graduates longed to establish themselves within the system, taking advantage of the openings which Gierek's "mini stabilization" offered. It was toward them that the "little Fiat" slogan, the loans for buying furniture and TVs were directed, together with the promise of acquiring their own apartment reasonably soon. Such baits were intended to stop questions about the meaning and purpose of their lives, to suppress memories of the recent past; and they partially succeeded. But vexing questions posed by high school students recurred.

The way in which ideological values were discredited in the minds of the young is well illustrated by the example of High School No. 1 in Gdansk, which is located in front of the second entrance to the shipyard. The events of December 1970 took place right under their eyes and their aftermath provided a lasting lesson. At the time, the students regularly attended pastoral meetings organized by the churches. No politics were discussed at these, but alert students did attempt to find answers to various social, moral, and spiritual questions, forbidden subjects for discussion by the official youth organizations. Voices were already being raised in Party circles to the effect that the Party was about to lose the fight for control over the young. And they weren't far wrong: these young people were about to create an opposition movement called the Young Poland Movement (RMP), which would exercise considerable influence. The name was inspired by a literary and artistic current that revered the best of Polish culture. Aleksander Hall was to become leader of the group, assisted by Bogdan Borusewicz, a young historian (later labeled a "born conspirator" by the secret police) with a degree from the Catholic University of Lublin.

The year 1976 was a turning point on the road to change in Gdansk and elsewhere. Organizations began to appear which were totally independent of the Party. Among these, the Movement in Defense of Human and Citizen Rights (ROPCIO) aroused the most interest. This movement was dedicated to publicizing human wrongs, violations of individual rights guaranteed by the Helsinki Final Accords, which had been signed by our country in 1975. The movement was also to give rise to the idea of an independent trade union, whose mission would be, along with KOR's, to defend the rights of workers.

One of the central freedoms at stake was freedom of expression (a direct corollary of the Helsinki agreement). Without this basic freedom, human life becomes meaningless; and once the truth of this hit me, it became part of my whole way of thinking. From that moment, I began to see myself as part of a vast pattern, woven from scraps of knowledge of our own history and tradition and from everyday experiences, informed by the tragic lessons of December 1970.

We began to recognize an international dimension to our problems and learned of the existence of human rights groups abroad to whom we could appeal. It was clear as well that the church, with its newly awakened social values, provided an activist, non-violent approach that allowed us to deal with the explosive situation that prevailed in Poland without resorting to destructive confrontations.

I wasn't present when the declaration announcing the creation of the Free Trade Union in Gdansk was drawn up; it was left to others to translate into words our various thoughts and inspirations. The same idea had, after all, worked its way to the surface in different parts of Poland: Kazimierz Switon and his friends had organized the first trade union of this type in the industrial region of Silesia. Thanks to my dismissal from the yard, I had been effectively cut off not only from my work but from my co-workers. When our incipient movement had been temporarily thwarted, I concentrated on seeking out new contacts outside the shipyard. I was fully aware that I couldn't be involved in the formation of an independent union: I was under close surveillance and had been described in the official press as someone who "has acquired a serious experience of leading strikes and knows how to interpret the interests of the workers." Excellent references, but there are people in the security forces adept at flushing out a particular

98

meaning from behind the tone and the manner of things said and written, and they had already compiled a fat police file on me. In those circumstances it would have been a serious mistake to have turned up anywhere where plans for organizing an effective opposition were under way.

At this time I came across an issue of *Robotnik Wybrzeza* (*Coastal Worker*) which contained a declaration announcing the creation of the Free Trade Union. The editors gave their names and addresses, in black and white: I could scarcely believe that it wasn't a hoax. At the same time I learned of the existence of the Young Poland Movement, and its involvement with union activity. This was confirmed when the group placed flowers in front of the entrance to the shipyard on May Day, 1979. Many of the movement's organizers, both workers and outside supporters, were running serious risks. Blazej Wyszkowski was under arrest at the time and I had doubts about the movement's long-term effectiveness. Nonetheless, I decided I had to cast my lot with them, especially so after shipyard worker Anna Walentynowicz joined the group. Her organizational skills were a godsend.

Some background: in October 1956, the authorities tried to counter the increasingly turbulent mood among the workers by setting up KSR (Konferencje Samorzadu Robotniczego: Conferences of Workers' Self-government) in the larger enterprises. In order to keep appearances of legitimate worker councils, Gomulka created KSR, which consisted largely of Party and management representatives and made no more than a pretense at self-government. Theoretically, these bodies existed to implement a degree of worker autonomy, but by the seventies they served no real purpose at all. Since their members were mainly representatives of the Party leadership and the official trade union, they obviously precluded any real opportunity for independent self-management.

When I was working at the ZREMB, I was elected by the employees in my sector as their delegate to the KSR. During a meeting of the general assembly, the president of the general assembly, who represented the Party at the district level, proposed the Party secretary as the president of the KSR, the union president as the secretary of the KSR, and so on. Everything was proceeding along well-worn lines. Thus the KSR was no more than a carbon copy of all the existing Party organizations, whose usefulness to us workers was nil. We were only being asked to do one thing: confirm officially that we knew what was going on and that we accepted it. At this point in the meeting, I stood up and asked what they thought I was doing there, since everything seemed to have been arranged in advance? Then I went on to quote Jacek Kuron—later a key figure in KOR and in Solidarity—who had already pointed out the absurdity of the KSR. They were unprepared to respond, but I seem to have hit a soft spot, because I was fired shortly afterward. My job, the only electrician's job there, was abolished.

I knew very well, of course, what the real reason for my dismissal was, even if it wasn't declared. The management merely spoke about "restructuring" the works, they said that my job wasn't needed anymore. I tried to take the case to arbitration, but got nowhere; my police file simply grew heavier still and grew even larger when I took part in the celebrations for the ninth anniversary of the tragic events of December 1970.

We had decided to celebrate the day with solemnity. But when everything was ready and the bunches of flowers had been brought to the yard, the police pounced. They even arrested the people who attempted to place flowers in the nearby cemetery. They searched us, then put each of us behind bars. My colleagues were freed later that afternoon after the best time for a demonstration had passed, but I was kept for forty-eight hours.

Three days later, as soon as I was free, we were ready to set off again. Bearing our flowers, we got as far as the shipyard perimeter, only to fall once more into the hands of the security police. Back in prison again, it was my friend Borusewicz who this time was held for forty-eight hours. I was then charged with "hooliganism" and brought before a magistrate. But by this time our group was large enough to be reckoned with: during the last weeks of 1979, the militia carried out around seventy searches and a hundred and forty arrests in the Tri-City region.

Five days later, I received my letter of dismissal. It came at a very bad moment. Danuta was going to have a baby in a few weeks' time, our youngest was just two and the eldest only nine. We lived from day to day, scarcely managing to make ends meet. And my two recent arrests had only added to Danuta's distress. I was thus faced with a dilemma: whether to withdraw from an active role and concern myself exclusively with work to support my family, or whether to push on, and become totally involved. It turned out that the authorities made the choice for me. I had already crossed one psychological barrier and had broken with the pernicious convention that requires a prisoner of conscience to be ashamed of being behind bars. Returning home at dawn after my various arrests, without a penny because my pockets had been emptied, I got into the habit of telling people on the streetcar about the various things that had happened to me. I would tell them about the times I'd spent in the cells for having wanted to celebrate the memory of my shipyard colleagues who fell in 1970, or for celebrating traditional patriotic anniversaries the authorities passed over in silence. Surprised at first, people would react strongly: most of them were kind and would give me tickets so I could get home. Many would demand further details. Then I would tell them of the need to create an organization capable of defending human rights and a Poland we could believe in.

I remember clearly the three months following these events. I had decided to take advantage of the fact that I was unemployed and obliged to sign in daily at the employment office. I already knew where I wanted to be employed: the Elektromontaz enterprise not far from the ZREMB site and well placed for public transport. But I could afford three months of unemployment without losing benefits or seniority. I decided to use those three months in my own way. I would go to the employment office and pick up my interview sheets for various jobs, and in this way comb the whole of the Tri-City, from Gdansk to Gydnia. I wasn't impatient, and I wasn't especially worried, knowing that, with my qualifications, I would eventually land the job I wanted. I set off every morning with my toolbox bulging with underground literature, including copies of the *Coastal Worker* and various leaflets. Clutching my interview card from the employment office, I would turn up at the factory in question for an interview with the personnel officer, the foreman in charge of a particular sector, or even the director. I wouldn't conceal from him the real reason for my dismissal; I would talk about my growing opposition to the authorities and, if, in spite of everything, they seemed prepared to take me on, I would then start getting more vehement, warning them that I wasn't prepared to give up my opposition activities, implying that they'd soon have the security police with their listening devices all over the place. In the end, I was prepared to admit that I simply didn't want the job. During the course of my visits, I would distribute my leaflets and place a copy of the *Coastal Worker* on the boss's desk. Then I would return to the employment office to get another letter of introduction. In this way, I managed to spread leaflets in a number of factories in the Tri-City region, continuing right up until the second to last day of the three-month period, when I turned up at the Polmozbyt works in Mialki Szlak Street. The assistant manager was named Wojtyla, like the Pope. As soon as I went in, everything looked a bit fishy to me, as if they were expecting me. I displayed my papers and letter of introduction and was just starting to say who I was when he interrupted me and said abruptly: "You're hired." I told him that I was a militant member of the opposition movement in favor of independent trade unions. "I'm hiring you," he repeated. I showed him my leaflets, and when he'd calmly read through them he looked up and said: "You know, two men were here a moment ago. They told me that a loony was going to turn up, an expert electrician, one of the best around, and that I must sign him on. 'He rattles on,' they said, 'but that's as far as it goes, he's harmless enough. He'll talk about the opposition, it's his pet subject, but he isn't a member of any opposition movement. You must take him on, offering him the terms he wants.'"

The militia, housed next door to the employment office, had apparently decided to put an end to my factory pilgrimages.

After a few minutes, the assistant manager began looking closely at the material I'd handed him and said: "I can see that it's not you who's the loony. What are we going to do?" We discussed rates of pay and such, but I ended up by refusing his offer. I returned to the employment office for another letter of introduction and on May 1, 1979, the last day before the end of my three-month period, I was taken on at the Elektromontaz enterprise.

There followed a period of creativity and growth for our movement, as well as for others with which I was in contact or was about to make contact. We began to draw up a plan of action in which all the various groups would find their place. In commemorating great historical events which had given expression to our national ideals, we echoed our celebrations of the anniversaries of more recent events, linked to our own experiences. We were no longer concerned about the searches, the arrests, and the spells in prison. We took them in our stride as occupational hazards, disturbing, yes, but by now commonplace. Sometimes this involuntary "unemployment" came as a relief when one could sleep the clock around and think about the future. As the ninth anniversary of the events of December 1970 approached, a number of people were arrested. Borusewicz was first and he was kept in jail for two weeks. I was on my own, except for the members of the Young Poland Movement. On the night before the anniversary, I avoided sleeping at home, where the security police were waiting for me. When I got to work, they surrounded the factory and were combing the workshops for me. The workers hid me in a container and in this way I managed to get out of the building and to the yard entrance in spite of the surveillance.

I arrived in time for the celebration in front of the second entrance. Dariusz Kobzdej and Maryla Plonska had just finished their speeches. When it came to my turn, I called on them all to take part the following year in erecting a monument to the victims of 1970—each of them was urged to contribute a handful of pebbles so that we'd end up with a huge mound, like the one raised in memory of Tadeusz Kosciuszko at Cracow—the patriot who had led uprisings against Russia and Prussia at the end of the eighteenth century. For the first time since we had celebrated this anniversary, we had some priests with us; they encouraged us to prayer and meditation. The militia, who had us surrounded, didn't intervene.

But when my co-workers from Elektromontaz who'd taken part in the celebration were subsequently fired, we decided to strike. It was to be my first strike for quite some time. It was then that the management announced that, because of an electrical breakdown, everyone had permission to go home; the buses were already waiting outside. In this way they got rid of the whole work force and preempted our strike. Nobody was arrested (though, inevitably, we were followed by the security police). Given that we'd provoked a work stoppage, our first strike could almost be said to have been successful; but then I was fired again.

I decided to go from one factory to another, until I was taken on again, whether my search for a job lasted three months or more; the fact is, I didn't get another job until August.

This was a particularly eventful period in my life. It soon became obvious that the walls in my apartment had ears. I had confided in my own home to a circle of reliable friends that I was going to make a speech, a well-thought-out one this time, about "social justice," and the secret police knew it word for word. The employment office wasn't giving me any more letters of introduction; they obviously didn't like the idea of sending me (and my propaganda) to any more large factories with large work forces. My children were hungry and I decided that, that very afternoon, I would take them into a shop and let them take all they wanted to eat. Then I would go up to the cash register and show my identity card, saying, "Madam, I'm sorry to trouble you, but we haven't anything to eat. Take down all the details, and as soon as I get some work and some money, I'll pay for everything they've taken."

When I arrived at the employment office, however, the boss ran up and told me to wait. A moment later, the cashier came along with 6,000 zlotys, saying, "You've been granted some assistance. We know about your situation."

During this time, we were conducting meetings throughout the region: on the beach at Stogi, in the woods of Wrzeszcz, at Morena— a quarter of Gydnia. And, always, the militia hunted for us, constantly setting traps which we managed to slip through. The map of Gdansk at their operational headquarters must have looked like a battlefield plan or, rather, an urban warfare map. There was hardly a place where there wasn't some kind of secret meeting or operation in progress.

The decisive moment came on May 3, 1980, the date of the arrests of several members of the Young Poland Movement and of the Movement in Defense of Human and Citizen Rights—among them, Dariusz Kobzdej and Tadeusz Szczudlowski—following their speeches in front of the Monument to King Jan III Sobieski.[7] We began openly to distribute leaflets demanding respect for the rights

7. An equestrian statue in Gdansk, dedicated to Jan III Sobieski (1629–1696), who became king of Poland in 1674 and stopped the Turkish army at Vienna in 1683.

of citizens and recognition of the political rights of all Poles; we called for honesty in the conduct of public affairs, for an immediate overhaul of the economy, for a halt to the price rises and inflation, for effective implementation of one of the slogans for "Gierek's decade," "decent housing for all Poles." "There's no bread without freedom"—such was the leitmotif of our crusade. In Gdansk the front line had been drawn up with us on one side and the militia on the other. The authorities turned a deaf ear to our demands, leaving us face to face with the militia. It was a stalemate.

In August 1980, the curtain was raised once again to reveal a major Polish drama. There were stirrings of life in government circles. It was then that we learned of the conflict between the Gdansk team—with Party Secretary Tadeusz Fiszbach and District Governor Jerzy Kolodziejski—and Gierek's team in the capital, over the deteriorating situation along the Baltic coast. In the analysis of the former, the events of December 1970 fostered the general belief that if "the working class pushes on to the bitter end, it could secure enormous concessions." The Gdansk authorities knew that tension had been mounting since 1976, that Gierek's program was a fiasco, that they could therefore only help to temporize by playing down the dispute, so as to delay a new explosion for as long as possible. They decided to operate on two levels: to concentrate on increased productivity along with wage increases, and also to try to reduce the disparities between conditions for coastal workers and the more advanced inland industrial centers.

In 1979, at a meeting of the Politburo of the Party Central Committee, Fiszbach and Kolodziejski had presented a highly alarmist report on the region's economic and social situation. Their efforts were ineffectual, however, in political terms, and went almost unnoticed. They had run up against the intrinsic problem presented by the Communist government: "The center knows better; the central organization knows everything." But the way the people at the center look at things is purely from the point of view of power; the alarmist reports coming in from Gdansk could only be explained in their eyes as an attempt to introduce newcomers into the privileged circle of decision making. The reports were, in any case, at complete variance with the optimistic image which was being transmitted by the propaganda of "a Poland growing stronger every day and providing better living conditions for its people."

The Gdansk team had picked up rumors about the wish to raise a monument to the shipyard victims of 1970, and had informed the government. Although Gierek had theoretically given the go-ahead, he took care not to keep his promise. Warsaw's reply was always the same: forget it. The Gdansk team attempted to point out that the erection of such a monument would enhance the credibility of the authorities' own reform program and help to ameliorate relations with the workers; but their words fell on deaf ears.

Absorbed by events in our daily lives—arrests, searches, and dismissals—we were scarcely aware of these differences between the central government and the local authorities in Gdansk. We found it difficult to believe in the information brought to us by sympathizers, such as Lech Badkowski, according to which the district authorities wished us well, but couldn't do much to help us. They were apparently waiting for us to modify our actions, promising in return that the severity of the reprisals would be alleviated. These were difficult conditions to accept, though we did give them some consideration.

These calls for moderation were aimed in particular at the anti-Russian slogans which frequently appeared during demonstrations and anniversary celebrations such as those held for the Liberation of Poland (1918), the Constitution of May 3, 1791 (after the first partition of Poland), the "Miracle on the Vistula" (1920), and the execution of thousands of Polish officers at Katyn in 1940.[8] It was recommended that we avoid phrases likely to annoy the Soviet consul in Gdansk. I learned later that the Gdansk authorities were under pressure from Russian consular officials, who knew perfectly well what our opinions were and accused us of being "counter-revolutionaries." Our activities and slogans, and all the names and addresses of those who had taken part in demonstrations, were carefully recorded and there was a strong demand for our removal.

For more than forty years now, no one has managed to work out a system in our country that would allow direct contact be-

8. A massacre for which the Soviet authorities were responsible and which Stalin attributed to Hitler's troops, an assertion the present Polish government has not corrected.

tween the people and the authorities: this is our particular dilemma. During all my years of political activity, I have never managed to exchange more than a few words with government representatives, and then only in extreme situations, when we were only a step away from catastrophe. I was greeted as an "authoritative spokesman" when I represented the Shipyard Strike Committee in December 1970, and again when I was arrested for the first time by the militia: on that occasion they even listened to me with a certain interest. On most other occasions we were met with a wall of silence, as I was to experience again in 1979 and 1980. So we knew full well what to expect when we again came face-to-face with these same authorities shortly afterwards; their methods no longer held any secrets for us. But we knew our Poland, and ourselves, too, by now, and what we knew didn't encourage us to retreat.

Thus the trickles of water meet to form streams, and the streams join to produce a river. Sometimes it's a majestic and irresistible force, at other times it's blocked, compelled to go underground. Our movement was like that river.

Some Other Witnesses:

Andrzej Gwiazda

Lech, for the first time, participated in distribution of the *Coastal Worker*, together with leaflets, and we had prepared our plan of action. We had opted for Sunday mass as the time to distribute our leaflets in front of the churches. We set off in Lech's car. My wife Joanna and he stayed in the car, while I walked to the church. I went in, but all I could see were members of the security forces. We didn't know it at the time, but one of their agents, Edwin Myszk, had in fact infiltrated our group. (Today Myszk is in prison, probably in Kurkowa Street jail, for dealing in stolen cars.)

They were obviously waiting for us in church, so I quickly got back in the car and we drove off again. They didn't have a car with them, and we drove to Gdynia-Demptowo unimpeded. We then parked behind a church there; distributed maybe as many as a hundred copies; nobody bothered us.

Lech was also giving out leaflets and only an experienced eye could have seen that his hands were trembling slightly. This was normal with beginners: your hands tremble out of nervous excitement. The second or third time, it becomes routine; but the first time's a true baptism of fire.

Everyone took his copy, stowed it away, and disappeared. There wasn't time to hesitate, each of us kept to our own part of the crowd. Everything happened very quickly, as people were afraid of being seen to linger (and just as well, too).

Later, we could relax and breathe easily again: we'd done it! It wasn't so awful after all. . . . And how satisfied we felt: so many people were going to read, discuss, and pass on the message. What's more, the Demptowo parish included parts of town that depended on the shipyard: we'd struck it lucky, it was even better than at the church we chose first, there were new apartment buildings here with new tenants to join us.

We wanted our collaborators to find their own feet fairly quickly, to become autonomous and participate actively in meetings at their places of work. Lech took part in these meetings. He may even have chaired a few. He certainly organized his own group meetings at Stogi and elsewhere.

We tried to recommend a few books to him, in particular the works of the sociologist Florian Znaniecki and a book on economics, but he wasn't really interested in theory.

We never managed to get him to write much; he would never do more than draft his curriculum vitae at this stage. It was Anna Walentynowicz who surprised us most: we had never expected much in that line from her, knowing that her studies had been restricted to courses for illiterates. After much hesitation, she wrote her first article. "Anna, don't be frightened, we'll correct it for you," we told her. I remember how much we all liked it and how we didn't change a word. But I have to admit that we didn't get many nice surprises like that.

We were overworked. I'm quite unable to say, for instance, what the weather was like during the August 1980 strike. I didn't even notice it. I only remember the rain, in the early morning, when I would collapse in a corner and fall asleep—that's all.

It was the same thing in 1979 and 1980, when the Free

Trade Union was set up: the nights when we could sleep four hours at a stretch were few and far between. As underground publishers, we had to do the developing, prepare the ink and the frames for the silkscreen prints, write the copy—all that, though there were only a few of us. Did we already have the impression that we exercised some influence, of having power on our side? I think we really did.

We would sometimes fix two meetings per day, spend whole days without eating or drinking, because we also had to give the men from the security police the slip. We got more and more requests for meetings, and there simply weren't enough of us to cope. The time when only a few supporters turned up at our assemblies was over.

Paradoxically, at this time, the opposition in Warsaw had come to a complete standstill. I was struck, on a trip to the capital, with the feeling of general stagnation; the opposition was going around and around in circles, unable to find a way out. They needed new ideas and weren't finding any—just like today. . . .

Usually everything withers and dies within the narrow limits of a circle when the same ideas are rehashed over and over again. I couldn't believe what was happening at Gdansk, we were collapsing with exhaustion, barely able to carry on. And there was so much interest, such massive support; there'd been so many dynamic developments that we couldn't even fit in all those who came to see us anymore; and we even had to drop an edition of our beloved newspaper, for lack of time.

We don't really know what the driving force was that enabled our human rights movement to take off in this way: was our commemoration of the events of December 1970 a cause or an effect? The fact is that in 1976, there were only six of us; in 1977, thirty, with around a hundred sympathizers; in 1978, the number of our active supporters could be estimated at around six hundred; and finally, in 1979, at several thousand. Every demonstration, enthusiastically received by the public, clearly extended our popularity.

We had been discussing the problem of the Free Trade Union since September–October 1977, at Mariusz Muskat's place, I think. I remember declaring that such an organization was crucial, and that it was pointless making speeches about its relative utility; we had to go for it at once. Nobody really had any idea then how we could make such an organization work; we discussed at length what its possible activities might include. What was the point of a trade union that hadn't got the right to strike? And yet no one could launch a strike in our country, people just wouldn't follow, not after 1970.

We reopened the discussion on several occasions. And the project finally became fact in Silesia, where the Free Trade Union first saw the light of day.

Alina Pienkowska, nurse at the Gdansk Shipyard and wife of Bogdan Borusewicz (their marriage was celebrated clandestinely during martial law)

Lech continued to go his own way, putting his own ideas into practice, outside the group. On his own initiative, he went with Henryk Lenarciak to meet representatives from the episcopate, taking on the role of ambassador for the group. It was a private meeting, whose purpose was to inform the church about the situation and the climate of feelings in opposition circles. Lech never spoke to us about this interview, although we saw each other frequently. His attitude is still the same today: he refuses to submit to anyone else's anything. This isn't something I reproach him for—it's simply part of his character.

He brought new life to the Free Trade Union and gave us new confidence in ourselves and a great deal of information, in particular about the events of December 1970. We were younger than he was, eager for details about all that had happened. I'd heard my father talk about it, but his viewpoint hadn't even been that of a bystander: Lech, on the other hand, had been in the front line as a member of the Shipyard Strike Committee. He gave us a thorough account of events, and his information seemed to us valuable enough to justify his writing a pamphlet about it, his "Memoirs of December." He began giving his account in a (tape-recorded) working session with the Gwiazdas, but the project was interrupted by the events of August 1980.

His ideas about the future were also very much his own. I

remember our journey to Warsaw to meet Jacek Kuron and Henryk Wujec. It was at the beginning of 1979; Anna Walentynowicz and Lech took the train, the Gwiazda couple probably went by air. I was detained by the hospital guards, and was the last to arrive. In front of everybody, Walesa opened the proceedings by picking a quarrel with Kuron: unfortunately, I can no longer remember the motive. In the eyes of us the initiates, Kuron enjoyed absolute authority, but Walesa would defend his position against anybody. We tried to ignore the quarrel and continue our meeting, but the two of them went on arguing more fiercely than ever [the worker *vs.* the intellectual].

I took part in a meeting of the Young Poland Movement at Szczudlowski's place. Bogdan felt he was wasting his time and left early. Grand debates about grand causes were foreign to us! Our aims were much more down-to-earth. The tasks we had to achieve from day to day were of the most concrete kind: we had to prepare each new edition of the *Coastal Worker* and maintain the standard for each article (none of us was a professional journalist); we had to keep going at all costs, despite the fact that many of our collaborators had lost their regular jobs as a result of working with us. When I look back on it, the quality of our editing almost makes me blush. But the important thing then was to meet demands: people were desperate for information and they wanted an honest and uncensored newspaper.

Another of our tasks was to get hold of books, which we loaned out during meetings: more than forty people present at a meeting at Anna Walentynowicz's home had to share two copies of *The Gulag Archipelago* over the course of a month or two.

Bogdan felt very sympathetic toward Lech. Lech interested him as a worker activist, though it should be stressed that Bogdan respected a person for what he was and would never judge anyone solely from the viewpoint of the militant opposition. Foreign journalists were eager to talk to workers, and Bogdan would often bring them to Lech's home in Stogi; the creation of the independent trade unions and the appearance of the newspaper the *Coastal Worker* had caused a sensation and attracted them in droves. Lech even received a visit from the British consul. All these interviews took place in Lech's small two-room apartment. From the very first, Lech was completely natural and at ease, as if used to public relations, and the journalists and diplomats would go away delighted.

I often used to visit the Walesas. The size of their apartment came as no surprise to me: we all lived in much the same conditions. I myself rented a room nine foot by six for 1,300 zlotys a month, and I had to pay 700 zlotys a month for my one child to be looked after in a day-care center. This situation wasn't atypical . . . and Lech's position was similar; he was one of us. I formed my opinion of him at that time, and nothing that has happened since has changed it in any way, not even his winning the Nobel Prize.

It was an extraordinary period, in spite of the endless arrests. Young as I was, I think I must have seen the inside of every militia building in town. Women were rarely locked up, however. In Warsaw, they were never arrested, which allowed Grazyna Kuron, Zosia Romaszewska, Helana, Lutka, and other of our colleagues to work more calmly and much more efficiently than we could do.

But our periods behind bars had advantages: forty-eight hours with nothing to do but sleep and recover were more welcome than you can imagine, as the work was exhausting; we were worn out.

Dariusz Kobzdej, doctor of medicine and youth leader

In December 1979, when we were commemorating the events of December 1970, I met Walesa in fairly unusual circumstances. In the midst of our preparations for the celebration, all of the members of the Young Poland Movement and of the Free Trade Union, with the exception of perhaps three or four, and a few members of KOR—including Bogdan Borusewicz and Adam Michnik from Warsaw, and probably Jacek Kuron—were brought before the magistrate's court. I managed to evade arrest and reached the shipyard in disguise. At that time, there was a four-foot railing running along the top of the wall that stretched down the road from the second entrance. When I arrived, there were about a thousand people standing in front of the wall, a little way back from it. Behind them, in a semicircle, were the vehicles belonging to the militia. The crowd seemed disorganized; it was quite clear that there was nobody leading them. A few people, apparently tipsy, were shouting, but the rest of the crowd ignored them. I managed to cross the street and reach the wall; somebody helped me up. I was handed an amplifier—not a very powerful one—and a microphone, and I got out my notes and started to read my speech. The crowd drew closer to the wall and formed a semicircle around me.

Shortly afterward, we were joined by a Jesuit priest, Father Bronislaw Sroka. He had come specially from his parish in Swieta Lipka, where he had been moved recently from Gdansk. He was wearing his soutane. It was he, who, a little later, managed to calm the crowd by encouraging us to start praying.

Walesa arrived just as I was reading my speech. He asked me to help him climb up onto the wall. He then held on to me, and, being fairly short, climbed onto my shoulders. I could hear what he was saying, but I didn't know that he wasn't reading his speech. He spoke with great conviction. It was only later, when the speeches made at this demonstration—with the exception of Walesa's—were published, that I realized that he'd improvised. It felt as if his words were creating a sort of bond between himself and his audience, whose excitement was so intense that, for the moment, the security police didn't dare intervene or even move.

We then set off toward the station. There were no incidents. The militiamen who were following us seemed to be afraid of stopping us and demanding to see our papers; they could sense our determination. After a few minutes, they moved off.

Walesa didn't leave with us. He asked us not to accompany him.

When I got out of prison, I received a very warm welcome from Walesa. I really felt as if we shared a deep friendship. He had taken up our defense without being driven by any personal motive or self-interest whatsoever. We were freed at the beginning of August. Anna Walentynowicz, the long-time heroine of workers, was released shortly afterward. The tension at the shipyard was rising daily; in an atmosphere as heavy as this the strike had to be imminent.

Jozef Drogon, worker

Two days before the strike, Walesa said to me: "When you hear the warning sirens, it means the strike will have started." The next day, I went to see him and remarked that I hadn't heard any sirens.

"If you hear them tomorrow, that'll be fine," he answered. The next day, on my way to work, I heard the whine of the sirens: the strike had begun. It was August 14, 1980.

The Strike and the August Agreements

I went to work by streetcar that day. I was alone. One usually is at critical moments. I was in no hurry. The thoughts were buzzing around in my head: why hadn't I been arrested? I could see militiamen not far away: they were unmistakable. They could nab me under any pretext. The shipyard had come out on strike at six in the morning, and by eight everyone knew what was going on.

I had heard the sirens before leaving home: I knew then that it had started. I hadn't been able to leave any sooner because there were jobs to be done in the house: Danuta had given birth only a few days previously and she could scarcely stand. The birth of our fifth child—a girl—had worn her out. But it was because of my daughter Ania, and for her, that I decided that I would see it right through to the bitter end.

The militia had come to arrest me one evening just as Danuta was going into labor. I pointed out that she couldn't be left on her own with the kids and that I had to take her to the hospital and care for the children. She was shrieking at them not to take me away, her shouts echoing throughout the building. They didn't want to listen, but they couldn't bring themselves to take any action either: the order "Take him away!" was given at least five times, but they still didn't budge. Seeing how embarrassed they were, I decided to help them out: I didn't want to get them into trouble, so I pleaded with my wife to calm down and to ask our neighbor to come around. And then I left of my own accord. When I got back home forty-eight hours later, Danuta was in the hospital.

It was a decisive moment for me and I swore that, from now

on, I wouldn't let anything intimidate me. But when August 14, 1980, came, I didn't think I would be able to get to the shipyard.

The build-up to our strike had already aroused wide interest, but ours was nevertheless not the only strike in Poland. Everything had started on July 1 in Lublin: the railwaymen had welded an engine to the rails along the line leading to the border with the Soviet Union. They were protesting against the dramatic meat shortages that had hit Poland at a time that meat was being exported and food prices were rising. Rumors were circulating that the prices in the state shops were going to be brought in line with those on the free market, which was better stocked, more expensive, and consequently reserved for a richer, more privileged clientele. But even its stocks eventually ran out.

I caught the streetcar; I had a thirty-five-minute journey to make, and time to mull over all kinds of doubts. I knew I was being followed by the security police: I could see their unmarked car following behind. What if this strike was just what they wanted? What exactly were they plotting? Were certain changes being planned at our expense? And were the authorities counting on us to show our hand so as to be able to gun us down, the lot of us? Lukaszewicz, secretary of propaganda at the Central Committee, had published his estimate of the strength of the opposition in Poland. According to his recent statements, in Gdansk, he reckoned it at 12,000 persons, all known to the authorities, who had lists of names and addresses. It would take only a matter of hours to put us all behind bars.

I got off in front of the shipyard and walked toward the entrance. That morning, before everyone signed in, specially prepared leaflets and copies of the *Coastal Worker* had been distributed on the suburban line and on the streetcars most of the workers took to work. The vital information concerned the dismissal of Anna Walentynowicz on August 7, five months before she was due for retirement. The text of our protest ran as follows:

To the workers of the Gdansk Shipyard:
This address is directed at the colleagues of Anna Walentynowicz. Anna has been working at the shipyard since 1950: she spent sixteen years as a welder, following which time she drove an overhead crane in shop 2. She was awarded the

Bronze and Silver Crosses of Merit, and then, in 1979, the Gold Cross of Merit. The quality of her work has always been excellent. Moreover, she has constantly fought against injustice and inequality, which is why she decided to join the Free Trade Union. It was then that her troubles began: for her part in distributing the *Coastal Worker* she was shifted twice to other units and formally reprimanded. Though disagreeable, such sanctions are harmless enough. But the management isn't attempting to preserve even a semblance of legality now. While on sick leave, Anna Walentynowicz received a letter of dismissal, effective date August 7, for having infringed the regulations. . . .

If Anna Walentynowicz has become an undesirable element, it is because they were afraid her attitude would influence the other workers. She became an undesirable because she defended her colleagues and encouraged other workers to do the same. The authorities frequently resort to isolating those who show leadership potential. On the day following the strike of June 1976, many workers were dismissed for this very reason. If today we fail to make our opposition felt, there will be no one to contest the increase in working hours, the violations of security rules, or the compulsory overtime. The best way of defending our own interests is to defend one another. That's why we are calling on you to defend Anna Walentynowicz! If we fail, many of you will soon find yourselves in the same position. We have stressed to the management the senselessness of their action; it occurs at a time when a wave of strikes is virtually submerging our country.

Signed: Founding Committee of the Free Trade Union and the editorial board of the *Coastal Worker*: Bogdan Borusewicz, Joanna Duda-Gwiazda, Andrzej Gwiazda.

It was thanks to the efforts of three twenty-year-old supporters—Jurek Borowczyk, Ludwik Pradzynski, and Bogdan Felski—armed with posters, leaflets, and news bulletins, that the entire work force got the word and struck.

The crowd was milling about in front of the second entrance when I arrived; the guards were scrupulously checking every pass. I'd been banned from the yard for some years now; in order to get in, I had to jump over a nearby wall.

We had agreed that once the shipyard had come out on strike, I would become the principal "ringleader." The program I'd drawn up included the reinstatement of Anna Walentynowicz, Andrzej Kolodziej, and myself; the permission to erect a monument to the victims of December 1970, and a pay raise of 2,000 zlotys for each worker. The rest was to be elaborated on later, once we'd received the support of shipyard personnel. Only then did we include our central demand: the right to organize autonomous trade unions, independent of both management and government authorities.

I was haunted, nevertheless, by the feeling that August had come too soon, that we needed a year or two more of hard work to prepare. In my own forecasts I'd taken account of events like those of August 1980. But the members of the Free Trade Union themselves hadn't formulated their ideas clearly enough to enable us to deal with the problems we would soon have to confront. The declaration of the existence of independent trade unions implied that we had already worked out rules and guidelines for the members to follow in order to avoid basic errors of our own management. But events had overtaken us; we no longer had any choice but to go on. . . .

In our discussions with the management, we had to present our problems specifically. But among ourselves, we spoke quite a different language, debating the important questions (God knows there were enough of them!), such as autonomy, democracy, trade union liberties, recognition of the Katyn massacre, and other key events in our recent national history that had been distorted or glossed over. Our program was fundamentally educational: its primary aim was to change people's way of thinking (as the "Flying University" was doing[9]), rather than to overthrow existing institutions. Our organization was to be a sort of Noah's ark with room for all, bringing the entire Polish nation into calmer waters. But the strike was to collapse when, on the third day, following

9. Created in November 1977, under the inspiration of Andrzej Celinski, the "Flying University" continues to offer lectures on topics that are ignored in official courses.

1970—Confrontation in the North

Gomulka's tanks suppress uprisings on the Baltic, creating the martyrs who a decade later were to be recognized as the forerunners of a historic social revolution—Solidarity. Within a month of the strikes the Party secretary had resigned; and in less than a year, Gomulka's long and checkered career came to an end when he was expelled from the Central Committee.

Below: Striking workers seek shelter (left of platform) from machine-gun fire of troops positioned on overpass (not pictured) in Gdynia, where casualties were heaviest in 1970.

August 16, 1980.
The strike at Gdansk
shipyards ushers in
Solidarity and the
leadership of Lech
Walesa.

A striking shipyard
worker.

Lech and his counselor/priest, Father Henryk Jankowski, rector of St. Brigid's Church.

Jankowski with Anna Walentynowicz, shipyard heroine and valiant fighter for human rights.

Father Jankowski, shipyard priest, offers mass to strikers.

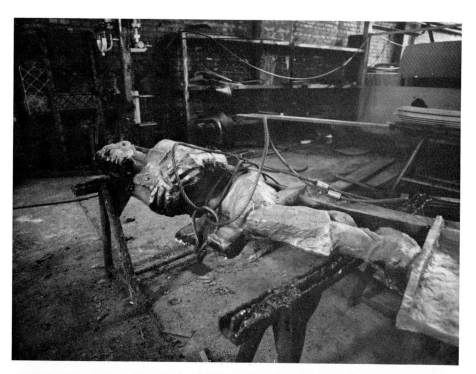

The Solidarity monument to honor the fallen strikers and their supporters of December 1970 is fabricated by workers at the Gdansk shipyard.

The signal that an agreement has been reached between Walesa's *Solidarnosc* and the Gierek government: the Gdansk Accords, August 31, 1980. Edward Gierek resigned as first secretary soon after the accords were signed.

The Solidarity leadership, Gdansk—after the 1980 accords. Left to right: Lech Badkowski, Lech Walesa, Bogdan Lis.

Lech composes himself before speaking during the 500 Days of legalized Solidarity. Lech's arrest and martial law followed on December 13, 1981.

The shipyard cross is transferred to St. Brigid's Church.

A decade later: the ceremony, December 16, 1980, to honor the fallen strikers.

The woman at right mourns the death of her son.

Shipyard worker and coal miner: what began as a free labor union in the Baltic blossomed into a national movement claiming the allegiance of seventy percent of the Polish people.

Above, survivors of World War II concentration camps honor Lech; *below*, the coal miners' band follows suit.

The shipyard workers, *above*, at Gdansk Solidarity ceremony; *below*, Lech and Danuta.

The elected president
and international symbol
of *Solidarnosc*.

From all walks of life: Solidarity.

Graffiti in the north: *above*, "Man is born and lives free"; *below*, "The Volga River's shores are foreign to us and its tanks don't frighten us."

Pope John Paul II's visit to Gdansk on June 12, 1987—it was clear that the spirit of Solidarity still ruled the people. Disappointing the Jaruzelski government by his new outspokenness, the Pope emphasized *Solidarnosc*'s "eternal significance." He continued, "The word was uttered right here, in a new way and in a new context. The world cannot forget it. This word is your pride." During martial law, four years earlier, the government had barred the Pope from visiting the Baltic on his last trip to his native Poland. *Both photos, Bettmann Archive*

a general vote, I was forced to announce its suspension. Henceforth, we would have to adopt a radically new attitude, finding the exact expression of our aspirations in "a Strike in Solidarity." We were only one step away from Solidarity itself.

In our talks with the management, we stuck to our demand for a 2,000-zlotys pay raise as a precondition to all negotiations. We wanted to keep things simple, avoid unnerving them or the mass of workers who had joined our strike with complex arguments. I felt certain many workers were unsure of what they wanted and that they needed firm arguments. I knew they were watching me as if I were in the ring: if I got knocked down in the first round, only half of them would stick around for the second. I had to make sure they were solidly behind me.

Until then I had been talking, bluffing, playing "on credit." Although we pretended to be holding all the high cards, our opponents knew our game inside out, they'd been playing against us for years! But what they didn't know was the nature of our very last card: the determination that had been maturing for ten years now, since the death of three of our colleagues right in front of the second entrance to the shipyard. It was a subject the management merely skirted during our negotiations. They tried to give us the impression that our strike was based on a simple "misunderstanding," especially so because there was no problem at all about reinstating those who had been dismissed, or setting up a commemorative plaque, or honoring our dead in any other suitable way. They encouraged us to open negotiations with them in an "atmosphere of shared responsibilities."

One of the first decisions of the Strike Committee was to demand access to the shipyard radio station. We knew that our strength lay in being able to keep everyone informed of the progress of the negotiations. Each worker could then feel part of them and get to the microphone to give his point of view. From the outset, we connected a microphone in the Health and Safety Office, where the negotiations were taking place, and another outside the room; we were thus able to transmit to all the workshops and production areas. We subsequently arranged for the debates to be heard in neighboring shipyards and in the factories on Walowa Street, and later still, our delegates took recordings away with them to play at other work sites. The authorities in their turn took care to set up contacts with the Party District Committee and other governmental services, including State Radio and Television. In this way it was possible to follow the negotiations in Warsaw itself. This strike was to be conducted with the curtain raised.

While these negotiations were going on at the shipyard, life in Gdansk was gradually slowing down. On Friday, the second day of the strike, the public transport system was immobilized and people were forced to get around on foot, a diverting, if rather disconcerting, turn of events. The only means of transport still working was the fast electric train connecting the three cities (its terminus was located near the shipyard).

More and more people kept flocking to the shipyard perimeter, and all of Gdansk was eager to see for itself what was going on inside. Since the port was no longer operational, the authorities were obliged to inform the shipowners about the strike in order to avoid paying a penalty for making their ships wait in the roads, as international convention demanded. The Gdansk and Gdynia roads were filling up with ships, perfectly visible from the beaches and the rest of the city. Telex and telephone communications had by now been cut, and the blockade was tightening around the Tri-City area.

The official press continued to speak in opaque terms about "work stoppages which are a source of genuine anxiety, aggravating as they do an already difficult economic situation and reducing the production of essential goods, which are becoming increasingly hard to find in the shops. Solutions to a number of questions raised in the course of these discussions reside in the workplace itself. Certain legitimate demands are receiving satisfaction, others require more detailed analysis, and still others, despite their current and possibly future importance, can unfortunately not be satisfied. The authorities quite simply lack the means."

At the shipyard itself, the situation was confused. That Friday, new blood came to swell the ranks of the Strike Committee, which had consisted up until then solely of the workshop delegates responsible for provoking the strike. The workers gathered in the hall of the Health and Safety Office were joined by others who didn't have the imagination to think any further than the problems affecting them personally. In the course of the discussion, they restricted themselves to three points (two of which had practically been resolved): reinstatement of the dismissed persons, commemoration of the victims of December 1970, and a pay raise. They were inclined to accept a compromise pay offer by the management—a raise of 1,500 zlotys per person.

That Saturday, after the majority had adopted the new pay raise and the strikers had been given a no-reprisals guarantee signed by the president of the District National Council and the first secretary of the Party in Gdansk, Tadeusz Fiszbach, the strike was more or less over. As for the rest of the demands—control of trade union activity in the shipyard, improvement in the food supply, abolition of "floating" prices, alignment of family allowances with those of the civil service and the armed forces, continuation of wage payments for the duration of the strike—the management promised to bring them before the competent authorities.

From then on, the strike was to take a different turn. The delegates at the Health and Safety Office allowed their demands to be reduced to the few points which already rang in their ears like a declaration of victory.

I got up, sensing the workers' mood, and speaking into the microphone, said that the strike had ended. As I moved to the door, I brandished my fist and shouted to the supporters of the Free Trade Union, "We've won!"

But that wasn't how others saw things just at that moment. This is how a witness summed it up:

> I was standing with Zdzich Zlotkowski near the main door to the assembly hall of the Health and Safety Office. While the agreements were being signed at the central table (there were three in a row, and the delegates of the Free Trade Union and the management were all grouped around one of them), the room was already half empty. On seeing me with Zdzich near the door, Walesa gestured at us and said again, "We've won!" I replied, "My ass! You've lost," explaining, "just take a look at what's happening in the yard: cables cut and loudspeakers split with axes; they're writing 'Traitor' and 'Informer' on the walls, they're spitting at the very mention of your name. If you go out the door, they'll stone you."

> Lech was completely at the end of his tether.

"Jesus, what have I done?"

Zdzich replied: "What have you done? You've sold the lot of us, that's what you've done. You've only looked after yourself. You're among those who'll be getting the 1,500 zlotys pay raise!"

"What should I do now?" Lech asked.

"Get a real strike going, to defend all the small factories that supported you."

Lech murmured, "Help me!"

The people standing outside, by the second entrance to the shipyard, saw the electrically powered cart draw up with Lech standing on it. Walesa grabbed a microphone and began speaking over the gates. He reminded them, as he'd said before, that he would be the last to leave the yard. "If you want to go on with the strike, it will go on!"

"Who wants to go on with the strike?"

"We do!"

"Who doesn't want to go on with the strike?"

Silence.

"So the strike goes on! I'll be the last to leave the yard."

The gates were closed again.

No, the strike had nothing harmonious about it: moments of enthusiasm were followed by compromises, and even fear.

A strike is a crowd reacting in its own changeable and unpredictable ways. I was aware of that crowd: in the midst of a crowd, before it became a mob, I know instinctively what most people want. It's a question of experience: you have to have been through it often to understand what is happening. At first sight, everything may appear to be going smoothly, yet the cracks are there. The odd person starts going out of his mind, thrashing around like a wild animal, because after a few days he can't stand it any longer. And when the cracks appear, you have to know how to patch them up; know what to look out for, know what to defend at all costs, and what to say. I'd probably have done things completely differently if we'd had to start all over again: I misread the mood; it's only with time that one can see one's mistakes.

My experiences during December 1970, and at the Elektromontaz, nevertheless stood me in good stead. I knew now what to avoid; I was wary of being overconfident. And during the strike of August 1980, in front of the second entrance to the yard, I surprised myself by the quality of my speech: for the first time, my words were entirely in step with my thoughts, and with the plan which I was trying to communicate to my audience. Previously, I always spoke faster than I could think, and my speeches were often a flop as a result: I would start off well, the argument would be a good one, but then, gradually, I would lose the thread of what I was saying.

At the same time, I had to watch the details, the small print: the shipyard almost went back to work at least four times; whole workshops would lose their grip and collapse. There were terrible arguments, too, between the different shipyards. Access to the naval repairs yard was banned, and we had to resort to all sorts of stratagems, such as speaking from the top of an electric cart using loudspeakers. Nothing was easy, but I really felt, however arrogant it might sound, that if anything was to be achieved, it was up to me to achieve it.

Paradoxically, it was the yard's director, Gniech, who replaced Zaczek, who himself first used the expression "Strike in Solidarity!" "Strike in Solidarity"—the words rang out like a living reproach to our caution. We had previously resolved to limit our discussions to problems concerning the shipyard workers only. SOLIDARITY was born at that precise moment when the shipyard strike evolved from a local success in the shipyard, to a strike in support of other factories and business enterprises, large and small, in need of our protection: moral reasons impelled us toward solidarity with our neighbors and our co-workers in every line of endeavor. The result was that, in spite of having declared the strike officially over, that very Saturday afternoon I announced that our movement would continue and the next phase would be put into operation.

This was the decisive turning point. On that third day, our own strike lost its impetus. I had been dealing with a director who was generally considered to have faced up rather well to a situation that, for him, must have been absolutely unprecedented, and I felt obliged to contain our conflict within certain limits. Our movement had been in no way disorderly; each of our objectives had been submitted to the judgment of the general public: I would not and could not go further than that. In the meantime, however, I had given the director my word and we had to face the consequences.

The next day I read the leaflet in which the director set out the situation as he saw it, and I told him straight: "This is by far and away the best thing you've written. But for us, the struggle must go on, because that's what the people want." We founded an Inter-enterprise Strike Committee, and that was the start of a significant new phase. I should stress that, after an initial confrontation, the director came to sympathize with our cause and that no bad feelings persisted between us.

There was a writer at the shipyard (a friend and translator of Günter Grass, who himself was born in nearby Sopot), employed in the yard since 1950, who took part in the events of 1980 and later wrote them up. This is what he says:

The negotiations lasted from Thursday to Saturday. August 17 was a fine day. Too fine, perhaps. It looked like being a jolly weekend. People were all looking forward to doing their own thing: angling, gardening on the allotment, going for drives, hiking, etc. "If only Walesa would leave off, if only he'd agree; it's a success anyway!," they were saying. Washed and ready and waiting for the final announcement, they stood by the gates, near to the loudspeakers. And here it was at last: "I declare the strike ended. Everyone back to work on Monday!" What a relief! And then the national anthem, struck up by Walesa (who sang flat). "He's no singer," some of them said, "but he *can* talk," others replied. "Yes, you can't deny that; he hasn't let us down. . . ."

Most of them went home. And that's when Walesa's troubles began. He doesn't like talking about them. The new situation arose behind his back, outside the assembly hall. There was a podium with a microphone and loudspeakers, which we had christened the "public disco." Anyone could get up there and speak what was on his mind. You could even recite poetry, and some did; I remember one who could not be torn away from the microphone. A messenger from the transport base at nearby Oliwa also managed to get himself heard on that podium. His work force wanted to join the strike, without really knowing how to go about it. The messenger wasn't very clued into the proceeding. To begin with, he just stood there, looking puzzled at just about the same time Walesa was calling an end to the strike. Then right next door, in the Health and Safety Office—a representative of the transport employees found himself propelled onto the podium and a microphone thrust in front of him. He finally succeeded in setting out their cause, ending his speech with a plea for support. A moment later, the streetcar workers came out of the building and joined him. The podium was surrounded by young men—a hundred, two hundred, five hundred people shouting "Solidarity!" "Solidarity!" "Solidarity!" Several dozen more came to the windows of the assembly hall and began to chant "Two thousand!" "Two thousand!" "Two thousand!"—questioning the concessions which had been made during the negotiations. The thing should be made clear: the whole business began outside the shipyard. The shipyard workers were satisfied with what Walesa had negotiated. They didn't think of the success of their strike as the successful vindication of all their claims; on the contrary, they felt that the outcome of the shipyard strike should serve as an example to other factories in Gdansk. By Monday, they would be clear in their own minds about their future; in other words, they would see what the authorities really meant to do, and how strong the strikers of Gdansk and Gdynia really were. We—at least many of the shipyard workers—were ready to strike again on Monday in support of, for instance, the streetcar workers, and possibly others.

As soon as he came out of the hall, Walesa saw at a glance that the shipyard strike couldn't be allowed to end in that way. The cracks were appearing and by Monday there would be nothing left of the strike; Walesa decided to resume it.

"So, we're still on strike, is that it?"
The question was a pure formality, although there were scarcely more than a thousand people left to do battle. That Saturday night was difficult for those who had stayed on at the yard. They told us afterward that there weren't enough of them to station guards at the gates and along the perimeter wall. By Sunday, things were looking better: part of the work

force had returned. But, until then, there must have been some bitter moments for Walesa. That night graffiti had appeared on the walls calling him a "traitor." And on Saturday afternoon, in the repairs yard, two "messengers," wives of Gdansk strikers, had made exhibitions of themselves, attacking Walesa and the strikers with harsh language, calling them names and accusing them of having "done themselves a good turn" without concern for other workers. Their excessive language made the workers in the repairs yard acutely uncomfortable. It was an unfortunate episode (it took place on the Saturday during the discussions with Deputy Premier Pyka). Though the intentions of these women were probably good, their actions, fueled by anger and disappointment, were misguided: it's not just what is said that's important, but the way in which it's said.

Never, under any circumstances, did Walesa employ language of this kind against anyone. This was a feature of his speeches: his harshest remarks never jarred his listeners; even when expressing himself most vigorously, he was never offensive. He never used insults and never swore. This was no doubt the result of his civilized attitude to life, closely linked to his Christian faith.

People are generally not moved by insults and curses. For a few days, the repairs workers lost their trust in us, not because we left the shipyard that Saturday, but because we hadn't been able to get our message across to them in the right words.

On Sunday, August 17, Walesa took up a wooden cross, like Simon of Cyrene, and carried it in front of the entrance, to the spot where we meant to erect the monument. The cross was cemented into the ground and marked the cementing, for many days, of a communion of strikers, involving several hundred different enterprises—shipyards, factories, offices, universities, right down to the various unions, associations, and societies. During that Sunday night, we got rid of the inscriptions defaming Walesa. And that same night, he consolidated his position by officially assuming the chairmanship of the Strike Committee created in solidarity with the interests of the various enterprises of Gdansk, Gdynia, Elblag, Pruszcz, Tczew, Lebork, and many others.

On Monday morning, the director, who, on Saturday, had

co-signed with Walesa the agreement regarding the shipyard, tried once more to appeal to the loyalty of the work force and reproached Walesa for having broken their agreement. Walesa could only agree with him: "Your petition is the best thing you've written," he said, adding ironically, "pity it isn't signed," his good nature tempered for once with an ounce of malice. The director lowered his arms: "It isn't up to me anymore. It's not a shipyard strike anymore. It's a STRIKE IN SOLIDARITY."

This was when a "technical breakdown" prevented both sides from putting out communiqués, proclamations, appeals, and speeches on the local radio. Before the "technical breakdown," the director had succeeded in addressing a new appeal to the work force. He shut up after that. The workers were deaf to his words by then anyhow.

The crowd refused to believe that the radio had broken down, and nagged the director to allow them access to the transmitter. The director was powerless to do anything, but the crowd had the answer: "Walesa! Walesa! Walesa!" chanted several thousand people, either sitting or standing in front of the management building. The same shouts continued, alternating with "Lech! Lech! Lech!" They thought Lech knew everything, could achieve absolutely anything. He had become a myth, a legend. It was a naïve faith which sprang from the fact that through his personality, his presence, his words, and his actions, Lech had cemented a movement previously diffused and achieved unity that had seemed impossible. The tiny seedling had grown to gigantic proportions; the larva had sprouted wings; in his mouth, vague and uncertain words became magic formulas and incantations.

Walesa gathered the crowd in front of the building. It was not for the first time, but this time, all fear had gone; they held their heads high. There was power welling up in this crowd, it was almost tangible, flowing from one person to another, limitless.

Walesa had to sort out with the director the problem of getting the local radio going again, so that it could be at the strikers' disposal. He went up to the first floor, reserved for "interviews." Those who were in the know already were aware that the director couldn't do anything about the "breakdown," that he didn't have the slightest power to intervene. Maybe he'd already been divested of his authority? Maybe someone else was making the decisions instead of him at this very moment? A hundred Walesas couldn't do anything about it either. But the crowd firmly believed that Walesa would sort things out. He had to pass this second test. I watched him. He came back with a gloomy face. How was he going to explain his failure? There would be no point in launching into a speech about the limits of human endeavor, and the fact that the decision-making bodies in the shipyard had virtually no real power. He heaved himself onto his electric cart and, with the gesture that everyone knew, silenced the crowd. "Listen! I couldn't do it! No, no, no, I couldn't do it!" (All at once, there was a terrifying silence. Everybody was staring at their leader.) "I went to the director. I demanded access to the radio, and he raised his arms above his head and said: 'Mr. Walesa, you can have me arrested, but I can't do it. I can't do anything.'" Walesa's tone became dramatic: "And could I, myself arrested several times, arrested at the very moment my wife was about to give birth, could I really arrest anyone else? No, of course I couldn't!" When he had said this, he covered his eyes with a dramatic gesture, as if the very idea of doing anything so despicable left him feeling paralyzed. "Should I have done such a thing? Would you have wanted me to do it?" "No-o, no-o!" the spectators chorused.

Was he merely being skillful, or had the director's simple gesture affected him so deeply? Either way, he had just passed his latest test, and hung on to his authority.

The Inter-enterprise Strike Committee (MKS), a key organization that allowed Solidarity to express the many demands of many different types of workers in concrete terms, was created on August 17 and 18. The government recognized the MKS's significance at once, threatening to end the shipyard strike by force once it heard of the committee's existence. The government did not want to acknowledge the legitimacy of an independent strike committee that might eventually speak for the majority of Poland's work force.

The local government negotiators in Gdansk were instructed "to continue talks with the strikers, not with the MKS." Even before the appearance of the MKS it was clear that the central government realized it was losing control of the situation. Fearing the worst, the central committee began looking for scapegoats. The first identified were the local authorities in Gdansk, who were blamed for letting the strike get out of hand and then, later, for not using force when it might have stopped the strike. First Secretary Gierek inadvertently provided another scapegoat when he sent his own emissary, Deputy Premier Pyka, to Gdansk to break the strike. The Gierek-Pyka tactic was to avoid discussion with unified strike committees and instead attempt to split up the strikers by negotiating directly with each of the shipyard's workshops. When this tactic failed and a dejected Pyka left the Gdansk airport for Warsaw, he made it clear that he knew his own days of government privilege were over. Some suggested the Gierek himself would be the strike's next victim.

Politburo members Stanislaw Kania and Henryk Jablonski, president of the state council, arrived in Gdansk the night of August 18. In a series of meetings with other government and Party officials the Politburo members spoke of the emergency conditions in the Baltic, suggesting that the Party leadership had lost contact with the workers and Polish society generally. This sounded the death knell of the Gierek regime. Party hard-liners at the meetings suggested the strikers were antisocialist and that their leaders were terrorists. A special target of this group was Bogdan Borusewicz, one of the leaders of KOR, who was thought to be responsible for radicalizing the workers' demands. A surprising event occurred at the shipyard when Borusewicz, who was receiving news of the various points of view of the government officials from a journalist friend covering the meetings of Party leaders, arranged to have a detailed account of the meetings transmitted over the shipyard's loudspeakers. Thus the workers were able to hear directly how the government was responding to the strike and to understand that some officials recognized the strike as a legitimate workers' protest, while others saw the strikers only as counterrevolutionaries. The most discredited official was a Politburo member and president of the Central Council of Trade Unions by the name of Szydlak. He had made it clear that he had no interest in sharing power with anyone, certainly not with workers represented by an independent union.

As the MKS strike committee began to consider the final demands we would submit, it was clear to me that I would have to depend on the thinking of a good number of experts who had not been part of earlier strike committees. Some of my closest friends and advisers worried that an elitist committee was taking over and that the original strikers would be excluded from the deliberations. On the other side, as the "twenty-one demands" were being formulated, several members of the new committee seemed to have serious doubts about my leadership. One night before drifting off to sleep, I thought that all committee activity is shot through with personal factors. Each of us who had organized the strike was driven by our own unique sensibilities and particular experiences. It was therefore no surprise that when some of our number felt that they, along with their positions and experiences, were being pushed aside, they reacted with considerable bitterness. I recognized that the leadership could not individually assess and take account of every need, however justifiable that need might be. More important, I knew at this critical juncture, as we articulated the "twenty-one demands" and prepared to present them to the government negotiators, that the strike leadership, and by that I now mean the MKS, had to remain moderate. We had many tricky questions to resolve and we could not afford to be sidetracked by unrealistic demands. Fortunately, most members of the MKS shared this view. Borusewicz, the supposed radical, reminded us how the attempt to abolish censorship in the Prague Spring of 1968 had ended so tragically: he advised moderation. Aleksander Hall, the brilliant youth leader, stressed that we had to formulate our demands so as to leave the authorities room to maneuver. As we completed the "twenty-one demands," an addendum was incorporated, at Borusewicz's suggestion, which was a request that the Catholic mass be transmitted on radio stations on a regular schedule. Some committee members worried that this could become a major stumbling block.

As we prepared to negotiate with the government representatives we emphasized to the workers that the discipline within the shipyard had become important. The men got the message and on their own account got rid of all vodka on the premises and presented themselves in an orderly fashion. As soon as our demands were written, they were distributed to the workers. Within a few days, the terms for the negotiations were established with the government officials and it was understood that our strike committee would be informed by a variety of experts from many different regions of Poland. This is how the "twenty-one demands" strike bulletin read when it was posted on August 22:

STRIKE INFORMATION BULLETIN

Demands by the work force of enterprises and administrations represented by the Inter-enterprise Strike Committee (MKS).

The Inter-enterprise Strike Committee also represents the personnel of enterprises and offices that have not joined the strike because their work is indispensable to society, and should not be disrupted. The committee's intention is to negotiate for all work forces on strike. The primary condition to opening negotiations with the government is their agreement to reconnect all telephone and telecommunication lines. The specific demands of the work forces on strike, as represented by the MKS, are as follows:

1. Recognition of the Free Trade Union, independent of the Party and of employers, based on convention No. 87 of the International Labor Organization, referring to the freedom to form trade unions, which has been ratified by the Polish People's Republic.
2. Guarantee of the right to strike, and of the indemnity of strikers and their supporters.
3. Guaranteed freedom of expression and of publication as set forth by the Constitution of the People's Republic of Poland, and consequently, an end to the suppression of independent publications and the opening up of the mass media to representatives of all political and religious persuasions.
4. Restoration of rights to persons dismissed for having defended workers' rights, particularly those who took part

in the strikes of 1970 and 1976, and those students excluded from higher education because of their opinions. Liberation of all political prisoners (especially Edmunt Zadrozynski, Jan Kozlowski, and Marek Kolodziej), and an end to repression for crimes of conscience.

5. Access to the mass media to inform public opinion of the creation of the Inter-enterprise Strike Committee and to make its demands public.

6. Initiation of efficient measures for relieving the country's economic crisis by mass circulation of all information relating to the socioeconomic situation, and granting, at every social level, the opportunity of citizens to take part in discussions concerning economic reforms.

7. Payment to all strikers for days on strike, to be counted as a paid vacation period: funds to be taken from the Central Trade Union Council treasury.

8. Monthly increase of 2,000 zlotys to every worker's base pay to compensate for latest price increases.

9. Establishment of salary scales for all positions.

10. Assurance that all foodstuffs are available to the home market; export of surplus food only.

11. Introduction of rationing (with books) for all meat products (until market stabilizes).

12. Suppression of government-sanctioned "floating prices" and the payment in foreign currencies for scarce items in special "hard currency" stores (known as "internal export").

13. Appointment of management staff according to merit, not to Party membership. Withdrawal of privileges from militia, security forces, and Party members by making family allowances the same for all citizens. Elimination of "reserved sales" system.

14. Lowering the retirement age (to pre-Revolution age).

15. Payment of pension benefits (to post-Revolution level).

16. Improvement of working conditions and health services, plus full medical assistance for all workers and families.

17. The creation of adequate day-care centers and nurseries for the children of working mothers.

18. Paid maternity leave of three full years to allow mothers to raise their young children.

19. Reduction of the waiting time for apartments.
20. Increase in travel allowances from 40 to 100 zlotys and introduction of a cost-of-living allowance.
21. Saturday as a work-free day for all, whether workers are on scheduled production lines or on one of three eight-hour shifts. Compensation for work on Saturday: extra vacation days or the granting of other free days, with pay.

Inter-enterprise Strike Committee
Gdansk, August 22, 1980

The specialists who had come from all over Poland to advise us on the negotiations with the government turned up at various times during the strike. Lech Badkowski, for example, had been with us since the announcement of the strike, but by the ninth day of the strike he was with us officially, as a representative of the Union of Polish Writers of the Gdansk region. When Badkowski later joined the leadership of the MKS, he was warmly received and became the strikers' first spokesman and, later on, an important voice for Solidarity. His contribution to the negotiations with the government commission was crucial, as were those of many other experts.

The turning point in the strike occurred on Friday, August 22, when Mieczyslaw Jagielski, the new deputy premier, arrived in Gdansk to replace the discredited Pyka. When he met our delegates that evening we realized we had won a major victory for the simple reason that the government was ready to negotiate with the MKS on the basis of our "twenty-one demands." To prepare ourselves for the negotiations, our committee studied the demands closely with a view toward eliminating loopholes and any language that would seem to make our position appear unreasonable; in other words, the experts were advising us on the formal conventions of labor negotiations. After the first meeting, several of them advised me of appropriate procedures to limit the number of demands in each negotiating session. Once these had been accepted, we could then move on to the next group of demands. They made it clear that if the authorities were pushed too far in any one session, they might end up by accepting some demands while eliminating others, establishing trade-offs that would be disadvantageous to us. All of our strategies and tactics for the negotiations were discussed at great length in a secure building where we could be certain that our deliberations could not be overheard. During our discussions, the more cynical among us maintained that the government would never authorize an independent trade union. This group believed that we would be better off if we insisted instead on safeguards in the form of worker-controlled committees. Other members of the MKS thought such safeguards would be meaningless as they had been in the past, and, thinking back to the memory of December 1970, the majority pressed for independent unions.

Saturday, August 23, was the start of the negotiations. At 8:00 P.M., the bus containing the government representatives arrived and the crowd of workers reluctantly allowed it to pass through the second entrace into the shipyard. As the bus drove inside the yard, its progress was impeded by a wall of workers dressed in worn blue overalls who stood silent with folded arms and grim faces. Before the bus came to a stop, the workers had moved forward, shouting, "Get out! Get down on your knees before the workers!" Naturally I recognized this as an ominous welcome and quickly moved out of the Health and Safety Office with Gniech, the yard's director, making our way through the crowd to the bus. As Jagielski stepped from the bus, pale and drawn, I walked toward the deputy premier, holding out my hand to welcome him to the shipyard. The crowd responded by chanting, "Le-ch! Le-ch!" and waving their arms and clenched fists. They allowed us to pass as we moved back together toward the Health and Safety Office. After the deputy premier and I entered the building, guards had to extricate other government officials from the crowd, one by one, and lead them into the building. The negotiations were to take place in a meeting room to the left of the building's main entrance. I chose instead to lead the group in single file up the stairs and into the great hall, where delegates, journalists, and others who had succeeded in getting a pass were assembled. Gathered around the podium stood the members of the MKS, who introduced themselves and shook hands with the government officials. Jagielski tried to lighten the tone, and win over the delegates by moving toward a woman—a streetcar operator named Henryka Krzywonos—and stooping to kiss her hand. After a few mild pleasantries, the negotiations began in the downstairs meeting room.

Danuta did not see me for the first four days of the strike, but by Saturday she couldn't take it any longer and, with a neighbor, who worked at the yard, made a visit. The neighbor parked some distance from the yard, leaving Danuta to walk to the entrance on her own. She later said that she found me confident of victory, though tired and plagued by a sore throat. On the following days, Danuta returned, either with our oldest son, Bogdan, or with our second son, Slawek. From that first Saturday, she took part in the masses and less formal prayers that were said each day inside the shipyard.

Danuta

After each visit, Lech would escort me back to the gate. As soon as people heard that he was coming, they chanted his name, and he would climb up onto the gates to greet them. There were some drains below, and on top, a plank balanced between stones. People were sitting on the plank, and one of them, a woman over fifty years old, saw Lech climbing onto the gates, and stood up on the plank. I wasn't looking at Lech, but at this woman, who, in spite of her age and her figure—she probably wasn't aware of where she was standing—started moving up and down like a ten-year-old girl on a seesaw. Lech was speaking in very simple sentences, making jokes, and people were laughing and clapping, enjoying themselves; some were even crying. I was in a different world—afraid, more than anything, but it's difficult now to describe precisely what I felt. I knew Lech was drawing away from me, he was with all those people, and I realized life was going to be different from then on—unknown territory stretched ahead of us both. Would it be for better or for worse?

That Sunday, after the first round of negotiations, we received news from Warsaw about changes that were occurring in the Party leadership at the Central Committee meeting. My first reaction was to try to decode the meaning of these changes, but it was difficult, forcing us to drift without a compass. None of us had considered it our duty to support particular government leaders, nor to attempt to exercise influence in Party matters. In the present situation, it was clear that if we backed someone it would only have undermined his position. Therefore we concentrated on our own business, leaving the government leaders to jump through their own hoops.

From the beginning of the negotiations, Jagielski took a reasonable position in response to our demands, and he was supported in his efforts by the Fiszbach-Kolodziejski tandem, from Gdansk. They had become virtual allies, partisans of an agreement. The district Gdansk leadership suggested that the government must resign itself to the fact that it was in the country's best interest to negotiate in good faith and to support an independent union. The difficulty lay in the wording of the "twenty-one demands," whose implications in a few instances were unmistakably political. The addendum about broadcasting mass on the radio had become a problem, especially so when the minister of religions arrived from Szczecin to interrupt the deliberations with word that the addendum was nonsense and wasn't provided for in the Constitution. The minister suggested that the church itself would oppose the addendum, because radio broadcast would cut church attendance. When it was pointed out that we might consult the Primate on this matter, the minister barked that Gdansk stood alone on this issue and that the government had already concluded its agreement with Szczecin. Bogdan Lis responded, "I guess we're stuck. I'll inform the committee presidium and the delegates that the negotiations with the government commission have been cut off by the government representatives." Kolodziejski, the Gdansk governor, stated calmly that mass could be transmitted by radio. He had made a decision that could later cause him trouble, especially so because in such situations no one usually takes the responsibility for a decision of that magnitude. Anyway, the problem seemed to have gone away and a few other tricky points were soon resolved to our mutual satisfaction and we were at the end of our list of demands. What we didn't realize at the time was that the other negotiations then under way in Warsaw would soon reveal a new leadership in top Party and government circles. During the last two days of our negotiations press reports appeared accusing us of stalling and allowing "bananas to rot in the holds of ships waiting to enter the harbor at Gdansk." Obviously the government commission was trying to intimidate us and "the bananas" became a constant reproach. The next day we handed over an MKS declaration to the deputy premier to the effect that the responsibility for prolonging the strike lay with the government, not us. We knew the Party propaganda machine had been cranked up again, and we wanted to be certain that the agreements were signed before a new government came into power. One disturbing report broadcast on radio and television quoted a recent Wyszinski sermon at Jasna Gora. A passage was taken out of the sermon's context to support the government position that the strike committee had become unreasonable. We later found out, when we saw the uncensored text of the Primate's sermon, that he had not sided with the government at all. In fact, on August 28, the Primate met a delegation of strikers and handed them a communiqué from the General Council of Polish Bishops together with a declaration from the Pope that approved all of our demands. This information had been censored from the official media.

The last negotiating session occurred on Saturday, August 30, and it was obvious that Jagielski was in a great hurry to conclude the talks. He suggested that he hoped to return to the shipyard with the agreements "politically approved" by the Central Committee later in the day. He was even ready to discuss the wording of a final communiqué as an announcement of our agreement. I realized after he had left that we still hadn't agreed on the release of political prisoners, and when, on Sunday, I raised the issue of the prisoners with Jagielski, not so much as an ultimatum but as a simple question, he answered, "All the political prisoners will be released the following day."

Though all signs were positive, some of the members of our committee worried that though it appeared the Gierek government would approve the agreement as negotiated by Jagielski, what would happen if another government immediately invalidated it? As it turned out, we were a little slow in getting our papers in final form, in large part because we had some problems with our typists. Jagielski didn't know about this and assumed our delay was a manifestation of our distrust. When Bogdan Lis told him that we were making progress but were a bit behind schedule, Jagielski, who obviously was under some strain, responded, "Excuse me, but I don't know if I'll be able to sign the agreement in one hour's time." We then realized that there was more bluffing going on than we had realized, and it was Jagielski who at this moment was playing on credit. He must have known just how serious was the political struggle at the top levels of the Party, but—much to his credit—he pushed on without knowing what the outcome would be. The actual signing of the entire list of demands together with the overall agreement was scheduled for the great assembly hall on Monday, August 31. With a minimum of ceremony both sides signed the papers, even though neither had any notion of what was happening behind closed doors in Warsaw.

Hardly had the ink dried when we received word that Gierek had been forced to resign.

500 Days

If I were looking for a metaphor to illustrate the situation Poland confronted after Solidarity was legalized in the late summer of 1980, I would compare Polish society to a pauper who, for most of his life, occupied a small corner of a fine house only to learn, quite suddenly, that he is in fact master of the house, not its tenant.

Now what happens to our pauper? Overnight his status switches from that of nervous tenant, uncertain of his rights, to that of an owner—master of his property and his destiny. He sets about discovering what the house was like in the time of his father and his grandfather, where the furniture used to stand, the location of the family silver and other heirlooms, the condition of his fields. As master, he wants to replace the provisional order with what he now sees as the natural order, and to put his own plans into effect. He moves the furniture back where it belongs, lays the carpets, hangs the old pictures, and sees to repairing the decay he had noticed as tenant but didn't much care about until his fortune changed.

As for the temporary owner who had apparently taken advantage of the situation, what can he do now? Inveigh against the care which our pauper lavishes so passionately on the house that is now his? Restrain him in his devotion to his property? Unlikely, for if he's to stay on he must begin his new position by drawing up a persuasive report of his earlier stewardship, and in his new role he must be responsive to his new master.

On the face of it such a reversal of roles, is, psychologically speaking, difficult, perhaps impossible, for the former steward and for the new owner. Their respective temperaments will govern their reactions and chances for mutual success. This is how things looked to me during the autumn and winter of 1980–1981. The Gdansk Agreements had opened up the possibilities for a new phase of co-existence between workers and management, between citizens and their government, and they had demonstrated the necessity of a sharing of power.

A short film made in Gdansk gives some idea of the atmosphere of those early days at the trade union headquarters. The film is in black and white and the countless copies that have been made from it have certainly not improved its technical quality. As the camera moves down the corridor, through the door, it closes on the desk where I am sitting. Someone puts a poster on the desk, points to it, and asks if the decision to strike is irrevocable. We are in the period September–October 1980, the time of the first token strike, the first test, for the government as well as for our-selves. Will the August Agreements prevail? We were constantly being scrutinized. Did we represent a force to be reckoned with, the authorities wondered, or would the August storm blow itself out by late autumn?

The fellow seated at the desk, though there's no doubt that it's me, looks very much younger—ten or even fifteen years. Yet it's scarcely five years since the film was made!

It all started off quietly. For most of that first Sunday afternoon and night I had only one thought in my mind: this was just the beginning.

On that Monday morning, the first trade union office was opened in Marchlewskiego Street, in the old part of Wrzeszcz. The rooms were on the first floor of a decrepit office block with creaking floorboards. At 10:00 A.M., the keys were handed over. Someone hung a red and white flag outside the main door. By late morn-ing people began arriving, and within an hour a line stretched to the street. It was obvious that it would be impossible to work there. Luckily, we soon obtained new offices, two floors in the former Hotel Morski, on Grunwaldzka Street, the main street in Wrzeszcz.

The film re-creates the first moments in the life of the independent trade union. My Grunwaldzka Street office was at the end of the corridor; everybody who walked to the end landed there, and the flow of people, transactions, and suggestions seemed endless.

It was some months before the rest of the country was prepared to recognize the idea of free trade unions. Large numbers of people kept arriving in Gdansk with a variety of complaints and demands for intervention in cities and towns throughout Poland where attempts to set up the new organizations were meeting obstruction. In some places, the authorities simply refused to take on the difficult task of initiating a dialogue with workers. Others spent most of their time waving the bogey of "Big Brother," promising early punishment and a reestablishment of the old order.

Gdansk had to explain, defend, organize, and approve these various appeals. The capital of a new worker's Poland had moved to the Baltic Coast. The authorities on the spot showed a genuine understanding of the movement, having participated in the events that had led to Solidarity's legality. Their most recent statements had been straightforward, devoid of any self-justifying undertones. This openness was particularly evident in the attitude of Klemens Gniech, the director of the Gdansk shipyard, with whom we had nevertheless had tough talks in the first hours of the strike. At the first meeting of trade union delegates in the shipyard, he declared:

According to what I've been told you represent some twelve thousand people right now. In my eyes, therefore, you are the genuine representatives of our work force; it's with you that I shall collaborate. The management of every yard or factory or business enterprise needs its work force to be represented in a responsible and trustworthy fashion; I cannot now envisage working without such representation, without the possibility of consultation on the progress of the yard or on particular measures concerning the workers. Our yard has become a symbol of the strike. Everyone's eyes are fixed on us. The procedures we work out here will provide a model for other workplaces. So let me stress to you the immense responsibility we shall be taking on in every decision we make.

We were in contact with Jerzy Kolodziejski, local governor[10] in Gdansk, who had to deal with all the difficult cases that came before our standing commission regarding opposition to local trade union branches in other places of work. These brought to light long-standing abuses, hitherto carefully covered up, by certain managements, especially of small plants, who had never been subject to any form of social control. These abuses added to the problems of organization and impeded the development of our trade union structures, while also resurrecting some awkward and powerful ghosts for the managements involved.

Trade union locals proliferated at a dizzying speed in places of work, in schools, and in hospitals; trade union members naturally sought to influence decisions regarding pay and productivity, and also the settlement of individual grievances, though most managements opposed their aims. There were no precedents with which to interpret the August Agreements, many clauses of which were drafted in general terms; within days, controversies multiplied about which specific powers the Constitution granted to trade union members. Although the Constitution did deal with this question in broad terms, it turned out that the right to interpret the texts and to apply them was reserved for the government alone. And now the government had to give up, one by one, all the privileges it had appropriated over the past thirty-five years in violation of the Constitution, and of agreements, then in force, which contravened legitimacy and justice. The church, meanwhile (whose power, as a symbol of Solidarity, was growing), stressed the fundamental nature of the civil rights that the government had flouted.

The problems that arose had to be settled by the MKZ—the Inter-enterprise Founding Committee of Independent Self-governing Trade Unions. There were only eighteen of us—the leadership of the MKZ—to carry the burden of reforming, there and then, the entire system, for which our sole training was a few years'

10. Poland is divided into districts, whose executive head is appointed by the central government. Members are elected to the legislative branches of local government—the District National Council, or, for the city, the Municipal National Council; each has its own presidium. Each district also has its own Party secretary. To limit the power of Party secretaries and the autonomy of the districts generally, the Gierek regime increased the number of districts in Poland from 17 to 48. When Solidarity established its national organization, it did so on regional lines to avoid any possibility of district control.

activity in the fledgling Free Trade Union. But when it became obvious that the experience we had acquired was not enough, I found new resources, in the activist church leadership, and in the faith which I had turned to in the darkest hours of the strike.

Every morning, before breakfast, however late I had gone to bed the night before, I would go to seven o'clock mass at the church in Przymorze, which Lenarciak had had built to commemorate the riots of December 1970. My day began with silence and calm, and it was this half hour of devotion that helped me face the rest of the day, including the hopes and expectations of others that we would never be able to satisfy.

In early September, we received a message from Warsaw to the effect that Cardinal Wyszynski wished to meet me and the group who had directed the strike and negotiated the accords. At last I was to meet, face-to-face, the man who personified the Polish church and who, as a prisoner of conscience for three years, had represented the principal link with the best of our living national traditions.

It was the first time I had left Gdansk since the strike. The Primate received me warmly, clasping me in his arms, like a father embracing a prodigal son. Stefan Cardinal Wyszynski was a powerful Primate. Each of his gestures seemed to express the two millennia of the church's existence. It was as if all the hustle and bustle of our daily lives stopped, as if everything took on another dimension in his presence. And this order and harmony spilled over into our meeting. It was Sunday; we had begun with an early mass, during which Cardinal Wyszynski, addressing himself to our group, said: "Nothing insignificant can ever achieve freedom. We must strive with all our might for the welfare of the workers, who are themselves making an immense effort in our Fatherland. But we must be wise; we must prove ourselves capable of embracing both the present and the future of our beloved country in order that, after so many vain attempts to free our countrymen in Poland, this attempt, which is founded on love, may triumph."

In the course of a private conversation, I was able to understand more clearly what the Primate meant. He believed that in times of rapid social change there is a danger of concentrating excessively on certain closely held points of view and prejudices. A little later, he said: "It's not a question of wanting to change the leaders, it's they who must change. We must make sure—and I make this comparison quite deliberately—that one gang of robbers doesn't steal the keys of the state treasury from another similar gang. What is at stake is the rebirth of man himself."

It was an important point and one we had had in mind in August, when we refused to pick and choose from among the professional groups, including the journalists, who were interested in learning what had happened in Gdansk. The hard-liners among us often reproached me, saying that one should subject people to "verification," accept some and refuse others, and they said this at a time when we were showing such optimism, such faith in man by our openness and by the fact that everyone was being urged to "change themselves"—rather than "be changed" by our actions. I felt close to the Primate on all these concerns.

Shortly afterward, I learned with great interest of his attitude toward the people in high government circles. He viewed them as dependent creatures, condemned by circumstances to be no more than puppets. In his eyes, they deserved compassion; after all, they were his sons, too, like the rest of us. We had heard about his meeting with Edward Gierek in January 1978, before the Pope's first visit, when he said to the first secretary: "You should convert, change yourself. Otherwise you'll fall to pieces; you'll be smashed, destroyed."

There were then forebodings in the air, though nobody yet spoke of them openly. The Primate expressed his warnings without fear, serving notice on the authorities; their failure to meet their moral obligation toward the people, obligations inherent in the power of government, would lead them to catastrophe.

Tolerant toward politicians, whatever their ideological stance, he said that, in spite of everything, Gomulka had been a man with clean hands, a political enthusiast, inwardly convinced that he was following the right path. Gomulka had stood up to the Stalinists and was arrested, only to be returned to favor and power after Khrushchev had consolidated his own power. When Gierek's career suddenly ended with the signing of the August accords (as Gomulka's had ended a decade earlier with the 1970 strike), his successor as first secretary, Stanislaw Kania, asked the Primate to speak to a disillusioned Gierek. "Perhaps, in the course of our conversation, I might be able to give Mr. Gierek the comfort he needs," responded the Primate, who, when he visited Gierek, was distressed to find him disoriented and in a state of collapse.

I learned a great deal from the Primate, who had a strong sense of history and a profound notion of justice. He sometimes surprised me by the kindness and generosity that were so far removed from the summary attitude it would have been tempting for him to adopt at the time. In 1970, after the events of that bloody December, when the church was in a position to make demands on a government weakened by recent upheavals, the Primate had declared that one could not "win" grace through the blood shed by workers, that the church should be strong in itself, not because of the weakness of an apparent opponent. For me it was a new way of looking at life and one that gave me plenty to think about, expressing as it did a moral point that left no one indifferent.

Novice though I then was, it was from such elements that I was able to construct what was later called the "Walesa line." But at the same time our cause was a "worldly" one and to surmount the obstacles raised against us, we also needed other skills.

If I had to state what was the most valuable notion that helped me to deal with the complex reality of Poland from August 1980 onwards, I would say that it was being able to point to a third way in those situations where everybody says there are only two. In life, it's sometimes essential to be able to think out different ways around a problem, just as in some games—in billiards or tennis, for instance—the point cannot always be won by hitting the ball forcefully in a straight line. At times it is the ball that is skillfully or even cunningly played that will achieve its object; if you apply spin, the line the ball follows isn't necessarily the shortest but it can land in the right spot.

In August, our objective was obvious: we had to stop the strike, formulate our demands, and get the government to accept them. And we had reached this stage intact, without visible scars. When the Agreements were signed it was equally clear to everyone that they were "evolutional," that they opened an era of significant reforms, and represented an attempt to determine the prospects of advancement for a country in a concrete political context which had so far obstructed all change.

Party politics didn't really interest us. We had no desire to assume power ourselves and to reestablish order through a government of our own. Instead, we were looking for profound internal changes in the existing government; we had experienced somewhat similar situations before, and there was no guarantee that another government would be any better. It was a question, rather, of getting the authorities to recognize the needs and aspirations of the people and of creating safeguards to prevent the corruption of power. The new trade unions were to be the driving force behind these changes. And the changes were to transform the Polish society.

Our idea was immediately taken up by Czeslaw Milosz, the Polish poet then professor at the University of California at Berkeley who had just received the Nobel Prize for literature. Some months later, at a meeting at the Gdansk shipyard, he told us: "If you were a political party who wanted to regain power, world reaction toward you would be the same as toward other political parties engaged in similar rivalries and the one factor would be missing to earn you the attention of people of every country, race, and class—hope! The hope that these petrified forms of social life can be replaced by new forms, corresponding to man's real needs and true greatness. The hope that millions of people, united by a common will, can find new forms of coexistence between citizens of the same country and between the countries themselves, especially now when these petrified forms threaten our planet with a conflict of appalling proportions."

We managed to carry out a number of projects without delay, in particular the construction in Gdansk of the monument to the shipyard workers who fell in 1970. We had made a clear commitment on this and the government didn't have much chance of backing out. We put forward the preliminary design, sketched out by Bogdan Pietruszka, the man who had drawn up the construction plans for our own shipyard, and who had himself lived through the events of December 1970. But there were to be endless difficulties before the project was finally approved. To discuss it with us, the government sent the deputy minister of culture, who happened to be a teacher of architecture. The poor man only succeeded in arousing our pity by his clumsy attempts to substitute for our drawing, with its explicit symbolism, another object, which could have served only to blur the monument's significance. By picking up allies in government circles, however, we finally got our way.

146

But it was an exceptional success: other projects were much more complex and easier to undermine by distorting the original plan on which we had pinned our hopes.

There were endless questions to be answered. What sort of Poland did we want? What sort of Poland was possible? How were we to resolve the question of the Party nomenclature? How were we to change the system whereby the Party alone decided on the filling of key posts at all levels of government, not only in the political sphere, but in civic, police, and military activity where its word was law? How were we to resolve the thorny problem of censorship, which affected all forms of creativity and communication? How were we to deal with the problem of the monopoly of the mass media? What were we to do about an economy doomed to inefficiency, subordinated to the plan instead of obeying the workings of the market? What were we to do about all those people deprived of genuine participation in the decision-making process at their places of work?

During the strike, we had been the driving force, we had set out the problems to be resolved; the movement had followed a program which itself dictated the tempo of events. But now the situation had changed. It was a race against the clock and we no longer had control of events. The priorities had been switched, and we had to redouble our efforts just to keep on course, to be flexible enough to change directions if necessary, to avoid catastrophes, and to act as a buffer when the demands put forward directly threatened the existence of certain power structures. In the course of dozens of meetings, I had to combat the general inclination to settle accounts with bosses, compromised factory managers, and government representatives as workers were carried away by a passion to clean up everything all at once.

They turned first on those they rubbed shoulders with daily, especially the official who may have had something on his conscience. But who were they to say that he was better or worse than any other? In a speech I had made at my last place of work, the ZREMB enterprise, I had said: "I'm not beyond reproach myself. Are you? A secretary takes a fountain pen, somebody else takes a light bulb from the corridor. I swiped a screw which I needed and couldn't buy in a shop. People are like that, as is the system: given the chance everybody pinches things they need. What are we to do now? Go on forever settling old scores? I'll tell you the situation we're in. There's this supporting wall; if anyone takes one more brick out of it, the whole wall will fall down on top of us. And then we'll be guilty, though in fact we're not because we didn't start this system. Right now, we must all shake hands and create a good trade union, that's what's important!"

But what sort of trade union was it to be? A few days after the strike, I had a visit from Anna Walentynowicz, shipyard heroine and our daughter Magda's godmother. We'd just moved into our new apartment on Pilotow Street, in the newly built Zaspa housing estate. The district governor had granted me the apartment practically overnight. It was a happy ending to long years of waiting and countless written requests, in the hope of getting a larger apartment, suitable for the needs of a growing family; at the time, there were already eight of us. The decision was probably made after a number of Western journalists came to see me at Stogi and subsequently put out a report and a film of the life of six children in a home less than twenty square feet per person. They had been useful, perhaps too useful; it was immediately suggested that we move to a house in Sopot, the fashionable part of the Tri-City area, the resort which had been taken over by Nazi officers during the war. But all I wanted was what I was entitled to, the benefits to which all Poles were supposedly entitled; in other words, about 100 square feet per person. In one night, the authorities visited the Zaspa housing cooperative office, found the right rooms, and usurped a corridor to link up the rooms to produce thereby an apartment that seemed a veritable palace, compared to the one we had just left. (Incidentally, when my other little girls, Maria-Wiktoria and Brygida, were born and the largest room became Solidarity's office, the apartment was much too small and we were cramped once again!)

Anna Walentynowicz had come to see me, as a friend, with a concrete proposal: I was to offer my resignation from the presidency of the MKZ. According to her, my shoulders were just not broad enough for the job, the MKZ needed someone like Andrzej Gwiazda, Jacek Kuron, or Modzelewski.

It was clear enough what she was getting at. In her view, I was too weak, not "revolutionary" enough in my demands, too soft in my dealings with the authorities. And it wasn't only her idea:

she had behind her a small influential group, all members of the original Free Trade Union movement. Were they right to put forward such a proposal? Time alone would tell.

The Gdansk MKZ was obviously hard at work contesting my position (acquired, admittedly, as a result of the strike). In the eyes of some, I was a usurper. These views only surfaced in the narrow circle of the group, never outside it in public meetings; the group's members would have been too afraid of the reaction in the shipyard and elsewhere within the independent trade union movement. I knew I was supported unquestionably by the majority and could therefore ignore the views of the few, though I never for a moment forgot that these views existed.

The film about our trade union records nothing of these internal tensions; it shows the surface of our activity and its effects. The reality was much more complex, marked by the hopes and ambitions of people who were firmly resolved to influence the course of events and to leave their mark on this episode in their lives.

Jacek Kuron, for instance, was undoubtedly a man of fixed ideas, and the originator of radical concepts. It was with him that I had had an interminable debate when I first began taking interest in the Free Trade Union. It was to him, too, that I owed much, especially the help that KOR gave me and many others when unemployed or in personal difficulties. Now the time had come to repay the debt.

Those who had formed the opposition prior to August 1980 now found themselves obliged to make a difficult decision: either to pursue, on their own, their efforts to set up an overt political opposition party in Poland, or to participate in the current of change and operate within the framework of Solidarity. Bogdan Borusewicz, for his part, was in favor of our course. But when Jacek Kuron, released from prison the day after the signing of the Agreements, was asked at a meeting of fellow workers of KOR in Gdansk how he saw his role in the new situation, he simply replied: "trade union expert." I don't know whether he was unaware at that time of the existence of the official commission of experts that included Tadeusz Mazowiecki, Bronislaw Geremek, Tadeusz Kowalik, Andrzej Wielowieyski, and Jan Strzelecki, and of another less formal body, set up at the Primate's suggestion, in which

Kukulowicz and Tyszkiewicz were involved. But if I put myself in Kuron's place, I can see that he had some reason to feel himself slighted; to have spent many years of struggle and imprisonment, to have thought and fought so hard for Poland's future, and then to be overlooked by a committee of experts must have been galling.

The reactions of other activists were as diverse as the individuals involved. Adam Michnik, in the same situation, wryly observed: "Well, I wasn't planning to write about it in *Trybuna Ludu* [the official Party newspaper] anyway!" Always the intellectual, he later was to write an article justifying his policy, "self-limitation of the revolution":

> The truth is that without agreement between the government and the people, this country cannot be governed. The truth is also that, in spite of official pronouncements at national functions, this country is not a sovereign country. This is the truth: Poles should admit the fact that their sovereignty is limited by the national and ideological interests of the USSR. In the last analysis, the truth is that the only Polish government acceptable to the leaders of the USSR is one controlled by communists; there is no reason to think that this state of affairs is going to change overnight, if ever.
>
> What follows from this? It follows that every attempt to govern against the people's will leads inevitably to catastrophe, but it also follows that every attempt to overthrow the government of Poland strikes a direct blow at the interests of the USSR. This is our reality. One doesn't have to like it, but one must recognize it.
>
> I realize that many of my colleagues openly reproach me with the charge that I have abandoned our aspirations to independence and democracy. To them, I reply frankly: in our present geopolitical situation, I don't believe that access to independence and parliamentarism is possible. I believe that we can organize our independence from within, in other words, that in becoming an increasingly better-organized society, increasingly efficient, we will enrich Europe and the rest of the world, in turn, with what we have to offer; at the same time we can offer an alternative choice, demonstrating our tolerance

and humanity. When we accomplish this we will be on the road to independence and democracy.

Pluralism in all areas of public life is possible, the abolition of advance censorship is possible, a rational economic reform and a just social policy are possible, press and television subject to the rules of competition and relaying the truth are possible, the independence of science and the autonomy of universities are possible, as are social control of prices and a network of consumers' councils, along with independent courts of law and police stations where people aren't beaten up.

If we have to obtain all this by force, to wrest it from the government, since no nation has ever received its rights as a gift, let us be careful in resorting to this necessary violence not to tear to shreds the Polish state, deprived of its sovereignty as it already is.

Adam Michnik later joined the team of Solidarity experts for the Masovia region and Jacek Kuron was invited to join the group of experts of the National Commission (enjoying a more restricted or theoretical sphere of influence).

I could not and would not "come clean," as the authorities demanded of me, and as church circles would very much have liked, warning me against "excessive politicization" of the Solidarity trade union. Why couldn't I? Because I was afraid of being too categorical in formulating ideas. If I took over the terminology employed by the government and strictly separated out what was political and what was trade union, what was still acceptable to the government and what was "anti-socialist," I would be drawn into the quicksands of political polemics, where the gravest dangers lay in wait for me. I would have been drawn into using the same tactics as the government. Solidarity's strength lay in surmounting the political divisions so characteristic of Poland and of the entire Eastern bloc.

The radical groups, on the other hand, continued to demand even more intransigent action and opposition to the government from me. But it was necessary to raise once again the question of the legitimacy of Poland's government, if the real causes lay much deeper, linked to the geopolitical changes that had taken place in Europe at the end of the Second World War and whose prime movers were still physically present on Polish soil. Clearly, there were limits unless the militants favored an invasion.

This dilemma has always existed. During the war, the Germans demanded living space for their expanding population, threatening us with physical extermination if we refused to comply. The threat from the East was different; as always, it wan't our body it wanted, but our soul. Confronted by this age-old dilemma the communist authorities of postwar Poland opted for the Eastern proposal, adopting *en bloc* the theories and experiences of the Soviet Union. It was at this time that the government embarked on its insane project to transform our nation by wiping out our most long-standing traditions, breaking our cultural links with Western Europe, attempting to tear out our religion by its roots and to change the very soul of the Polish people. This is why the process of recovery, of independence, must necessarily be arduous and slow.

And now that a new opportunity presents itself, is it such a good idea to want to prove that one's adversary has seized power against the will of the majority of the population, taking advantage of a combination of military and political circumstances?

By the very fact of participating in workers' protests, the free trade union activists found themselves at the heart of all these problems. Unfortunately, every move that the government made—or did not make—brought this wretched question of its legitimacy back to our agenda; it was always "if the dialogue proves fruitful," "if the reforms which have been announced are put into effect." If, if. . . . So inflexible was the government that it failed to take advantage of the favorable climate that had developed during the strike negotiations. If our movement was to become the driving force of change and reform, we needed the government's support in the sharing of power; otherwise we had to ask ourselves what type of reform could we take and how should it be organized? Under these circumstances could we run an independent and self-governing trade union?

For the first ten days, it was as if all hell had been let loose. It was true, I had never learned to carry out my functions in the approved style, but once we were installed in the Hotel Morski, we did enjoy a certain degree of privacy; it wasn't the way it had been before, when more or less anyone could grab hold of me and tell me his life story, then plead his special cause. Moving into our new headquarters marked a turning point. Two secretaries worked with us in shifts: Bozena Rybicka and Magda Wojcik, and later, Anna Kowalczyk. The experts, who didn't all live nearby, proceeded to organize a duty roster. Their life was far from restful and they found themselves working in an atmosphere to which they were quite unaccustomed. The behavior of members of the MKZ, the frequent angry outbursts they had to put up with, the aggressive nature of many of the arguments, all combined after days of euphoria to make this a difficult time for them. I tried to protect them, realizing how much they were sacrificing, putting themselves personally on the line day after day.

In the beginning, there were two daily sessions. At the evening session, the shipyard management appeared in the role of host, intent on keeping an eye on everything that was going on. These sessions were hard going, but that, too, I thought was characteristic of the first period of any "revolution," and during these sessions it was up to all of us to make whatever decisions needed making. As a result, we were deliberating for up to five hours a day. The rest of the time was spent visiting factories and, though some of those conducting the meetings were good at explaining the trade union line, others hadn't the least idea how to go about it; they were quite simply oblivious to the difficulties. In addition to the members of the presidium, some of the activists came along on these trips and helped to build up trade union locals. It was also at that time that the university students first began lending a hand. All that I have retained of that whole period is the impression of a vast mosaic of events impossible to fuse into a whole. But should it all in fact form a whole, one monolithic organization?

On September 16, a delegation arrived from Wroclaw including Modzelewski and company, a lawyer, and a number of other experts. Leszek Kaczynski, who represented our presidium at the talks, told us that the knives were out. The following day, another team arrived, from Warsaw, including attorney Jan Olszewski and the other Kaczynski, Leszek's twin brother. Their idea, which they had set out in legal terms, was that we should create a unitary trade union, but provide it with such statutes that would make it, in reality, a federation. Their argument was that, if we did not unite, the government would have unlimited opportunities to manipulate the different unions.

On September 17, seeing the hall of the Ster (Rudder) Club full to bursting—it was on the ground floor of the block housing our headquarters—it struck me that, though there were only delegates from the committees of the large concerns present (two apiece) they already formed a vast assembly (and yet this meeting was taking place only seventeen days after the signing of the Gdansk Agreements). Lech Badkowski, who was in the chair, saw to it that the speeches were brief and concise. After five minutes, he cut the speakers short. These were not specially prepared speeches but simply "greetings from the heart": to Gdansk, to me, to the shipyard workers, and brief, almost telegraphic items of news relating how and where MKZ and MKS had been set up, how many factories they included, and how many registered members they had. From these reports, the picture gradually emerged of a new trade union organization which, though not registered and having no ratified statutes as yet, nevertheless included, at the very least, some three million members. There were frequent calls for unity— "Victory through union!" "Let's have a united front!" "Union is strength!"—and everyone making these appeals received unanimous applause.

The lawyer Jan Olszewski then presented a motion in which he declared that: "For the purpose of registration, we whould put ourselves forward as a single structure to include the whole of Poland." He was supported by Karol Modzelewski, who said: "Gdansk has gained victory, but let's not forget, thanks to the powerful support of strikers throughout Poland. It would be suicidal for the coastal region to cut itself off from the rest of the country."

We drew attention, however, to the necessity for a solid local organization to impart a feeling of strength to the other organizations. No, that wasn't the point, they said. I insisted that the new trade unions weren't prepared to fall back into the old rut and I rejected the idea of creating a new central trade union. I pointed out the weakness of the previous system, but was just wasting my breath. Finally I exploded:

I'll tell you one thing—when I went to see Cardinal Wyszynski, the CRZZ trade union (the government's central council of unions) called together a plenum and proposed to put me in charge, so I had every chance of obtaining this unification you talk of. But I didn't. I don't want that sort of unity. Obviously, we should set up a consultative commission, but we must remain complementary, so as not to deprive each other of any freedom of action. Strong centers, with strong inter-enterprise committees, will help out the weaker bodies, enabling them to have recourse to strike action, but none of them—not even Gdansk—should attempt to exercise a central influence on these committees. Of course, we'll get together on certain problems, but as a National Commission. This commission must have the task of passing on all that has been discussed to the different regions, and it's there, in the regions, that the decisions will be made. It's these decisions which will be valid, not the decisions made by the Commission. We must avoid rushing headlong into some form of unification that would only destroy us.

Once again the temperature in the hall went up several degrees. People were no longer making appeals, they were demanding a common front. Some were saying that though Gdansk was strong and could enjoy a certain autonomy for the time being, this was only a short-term view: after the smallest centers had been wiped out, it would very soon be Gdansk's turn.

We gradually began to visualize our trade union this way: what it needed was diversity and a solid contact with the foundation, with the people working in factories, offices, and other places, but a certain form of unity was also essential.

Another proposal was made that, under the Solidarity banner, the Regional Inter-enterprise Committees should all go together to the court to be registered. Individually, we would lose out, the government would quickly find ways of getting rid of us.

In fact, the picture that emerged from the delegates' report was varied and somewhat depressing. The authorities' tactics toward trade unions in process of formation varied from region to region. There was no lack of open hostility, but in some places there was also cooperation. "They give us an office and then just wait," some delegates told us; others: "They don't give us an office at all, but wait to see what we'll do next; they're just watching us." Some even went so far as to talk of Poland being divided up into zones of liberty and occupation. One person declared: "The coastal region is a blessed isle and Gdansk is a free city—really free at the moment—but when we go back, it'll be like retreating behind barbed wire."

People were paralyzed by fear, and the official press remained silent. The net result was that the authorities thought things were improving. Some days after our meeting, at a secret meeting with Party activists (a record of it came into our hands), the first secretary in Katowice, Andrzej Zabinski, spoke of the necessity for Party members to join our trade union:

> If we don't join the new trade unions, we make their task simpler by allowing a new KOR-type organization to spring up. Obviously KOR is behind these new trade unions. There's no doubt about it, any more than that all these organizations are really only one and the same. The clergy sympathize with them. How's it all going to end? In theory, it should end with the unification of all these trade unions, but that could take years. Our first objective is to prevent them from turning out loyal Party members, the second, to pressure them to turn out KOR members; if this were to happen it would simply be a matter of time before the whole movement would be broken up in stages. . . . They must be harassed—there are thousands of ways. . . . I'm sorry for them; they're good fellows, often quite young, but they've chosen to get mixed up in politics, so there's no other way. They must be taught what the taste of power means. Offices must be made available for them everywhere and furnished in the most luxurious way possible. I always say, and I'll say it again here, in this committee: I don't know any man who hasn't been corrupted by power. It's only a question of time and degree. You can see it in them already. Easy access to money, taxi trips to Gdansk, telephone calls— direct to the secretary of the Party District Committee, and the deputy premier . . . they're traveling, starting to throw money around. The ball has started to roll.

The government's intentions were rapidly becoming clear. But one question remained: how many members of the government were thinking along these lines and how many were in favor of the changes promised by the August Agreements? For the time being, the word Solidarity was our only guiding light. It made its first appearance during the strike and became the title of our strike bulletin, and it was to be beautifully drawn by a young Gdansk artist, Jurek Janiszewski, in the form of a logo, permanently identifying our trade union. The word had materialized spontaneously, at exactly the right moment (just as, earlier, the idea and the form of the monument to the shipyard workers had), and now it would be ours forever.

Our group of advisers and experts in Warsaw was working away at our statutes, which were to reflect our trade union experiences, the results of August 1980, and Polish traditions in general. This was to be a workers' constitution, designating our objectives, our methods, our ideas, and our modes of organization. In Poland, everything was in ferment, everything was changing under the impact of recent experiences; people were taking off the masks they had worn for years and revealing their true opinions; transfers of authority were taking place, temporary armistices being concluded. This great ferment brought forth new leaders and basic trade union cells—factory commissions—were formed. Toward the end of September, once work on the statutes—under the direction of Andrzej Stelmachowski, Wieslaw Chrzanowski, and Jan Olszewski—was completed, we went to Warsaw to submit them to the competent court, according to the registration procedure laid down by law.

Warsaw saw the first meeting of the leaders of all the Regional Inter-enterprise Committees (RKM), as constituted to date. It was held in the former building of the Apostolic Nunciature. For me, this was no easy meeting. In everyone else's eyes, we appeared as one group, united by the same ideal of Solidarity, and yet, we didn't really know each other at all. We had only shared a few weeks' experiences and there was a great abyss of mistrust between us: Poland is not a country where the practice of democracy comes naturally, enabling one to develop a ready knowledge of any one person's thought processes, opinions, character, and moral worth. We had found ourselves in the same boat overnight and the whole country was watching us now, hoping that we would give them the long-awaited lesson in democracy, that the miracle would finally happen. But the process was only just beginning and there were to be many occasions when onlookers would have cause to be appalled. There were quarrels and brooding resentments, the whole gamut of ambition, jealousy, and distrust. I was seen on television armed with an outsized fountain pen, signing the Agreements with the authorities, while similar agreements were initialed at Szczecin and in Silesia, without fuss or publicity.

We spent the autumn haggling with the government. It was a difficult dialogue between two camps who spoke different languages. Solidarity would not and could not start talking again in a language poisoned by political propaganda. For every term defining the growing trade union and its activities, the government insisted on resorting to the standard lexicon patented in the Eastern bloc. Everything departing, however slightly, from the wooden forms was suspect, treated as "counter-revolutionary" and "anti-socialist." The result was an exhausting struggle over each word, each definition. The government absolutely insisted on having the statutes translated into their gibberish while our experts endeavored to make them accept the people's way of speaking, the way of Solidarity. At the beginning, everything led us to think it would be possible, but progressively, this battle of words revealed itself as a battle of the ideas they embodied as well, and a wall built up between the two camps.

Behind this wall they remained enslaved to "petrified" forms, incapable, with rare exceptions, of taking part in the new dialogue. They did appear to understand us in private conversation, but their public declarations failed to answer in any way the people's expectations. They always trotted out the old Party theses, afraid to let go of the ideological lifeline that had supported them for so long. Instead of trying to engage in dialogue, they aimed at getting the support of the silent majority, whose ranks swelled with the passing of time. For them, it was only a matter of piling up the arguments, counting on people's weariness, and waiting patiently for the weakening or division of public opinion.

I knew we had to keep busy sowing, without ever thinking of the harvest: seed we had scattered would survive in the earth, it wouldn't be consumed by fire, and sooner or later, the plant would grow. This is why throughout this period I intensified my public contacts, willingly devoting my time and energy to an exhausting round of the regions of the country. What we, in Gdansk, grasped immediately, sometimes without having to say it, could come across differently elsewhere. I talked to people about myself, not to increase my popularity but, on the contrary, so that they could see that I shared the same motives as they, that I was worried about my children's future, that I wanted a better standard of living for my family, that I had a wife who expected me to behave reasonably and to whom I didn't wish to be a source of constant anxiety.

At a meeting in the shipyards, I told the workers:

> See to it that your Lesio [Lech] keeps his hands clean. Keep an eye on him and don't let him get away with anything. I'm like the rest of you, I feel the same temptations. Sure, I've got Our Lady's picture hanging on the lapel of my jacket, but it's just because it helps to remind me of you, and to keep me in line. I've got a wife and kids and I'm happy with them, but I've still got eyes. That's the way I am, just like the rest of you. I do know that one shouldn't hurt other people, that one shouldn't do things at other people's expense, but believe me, I'm really not a saint. And I wouldn't want to be, for then you wouldn't understand me anymore.

The contact with new people and new surroundings was an education for me. If people saw me as a sort of embodiment of their hopes, I knew I ought to be honest, and to hold nothing back from them. That's why I used to analyze myself, to see what sort of man I had become. And it was then that I became aware of something for which I thank God with all my heart: I was a man at peace with himself.

It was a good time and it lasted until the middle of 1981.

The break in the official existence of the trade union occurred, in my opinion, in March 1981. It coincided with the Bydgoszcz crisis which was sparked by the militia's attack on Rulewski, the head of Solidarity in the region, and the attempt to bring up the question of the independent farmers' union at the Bydgoszcz regional council meeting. Although the March crisis had been resolved, we had already reached the breaking point. I had the greatest difficulty in calming this stormy atmosphere; it was like a general mobilization that had built in the cause of Solidarity and which, given the government's attitude, threatened to lead us all to catastrophe. At the time, I had the feeling of having defused an enormous charge of dynamite, of having staved off something that would have proved irreversible. Solidarity was never again to enjoy such a favorable combination of circumstances but, on the other hand, the risk of general confrontation with this desperate government had never seemed so fraught with danger.

The March affair is a key date to understanding the history of the trade union. I maintained that in an explosive climate like this, we definitely could not proceed with such a complex operation as the reversal of the power relationship in Poland. I was still counting on an evolutional outcome, but the government drew, unfortunately, only one conclusion from the mobilization: that it was itself threatened and that, within the space of twenty-four hours, the whole population could rise against it. However, the aftermath of these events left me certain of one thing: as long as we could hold our course, as long as Solidarity continued to exist, it would be possible, if only very slowly, to consolidate the changes, to give people a glimpse, if nothing more, of what life in Poland could really be like.

This is why, from that time on, every month that passed was a month snatched from the fate hovering over our heads. All in all, it was not a comfortable situation. There were times when we would rather have everything fall on top of us; maybe it wouldn't be the end of us, if we acted reasonably; if necessary we could always turn back. . . . I always saw the future of Solidarity as a long march in stages, never as a straight run.

Our chances of achieving the objectives of August 1980 certainly hadn't disappeared, there was always at least one option, but one out of how many? Despite our great hopes, the chances of succeeding here and now were slight—indeed virtually negligible. They resided in the simple fact that August 1980 was a common cause for every Pole. They were founded on the hope that the government would represent the people at least to the extent of understanding their aspirations and that it would be willing to participate in this difficult process of conciliation. What was at stake for the government? In our view, something tremendous and unique: for the first time since taking office, it could have enjoyed the genuine support of the population, it could have sealed a historic compromise and one likely to achieve a better Poland, the best we Poles could expect in our particular political situation. It could have won support like this, instead of the short-lived flirtations that had from time to time linked government and society, as in the case of Gomulka and Gierek. But from now on such support seemed out of the question.

People might say that it was the country's profound economic crisis and the increasing financial deficit that caused the government to lose this support. Financially, we lacked the momentum necessary to enable our economy to take off again. But, whatever anyone may think, the attitude of Solidarity had at no time led to the aggravation of our economic difficulties, even if that was the version of the facts most current among the defenders of the government's interests. The strikers' main demand in August 1980 was the creation of the free trade unions, though pay claims had dominated earlier talks. The shipyard workers gave in on these claims, ending up with an increase of a few hundred zlotys, and agreeing more for the principle of the thing, so that they could be done with the purely economic aspect of the strike. We understood the country's difficulties and we were ready and willing to make sacrifices. The proposal was even made that those who still had the means should stick together to refund, if only a minute part, of the Polish national debt! Such facts are without precedent and one can only compare them with the spirit of sacrifice that manifested itself at the outbreak of the Second World War.

Why then did this enormous mobilization of effort, this willingness for self-sacrifice, remain ineffective? Why didn't the government want to take advantage of the workers' offer? Because if it did it would have to launch itself, with us, into a far-reaching program of genuine reform. And because the government thought that the demands for these reforms were the most dangerous thing of all. It denounced the reforms as "political," directed against the socialist order, and so obstructed all possibilities of advance in that direction. The government let it be understood, however, that increasing social pressure could result in certain demands being met if they emanated from the "apolitical," purely trade union side of Solidarity—its "legal" side. This possibility cleared the air a little, opening the way for negotiation of collective agreements, for talks on job-related pay scales, indices, and, consequently, on wages. So this wave of claims did reap some results.

Certain maneuvers and even what could be called a "government strike" brought a fresh outbreak of pay claims during this period. The government took the easy way out and merely noted people's reactions without taking any steps to check the situation. I was expecting the worst: the struggle for more money was going to cripple the movement and make life easier for the government. It could always accuse Solidarity of having been the cause of all the trouble and hold us responsible for any future catastrophe. In fact, this is exactly what the government did; it saddled our trade union with overall responsibility for a crisis, which was in fact the result of its own bad management throughout the seventies. It was a maneuver that enabled it to obtain a double advantage.

November 1980 dangerously extended the field of confrontation with the government. Two incidents contributed to this: the first linked to the registration of the trade union; the second, to the case of Jan Narozniak, a mathematician at Warsaw University, who had made public a confidential memo from the attorney general.

The first incident regarding the registration triggered off, in public, the hitherto muted discussion on the legitimacy of the government and the respect for legality in Poland. At the root of the problem lay the decision of the Warsaw court to introduce unauthorized modifications into the text of Solidarity statutes that had been submitted for registration. On its own initiative, the court added paragraphs affirming the "preponderant role of the Party," additions that would henceforward form an integral part of our statutes, although anyone could find them set down in the text of the Constitution. Our people took the addition of these paragraphs as an indication that the independent and self-governing trade unions were to be subject to the control of Party officials; in other words, that we were back where we started. And yet, during the strike, we had already included in the Gdansk Agreements the principle of the "directing role of the Party," thereby showing that we were ready to demonstrate our political realism.

The attitude of the court immediately raised the question of whether its role consisted in drawing up the trade union statutes or simply in ensuring that they were in conformity with the law. The attorney general caused an uproar by indirectly challenging the good citizenship of numerous activists and groups who had been involved from the start in the creation of Solidarity. In carefully chosen juridical terms, he declared that they were to be the subject of "measures of surveillance," seeing as they were not "taking part in an illegal anti-socialist activity." Our people then asked: "What good are our Agreements if thanks to them we can be locked up at any moment?" Such is the mechanism of the politicization of the trade union movement: with the right methods, an absolutely honest opponent can be made to appear an irreconcilable enemy, who is then forced to fight for his honor, his security, and his civic status.

At the same time, a wave of more general claims broke out in the country: in the mountains, in Bielsko-Biala, and in Jelenia Gora. People began demanding that the various organs of government should hand back the public buildings they had appropriated and turned into rest homes and luxuriously equipped leisure centers for the government's exclusive use. They pointed to urgent social needs, to the lack of hospitals, dispensaries, and educational facilities, not to mention the absence of leisure centers for their own use. Accusations proliferated, embezzlements and other illegalities were unearthed, but the government was in no hurry to tackle such delicate questions. Hence a wave of strikes broke out in every region.

I spent the whole of that period traveling backward and forward to attend the various meetings between the strikers and the authorities. Our advisers and trade union experts were with me, visiting every place where there was a dispute in progress. In the course of one of these journeys we made together, the sociologist Jan Strzelecki explained the pattern of events:

A certain kind of social demand is built up from below. If it is discovered that public money has been spent on satisfying the elitist aims of a small group, this money must be recovered. We are dealing with both a movement of revolt and a motion to restore this country to its people. The same movement soon spreads into other domains: censorship, the way in which power is exercised, the principle of self-management in economic activities. In this way we develop a new conception of the State: it is a State which no longer substitutes itself for the people but one which in carrying out its functions is served by a whole series of separate social organizations that together reflect an

163

active society. A new actor appears on the national stage—the old show of "bogus participation" is over! All these elements constitute a whole that could eventually stand for something quite new if we could only find where its center of gravity lies.

Somebody once said to me: "If I had to make a film about you during the sixteen months of Solidarity's official existence, it would be like the American film *Vanishing Point*, where you see the whole of America through the eyes of one man. In the first scene he gets into a car and the rest of the film shows him traveling."

I got into that car in October 1980 and didn't get out again until the declaration of martial law on December 12, 1981. Everything happened then. That was how I got to know my country and my compatriots in other countries, in particular the Vatican, France, Japan, Switzerland, and Sweden. I covered hundreds of thousands of miles and dealt with thousands of problems. The film, if there were one, would be of the early type, where everything seems speeded up, and where one has difficulty remembering the jerky images; I can remember only a few still shots.

There are some roads that Poles have used for centuries, on journeys or pilgrimages. I followed these same roads but not as a pauper seeking prosperity in foreign parts, as my own family once did. I wasn't arriving empty-handed; I was coming to bear witness to our movement before the whole world.

I set off in January 1981 accompanied by Danuta and my family. Our first visit was to Pope John Paul II, in Rome, to whom we brought the message of Solidarity. The public sanction he gave to our ideas was a gift, in its turn, of equal importance. Addressing us in his official speech, he declared:

> I believe that the cornerstone of your venture, which began in August 1980 in the coastal region and in other great centers of Polish industry, was a common impulse to promote the moral good of society. For without this, one cannot speak of real progress, and Poland can claim the right to progress just like any other country. At the same time, this right is to some extent peculiar to Poland, won at the price of great trials in our history, and more particularly by what Poland suffered in

the Second World War. In this respect what is at stake has been, is, and always will be a strictly internal matter for the people of Poland. The immense efforts which were made over the course of the autumn, and which must continue, were not directed against anyone. They were not turned *against*, they were directed *toward*: toward the common good. The right, which is in fact a duty, to make similar efforts is something which every country possesses. It is a right which is recognized and confirmed by the law of nations.

In this same address, the Pope expressed certain ideas which were later formulated in the encyclical *Laborem exercens* (On Human Labor). I can say, therefore, that I was present at the birth of this document which points the way to some long-term solutions to the difficult problems of labor.

My visit to Italy was exceptional in many ways. To begin with, it was my first journey to the West. I was also keeping a promise I had made in August 1980 that, if I survived and if a trade union saw the light of day and its right to exist was recognized in our country, my first journey would be to visit the Holy Father in Rome.

My stepfather came over from the United States to join us in Rome. I hadn't seen him for years, and the old resentment still smoldered between us. It went back, as I've explained, to my childhood, but recent circumstances had fanned it brighter. My stepfather, Stanislaw, hadn't come to my mother's funeral in Sobowo (her coffin had been flown over from the States in 1975). Admittedly, if he had come to Sobowo he might have had to stay, Polish laws being what they are; so perhaps I was judging him too harshly. In any case, at that difficult moment, Danuta came to my aid, and it was thanks to her that we were able to re-create something of a family atmosphere.

The day of our meeting with the Holy Father began with mass at the Polish Pilgrims' Hostel in the suburbs of Rome. Then we crossed the city by bus to the Vatican. My first meeting with the Holy Father was in private. His reception was warm and affectionate. Then I had to address him in public, in an official speech, with the whole world listening. I decided to do without the draft my advisers had written; I wanted to use my own words to say what I had to say from the heart. I had a terrible memory of the wretched speech I had stammered through at the inauguration of the monument to the shipyard workers. A text concocted in advance and typed out on a sheet of paper always had the same effect on me as attempting to speak a foreign language; it was as if in trying to be properly prepared I made a trap for myself and inevitably fell into it. That was why I improvised at the Vatican, confident that at the right moment I would find the words I needed. I admit that I did feel a moment of panic: when the lights came on and the cameras started to roll and everyone was waiting to hear what I was going to say, I suddenly had the awful idea that I might let the Pope down. Then I said in the simplest possible way why we had come, what ideals had inspired us, what human rights we intended to protect with the help of Solidarity.

Toward the end of our stay, on Sunday, we were again invited to morning mass and to breakfast in the Pope's apartments. These precious moments spent with the Holy Father had to last me quite a long time; it would be another two and a half years before I was able to see him again (with Danuta and the boys, in an entirely different situation).

This visit to Italy had been planned and organized by the three large trade unions and we had therefore been invited jointly by the Christians, the Socialists, and the Communists. At the meetings, along with the "Bandera rossa" and the "Internationale," we also sang hymns! I expressed the belief that there were certain ideals that could unite all workers, independent of their other loyalties, and I saw countless signs that people everywhere felt the need for international solidarity, and that it was precisely in this area that a new message was expected of us. The cordiality and understanding shown by Luciano Lama, Pietro Carniti, and Giorgio Benvenuto in the course of our conversations was to stand the test of time, and of later events in Poland. Italians have always given Solidarity heartfelt support and their feeling of common responsibility with us has survived to this day. In our eyes there is no gift more precious.

We then paid a brief visit to Sweden, where I received the peace prize awarded by the journal *Arbetet*. It would be from Scandinavia again two years later that I would receive tremendous support in the form of a Nobel Prize.

Japan was a big surprise. Poles picture this country in such exotic terms that it was hard to believe that people there are really like us. Japanese journalists were among the first to come to take a close look at our strike in the shipyard; their analyses of its significance (done with their usual meticulousness) were of great help to Solidarity. I asked them why they were so interested in a country so far away from their own, and they replied that they found many similarities in our two situations, both of our countries having suffered the brunt of international power brokering. Lacking natural resources and living primarily from trade, Japan, like Poland, is a country obliged to keep a watchful eye on all that is going on in the world.

The Japanese had arranged my visit like a railway timetable. Each minute of my stay was programmed, probably on a computer. We were received by Sohyo, the largest trade union central, and we effectively conveyed to them our belief that the trade union cause was something common to us all and that we should follow the Italian formula by meeting other trade unions as well. We had insisted that our visit should not become a vulgar trump card in anyone's electoral campaign; it would have been a great shame to have undermined the significance of such exceptional encounters.

It turned out that the Japanese saw me as a real samurai! They were deeply aware of the threats hanging over Solidarity and over Poland itself, and in their eyes, I was the embodiment of the man who fights in the name of others . . . perhaps also the man who risks defeat.

They began their speeches by saying that they admired Chopin (some of them even recalled the musician's birthplace at Zelazowa Wola), that they had been to Poland and admired the films of Wajda and Polish painting. When it was my turn to speak about Japan, I referred to the rights of the individual being trampled by progress and of the invasion of the home by computers, an enviable creation, and yet one concomitant with a relentless rat race. Where was it heading? Where would it end? I saw, as I had seen at similar meetings, that people understood me, they were listening to me more willingly than to their own trade union leaders, who had airs of belonging to elitist cadres. I wanted to convey to them, jokingly, what I thought of their misconceived ideas, so in the middle of a reception, I took a pair of scissors and cut off the tie belonging to Mr. Tamizuka, secretary general of Sohyo. This joke was taken in good grace, but it was ill-conceived.

The Japanese economy and organization of labor hardly needs any publicity. The experiences of Japanese trade unionists seemed to me of greater interest. It turned out that the main trade unions constantly carried on their own studies and investigations and, according to the conclusions they reached, submitted well-founded pay claims to the employers. All negotiations were begun on this basis, and if they failed the recourse could be the final weapon—the strike. The trade union campaign opened on a fixed date and took place regularly in the spring; April was the month set aside for strikes.

At the Diet we met the leaders of the main political parties in Japan, who declared their support for potential change in Poland, as well as promising us substantial economic aid. I was in an embarrassing situation—obviously I couldn't take the place of the government. The dilemma was brought home to us sometime later, when we were told: "Just don't push us into the arms of Japan: when it comes to foreign policy, we know what we're doing better than you do. We don't intend to build a second Japan!"

It was a pity, since Japan opened up new possibilities for our stifled economy, a chance that the Japanese locomotive would pull us along for a good stretch. The offer was staggering: it dealt with branches of the economy that were neglected in Poland, such as railways, agriculture, chemicals, the car industry, and computer equipment. I asked how Japan imagined that Poland could carry out its obligations as a partner. For them, reciprocity consisted of the possibility Poland offered Japan of penetrating the markets of the socialist countries.

It was in Japan that we heard of the dramatic attempt on the Pope's life. The news broke in the middle of the night May 13–14, 1981. We were in my hotel room in Nagasaki, discussing the events of the day, and our visit the next day to the museum set up in memory of the victims of the atomic bomb. The first news flash was terrifying: the Pope was dead! The next news flash retracted it: no, the Pope was still alive, he was fighting for his life. I was overcome by a feeling of immense loneliness; the whole world seemed to have turned upside down; with our lodestar gone, some of us were wandering in a wilderness without hope. The tragedy of the Polish Pope was also the tragedy of Poland and of Solidarity: they were inextricably bound together; this was just the beginning. Then the news changed, became less alarming; there was still hope. The Pope's condition was serious, but the doctors were doing everything in their power. We asked for morning mass and the Bishop of Nagasaki celebrated it for our delegation. The moment of the attack was in my mind when I wrote, in the golden book in the Nagasaki Museum: *Man, how could you do this?*

The Japanese reacted promptly, strengthening the measures for our protection, which were already rigorous. I was given an additional bodyguard and we moved now only as a group.

It was also in Japan that I received an invitation to go to Geneva to attend the next annual session of the International Labor Organization at the beginning of June. I wasn't terribly keen to appear at this forum, anticipating that the government would make it difficult. But I was told that the Pope would be addressing the assembly and that had decided me. The trip had been planned before the attempt in Rome; I had accepted and didn't wish to withdraw now.

We left from Warsaw in June with Premier Jerzy Obodowski and a small group of his advisers representing the "employers' side." I was accompanied by Bronislaw Geremek, Andrzej Stelmachowski, and by Ryszard Kalinowski, whose responsibility within the trade union was international relations. From the moment the aircraft took off, there was a good atmosphere between us: after all, we were going to represent Poland jointly at an international assembly, where people would be watching us closely. Apart from Solidarity, the delegation also included representatives of two other trade union organizations, ostensibly backed by the authorities and claiming, on the strength of this, to set themselves up as rivals. There was a delicate point at issue: the body of our delegation, according to the statutes of the ILO, had the right to only one speech (I delivered it on this occasion) and to one vote in any division that might be called. Our ten million adherents constituted a potent defense against this argument. During the course of our visit to Geneva, we obtained an extraordinary degree of support from the entire international trade union movement. I particularly remember shaking hands with 140 delegates representing the gamut of the different trade union organizations, among them an exceptionally beautiful young woman whom I asked to stand beside me; she appears at my side in most of the pictures that were taken—indicating once again my ordinary, unsaintly nature.

Then came October and my visit to France, a political testing ground. It wasn't like being in Italy, where the Pope's national origins had rebounded to our credit. In France, the interest in Solidarity had two sources: trade union and political. I had already been in touch with the French trade union movement during those unforgettable days of August 1980, when the French had come to bring us their support. They had demonstrated it in that extremely tense period when the authorities were doing their utmost to play down the political significance of our strike. The support from France proved to be vital, clearing up the misunderstandings on which the ideals of Solidarity were foundering and thereby revealing the malaise of the Polish leadership. It conveyed the real atmosphere and significance of the "Polish summer" to international political opinion. This is why I thought it necessary to begin my visit in France by expressing my gratitude.

The five major trade union organizations represented on that day covered the whole range of current trends of opinion, from the Christian-inspired movement to the Communists. However, they all stressed the significance of the Polish experiment for the international trade union movement and this unanimity was of capital importance. Naturally, each trade union put an emphasis on the aspect that best suited it but without straying from the general spirit of approval.

My friend Edmond Maire, president of the CFDT (Confédération Française du Travail), declared: "The bonds which unite us go well beyond ordinary friendship, even beyond a similarity of interests; they point to a destiny common to us all."

Georges Seguy, secretary general of the CGT, the organization linked to the French Communist Party, declared in his turn: "It is most important for all of us that your experiment should succeed." He recalled that it was precisely because of its attitude toward Solidarity that the CGT, co-founder of the WFTU (World Federation of Trade Unions), with headquarters in Prague, had withdrawn from that organization. "What we are witnessing today in Poland," he continued, "confirms us in our view of the role that trade unions should play in socialist countries. Such a role should

170

be possible in any country whatsoever. I hope that we shall all be able to draw conclusions from the experience you are going through now." By devious routes, we had established a dialogue with those who refused to have one with us directly.

Our meeting at breakfast with Prime Minister Pierre Mauroy turned into a discussion lasting two hours on various aspects of Franco-Polish relations. In a way, it was a continuation of the conversation we had already had with the Foreign Minister, Claude Cheysson. The French government was clearly eager to understand the real situation in Poland and Solidarity's potential role in it. All the contacts we made that October must have played some part in France's decision to grant aid on an unprecedented scale to the Polish nation during the difficult months of martial law and in their expressed support for Solidarity, which was outlawed at the time, by the French trade unions. Nor did Jacques Chirac, then mayor of Paris, fail to live up to the declarations of friendship he made to Bronislaw Geremek and to me.

This marathon of trade union visits continued at a steady pace but I still managed to begin each day with mass in the Polish church. I took only one trip on the Seine, in a *bateau-mouche*, and I enjoyed only one evening of relaxation, at the Olympia, at the invitation of Yves Montand and Simone Signoret, who invited us to have a glass of champagne with them afterward.

At the Charles de Gaulle Airport, when we were having our breakfast before flying off to the north of France to visit the Polish house of the Pallotine Fathers, we had an unusual encounter. A group of American businessmen on their way to Poland for a visit bombarded me with questions, so many questions, in fact, that I didn't have time to eat at all. They were interested in what had become of the credit Western banks had granted to Poland previously, in the conditions needed for strengthening the country's economy, in the role and attitude of Solidarity as a genuine social movement capable of influencing the workings of the state and of the economy. I gave my opinion, which I still hold today, that only reform could guarantee positive changes—the first stage of which would be self-management among the workers. The second condition for the success of these changes would be the will of the Polish people: nothing else could do the trick.

As these meetings abroad continued, the form that the idea of international solidarity should take became clearer, as did the areas in which this solidarity would best be able to express itself. Such solidarity appeared to correspond to an increasingly strong need, not only in the East, but in the West, too, where a number of political parties base much of their support on the existence of trade unions. In Japan, we had noted the gap separating the "officials" from the "rank and file." But now it seemed that the missing link could be forged, thanks to the ideals proclaimed by Solidarity. If not everyone in Poland had perceived this yet, the Japanese had been quick to do so, doubtless because the question was of urgent concern to them.

For me all these journeys abroad offered an opportunity to take a fresh look at our preoccupations and the events that touched us directly. The visits were also intended to repay a debt of gratitude to all those who had given us their support in August 1980. But throughout I kept in mind the view shared by Cardinal Wyszynski, that the key to these Polish problems lay in our own hands and that we had to look for the solution to them in Poland itself, relying on our own strength and efforts.

The trips I made in Poland date from October 1980. My tour of the southern regions made a particular impression on me, especially an October day on the Sukiennice market square in Cracow, where I made a speech and swore to uphold the cause of Solidarity on the same spot where Tadeusz Kosciuszko made the oath to his country two hundred years earlier. I would never have imagined that I would one day find myself appearing so full of anger and of hope, in this noble eighteenth-century context. And I recall the sequel to this meeting, in the stadium of Nowa Huta, the new industrial center near Cracow, where a typical "political" question was put to me: what was my relationship to socialism? I answered: "We're in the process of working out a Polish style of socialism. We're asking the authorities to serve, not to lead. What happens in our country should be our affair."

Most working people conceive of socialism differently from theoreticians and politicians. Every social group sees it in its own way: some reject it totally, others consider it to be of some use, but on the whole most people think that it would be fine to work in the socialist way while enjoying the fruits of capitalism. For the great majority of people, socialism boils down to things we are accustomed to, which we pay no more attention to than the blood circulating in our veins: social benefits, hospitals, schools, and so on—the basic essentials. But, of course, there has to be the money for these things and honesty must be the rule. What we have stressed in order to make socialism acceptable is that all that is best in the economy and in the domain of social welfare is socialist, even if it was part of the socialism we have known up till now (and which, frankly speaking, was merely bogus socialism).

During the course of my travels, there were other moments in utter contrast with those political meetings: at Jasna Gora, for example, where I made my profession of faith to the Holy Mother of Czestochowa. In the midst of upheavals, unable to obtain satisfaction on numerous points, but persisting nevertheless in our common aim, we had to understand ourselves better, to remain confident, and to look for help from forces beyond ourselves. This was why the stop at Jasna Gora was so important. The Primate himself had said: "The heart of Poland beats there." So, if that was the heart of Poland, I had to go to it, to become one with that heart; I wanted the whole country to beat in time to its heartbeat.

I still have notes from some of these journeys, taken hurriedly by my secretaries and by countless journalists who were working in the new, independent press agencies that grew up around the trade union. Originally I intended to give an idea of these sixteen months of Solidarity's official existence by arranging and recasting these notes in some coherent, chronological order, but I later thought better of it. The reader will be more interested in them just as they were written or taped, even if they seem to linger over small details and if, in analyzing the conflicts of that period, they sometimes err on the side of superficial judgments. That's why I have dug them up. In my eyes, they have a unique value.

Mieczyslaw Wachowski

For a start, Lech had a passion for journeys and crowds. For him, a crowd was like food, he drew from it the energy he needed to carry on. I've kept a recording of the speech he made at each of these meetings, with the ensuing questions and answers. He replayed them before each new journey and quietly noted anyplace where he had either made a mistake or found exactly the right expression for what he wanted to say; he was marvelous at analyzing that sort of thing. Coming back from these meetings he might doze the whole way, but after an hour's rest in his hotel he was as ready as ever to return to the fray; he recharged himself in no time at all. After listening to the tape of the last speech he had made, he would continue to think about it and at the next meeting would answer the questions raised in the previous one. People were sometimes a bit foxed by this and not sure what he was driving at. This sometimes resulted in some rather comic situations.

When Lech made his speeches it was as if he was riding the crest of a wave rolling in from the crowd and was riding it like a surfer. He was able to express what each one of us felt deep inside. This was what cemented the crowd together in his favor. At last here was someone who expressed the thoughts of the man in the street! That's why he did what he did so well.

After every meeting or every discussion with the government, he was on his knees, a wreck; he really gave everything. Then he would need to recharge. More often than not, he left the place where the meeting had been held in order to put some space between him and it, to be somewhere new, a hundred miles away, on the road, in a different environment. He knew that, behind him, each of his words had carried its own weight.

I noticed that he began to appear more and more harassed. On one side by the National Commission, on the other by the government and by the calls to Warsaw, where he was constantly summoned in view of possible talks.

They were already calling him "Lech the Fireman." He was the man who went everywhere putting out the strike "fires." We had been at Rzeszow, dealing with the independent farmers, then we went to Warsaw and after the meeting with the Primate, we came back to Gdansk. On the road, going home, the police had picked me up for speeding. I'd said: "I'm in a hurry. I've taken the president home and now I'm going home myself, to bed, I'm half dead with fatigue, but I've got something to give you," and I handed the cop the Rzeszow Solidarity newsletter and the Gdansk one as well. He asked: "What's this?"

"Well, instead of paying a fine, I'm giving you a little present," I replied. No more was said and I was able to drive on. That evening, I went back to Lech's and asked: "What's going on?" "We're going to Jelenia Gora," he said. "Lech, we'll never get there! I've spent the whole night—several nights—at the wheel. We'll never make it. I've had it, there's no question of going anywhere." "We've got to go!" he insisted, so I gave in.

Mounting problems and all the work were becoming too much for him, he was beginning to lose his bearings. It was in church that he recovered his strength. I think he would have been unable to define what he felt himself; for him being in church was another food; he really needed it. He was indifferent to cameras and the photographers lurking in the background. During mass, he was far away. You could speak to him and he wouldn't hear. He prayed in silence, cutting himself off. And when he took part in the service, you felt that he was utterly absorbed in its progress, that he was living it physically and spiritually. One day in church a woman who must have been epileptic fell down and made a lot of noise, but Lech didn't even notice. I left my seat to help carry the woman into the sacristy, but he was oblivious to it all, completely absorbed in his thoughts. But as soon as mass was over, it was as if he was moved by a spring; he was capable of coming to in a matter of seconds, suddenly quite a different person, as if he'd stepped back into another time or another reality.

He knew that it would all end one day, but he just wanted it to happen at a moment he'd been able to foresee. In mid-1981 he said that if things kept on in the way they were going, the movement would break up and come to a stop.

Lech's career is like a giant slalom. The first leap was from the shipyard and this was followed by a terrific run, an isolated one, that had its ups and downs, but which plunged on regardless. One day, Celinski said to him: "Lech, you're such a complex man that you'll never have any friends. You don't allow anyone to get close to you; no one can talk of comradeship or friendship with you."

Lech thought this over for a long time. Later, on one of our journeys, we spoke of it again and he agreed it was true. In fact, none of us could be of any help to him there.

Anna Kowalczyk

Together we covered hundreds and hundreds of miles by car, on journeys taking several hours, mainly at night, when Lech would sleep almost the entire time. We always kept a small cushion on our laps and Lech would curl up like a dog and rest his head on it. ("My God, what a head I've got resting in my lap!" we used to say.)

He never panicked. I remember we were going back to Gdansk one time and Mietek had been driving like a madman for hours when a deer leaped out in front of the car near Elblag, smashing the radiator. We found ourselves stuck—Mazul, Mietek, Walesa, and I. Mietek signaled the passing cars but nobody stopped; they didn't know who we were. At last a heavy truck drew up and when they saw who was there, my God! The truckers were actually going to Elblag, but they towed us right into Gdansk. As for Lech, when we were waiting on the roadside, he didn't show a moment's irritation, he didn't complain or grumble; he was calmness itself. When we stopped to eat, the only thing that interested him was whether there was a nice bit of liver on the menu. He adored liver, and pancakes; he always insisted that nobody could make pancakes as well as Danuta.

At Zyrardow, we had gone to see some women workers who were on strike and when he came out of the meeting the road was blocked with buses and streetcars and there were swarms of people everywhere. When Lech appeared people began to sing "Poland has not perished"—not "May he live a hundred years!" not chants of "Lech! Lech!" but "Poland has not perished." He stopped, bowed his head, and stood there, lost in thought. He told me later that it was at that precise moment that it had "hit" him, that he'd been overcome by emotion. On that same day, Jaruzelski claimed that people were putting the national anthem to any kind of use, for any kind of end.

I remember Poznan, too, and the preparations for the commemoration of June 26, 1956, the date of the first workers' risings. On the 25th, we were driving over from Radom, where we'd been celebrating another anniversary: the workers' demonstrations at Ursus, Radom, and Plock. These celebrations followed one after another. On the way to Poznan, Lech said that we wouldn't go to the Cegielski factory but would go straight to the hotel—he was too tired. We had stopped at a gas station outside Poznan, when we heard a radio broadcast of what was happening at that moment at the Cegielski factory. Lech immediately said that we had to go; the people were expecting him. We stepped on the gas; we were still a good way from Poznan. We got there in the end, but Mietek didn't know where the factory was, so we had to ask the first militiaman we saw.

On the way, he had said: "I'll tell them this and then I'll tell them that." It was the first time I saw him prepare a speech. I took it as his way of getting to know me, as if he were trying the speech out on me to get me talking. Our first journeys together had been rather silent—I was still a bit shy, though always delighted to be with him. After a time I began to relax and we would discuss whether he'd been any good at the last meeting; though in my eyes he was always good. So we got used to one another and he grew to trust me.

Lech was, and still is, a remarkable person but it seems to me that there are too few people around who are willing to help him. For example, I'm very fond of Andrzej Celinski, I have a great respect for him and in many ways we get on splendidly. But we didn't agree about this, and when I said to him: "Andrzej, you're the best friend he's got, you should do more for him, help him out with all these tricky problems," he replied: "So you want to make him into a marionette, is that it? He should stay just as he is. Nobody must make a puppet out of him and pull the strings and make Mr. Walesa wave his arms!" Of course, that wasn't what I wanted at all. What I would have wished was for someone to help him inwardly, deep down.

He loved meetings. He loved the "Ping-Pong," as he called it, of questions and answers. It fascinated him. Some people said that we collected the pieces of paper with the questions on them and slipped him the answers, all written out. God forbid! We did collect the pieces of paper people handed us but only to arrange them by subject, and he answered them like a flash. He had such presence of mind that his answers always hit the nail on the head; they were irrefutable. After meetings of this sort, he was always ravenously hungry. He thought one shouldn't eat beforehand, that he'd speak better on an empty stomach; he didn't want to worry about his digestion.

All the trade union structures were now in place and the national leadership, the regional bodies, and the factory committees were demanding tangible proof that the overall program as defined by the August Agreements was actually being applied. But all that transpired from the talks with the authorities was so contradictory, so vague, so watered down by compromise, that it was very hard to recognize the great plans we had started with.

My role as a middleman between Solidarity and the government was particularly complex. I could in no way count on the classic distribution of roles whereby one party is *for*, the other is *against*, and the dialogue proceeds according to constant and respected rules in which the strength of the arguments is decisive. No, that would have been too easy. I longed for such conditions. In these meetings, in general I spoke very little. I knew that the struggle was going on a long way from the negotiating table; we had to get the most we could out of it now that we had finally succeeded in gaining a modicum of freedom, of involvement in economic decisions and negotiations; now that we'd had a taste of these things, we no longer wanted to go back. And if this stage had to end (as it did), I wanted to learn as much as possible, right up to the last minute—learn about democracy, the art of negotiation, and all those areas which, for thirty-five years, had been closed to us, or with which we ourselves had failed to grapple.

Why were purely tactical reasons so dominant in this period? Why didn't Poland's interests as a country—so apparent to the rest of the world—prevail over other factors? In fact, none of the great conflicts that have broken out in our country over the years have ever produced two opposing camps with clearly defined attitudes. Neither a population dissatisfied with its lot nor a government anxious to put out the fires of unrest wanted to go to extremes, nor did either seem disposed to make a thorough analysis of the situation. The two sides confined themselves to mutual antipathy and distrust but failed to produce proposals for the future. August 1980 was the first time such proposals had been sketched out, but the Poles were still not yet ready to receive the good news. Some didn't want to hear it and all failed to understand it. It raised vain hopes in those who saw in it something other than what it really signified. This good news was like the Gospel: each one interpreted it in his own way—one afraid of losing his worldly wealth, the other with the satisfaction of finally being able to take revenge. And it was like the Gospel, too, in that, just as among the Apostles there were some who were unable to understand Jesus' words, the truth revealed itself only gradually to the Polish nation; people had to come to maturity in order to receive it.

When I look back on the men then in power, I feel no rancor or ill will toward them. Some of them saw that their own future was linked to the success of our movement. Some of them, sometimes quite spontaneously, took risky decisions we didn't hear about until much later. We now know that Deputy Premier Jagielski was acting on his own initiative during the tense situation preceding the signing of the Gdansk Agreements. His only supporters were the Gdansk authorities in the persons of Fiszbach and Kolodziejski; all the high officials from Warsaw accompanying him withdrew from the negotiations. Maybe this gesture saved their careers.

Whatever their opinion of our movement, those with maximum responsibility within the government did their utmost to block it. Some of them made a brief appearance, only to disappear almost immediately, like a small flame blown out by a breeze. Premier Pienkowski was one of these: an actor in a brief and tedious interlude who was then swept off the stage.

The principal personality of the period was First Secretary Stanislaw Kania. The concepts and solutions that were finally embodied on December 13, 1981, when martial law was declared, hardly sound like his style. I still think he was one of those who paid for having attempted—within the limits of what was then possible—to help the people make concrete all that they had achieved in August 1980.

All the same, I always came away from my talks with Kania feeling disappointed. I didn't have a high opinion of him—not as a man, but because we never got anywhere on any of the subjects we discussed. We often discussed the question of Solidarity's access to the media, a demand that received strong support because of the insulting tone of the official propaganda, particularly on television. We also discussed problems of education, hospitals, the status of teachers and doctors, and the discontent in professional circles, where there were demands for drastic changes. But for these talks to have been successful, we needed two people with a capacity for making decisions and the authority to carry them out. Kania seemed to have his back up against the wall; he was tense and the talks plodded on. This, incidentally, was the case with all the political leaders: they opened the talks by painting a general picture of the situation, the lack of means available, and the complex problems they had to deal with. This was the way they handled every discussion. But I was there to engage in detailed talks on concrete questions, on which I had a mandate to speak. And when Kania had briefed me on a situation that I knew as well as he did, without putting forward the merest hint of a solution to the problem I had come to resolve, the conversation dried up. These discussions were so frustrating that I quite frequently lost my temper. I wasn't going to feel sorry for a political leader just because he found himself in a jam, unless it was as man to man, for private reasons.

In February 1981, an important change took place. Pienkowski was replaced by General Wojciech Jaruzelski, who became premier while retaining the portfolio of defense, which he had held since 1968. At his initial press conference, the television showed a man who, for most people, was something of an enigma. We noted that he spoke faultless Polish. His expressionless face, partly hidden by dark glasses, his stiff figure, and his way of standing to attention were intriguing. All that was known about him was that he came from a large family of landowners and that in 1939 he had been deported with them to the depths of Russia, where he had lost his father. Living through Stalin's great terror seemed to have turned him to stone for life.

The General's language, on the other hand, was unexpected: lively, different from what we were accustomed to hearing. One of the first things he did was to appoint as his deputy Mieczyslaw Rakowski, editor-in-chief of the monthly *Polityka*, who had for years been trying, with some success, to present himself as a political man of European status. In outlook, Rakowski provided a strong contrast to the group currently in power and his appointment gave rise to general optimism.

In his first speech, Jaruzelski called for a ninety-day truce, while setting out a ten-point anticrisis program. Almost as soon as he was appointed deputy premier, Rakowski began negotiations with Solidarity. A number of steps were taken to counter strike threats throughout the country. At Rzeszow and at Ustrzyki, an agreement was signed that brought an end to a farmers' protest. The inviolability of farms was guaranteed; the restrictions on the sale and purchase of land were lifted, and there were amendments to a whole series of laws that went against the interests of independent farmers. Improvements were promised in the availability of farm equipment. There was a move toward setting up a trade union, but the plan was never implemented. In the text of the agreement, the words "Peasant Solidarity" were deleted; the farmers' representatives were to set up a national commission, which would itself be responsible for creating a farmers' trade union, but what form this union would take remained undecided.

At Lodz, a compromise was reached with students who were striking for the right to create a self-governing students' organization with the capacity—like Solidarity in the social and political life of the country—to ensure and guarantee changes in the life of the universities. The students wanted to transform their universities into pure academic establishments, independent of the political stance of the government and free from its interference in the programs of different disciplines and the statutes of student organizations. It was at Lodz that the Independent Association of Students (NZS) was at last officially recognized, but the solutions to a series of other problems were postponed pending further negotiations. Though far from satisfied with how their demands had been dealt with, under pressure from Solidarity the students agreed to respect the ninety-day truce.

The strike at the Gencjana works in Jelenia Gora was also short-lived. A holiday home, which had been the subject of the dispute, was subsequently designed for public use.

However slight these gains might appear, the opinion was that the General had shown good will and that we should therefore cooperate with him.

On February 18, 1981, one week after Jaruzelski's inauguration as premier, all strikes ended. But at the same time the government introduced a new regulation considerably limiting the right to strike. The government reserved the right to decide, alone, whether a strike conformed to the conditions laid down in the regulation and ruled that the strike warning period should be extended to at least seven days. If these conditions were fulfilled, the workers would receive an indemnity equivalent to half their wages; if not, they would be striking illegally and at their own expense.

Some days later we learned from an official source that legal proceedings were continuing against certain members of KOR. The premier had appealed for three months' hard work in our restored atmosphere of calm, but in the dark a time bomb was ticking.

We witnessed a new wave of reprisals against Solidarity's activists. There were unexpected dismissals among trade unions at Lodz and anonymous attacks on members of KOR; the police placed the leading KOR members and Solidarity advisers under surveillance; at the instigation of certain Party leaders one group, the Patriotic Union of Grunwald, started a noisy campaign—complete with anti-Semitic slogans—against circles they labeled "oppositional." Attacks were launched not only against the leaders of the March 1968 student riots, like Kuron and Michnik, but also against eminent cultural personalities, including the filmmaker Andrzej Wajda. This wave of intolerance awoke disturbing memories. It revealed deep divisions within the government and suggested that certain special services, as in the Stalinist period, might be playing a decisive role in the shadows.

Rakowski and I were engaged in talks at this time. As head of the government commission responsible for negotiations with the trade unions, he was in an ideal position to succeed in the political game he had chosen to play. In the course of our meetings, it soon became apparent that Rakowski's dealings with Solidarity were intended to propel him to the top, and that by presenting our demands to the Politburo, he was ensuring himself a privileged position within it.

But Solidarity's special role—its autonomous existence as a movement—was a long way from that forecast in Rakowski's scenario. Even I was unable to exert a determining influence on the trade union's behavior, and Solidarity's aspirations went far beyond the part the government wanted us to play within the framework of the established order. I wasn't an easy partner for

Rakowski either; I refused to let myself be won over by this type of negotiation.

Rakowski nevertheless succeeded in organizing a meeting for me with Jaruzelski. Hearing that this was to take place, I couldn't help asking jokingly if I might not receive a modest promotion for the occasion. (I have, in fact, an instinctive respect for a uniform.)

So it was that, on March 10, 1981, at the government's headquarters in Warsaw, in a room adjacent to the premier's office, I found myself, to my surprise, face to face with Colonel Wladyslaw Iwaniec, who had been my commanding officer during my military service.

I admire people who can organize things in advance, foresee everything down to the smallest detail. It was in just such a way that this incredible meeting must have been arranged. The General must have gone through my file and noted how I had spent my military service; he must have wanted to refresh my memory of a time when I, too, was in the army. Our conversation was to confirm that he was completely aware of my background.

Face-to-face with my former commanding officer—he had been a lieutenant at the time—I found myself thinking back to those days, so distant, so different, and yet already marked with my current preoccupations, as if each of us carried within him a pattern of his destiny. I was stationed at a big barracks in Koszalin, where at least a dozen units had been garrisoned. One incident stands out from the rest in my memory. One of my unit, a corporal like myself, called Jurek, had come back from patrol blind drunk. He was a powerful man—he carried a punch that would fell an ox— and on this occasion he was also armed with a machine gun. He was knocking down anyone who came within range (he'd already downed three of our unit), so the officer commanding our platoon asked me if I could deal with him. I said that I would on condition that he wasn't sentenced; they could lock him up at the barracks but there was to be no question of a court martial. The officer agreed and I went out to Jurek, who was standing in the middle of the parade ground facing a great crowd of soldiers. As soon as anyone moved a bit too much for his liking, he swung around with his gun—it was loaded with live rounds (a normal thing for a soldier going on patrol). I went up to him, warned him what a mess he was getting himself into, and persuaded him very gently to give up his weapon and let me put him to bed. He gave in.

Apart from this incident, there's nothing much to tell about my life in uniform. I had the good luck to get leave after winning the prize for target shooting. A little later, I was sent to NCO school at Swiecie, and after nine months I returned to my unit, where I was given a squad. I didn't mind the discipline and I didn't have any trouble from my men. I managed to get further with them through good humor and jokes than others did through shouting. I taught Morse code to the soldiers in the company and ran courses in electricity and radio navigation. I remember our general giving me my corporal's stripes. He took a good look at me, then he said: "I can see old Pilsudski was down your way." I already had a mustache and must have looked rather like him—or so I thought.

I won't describe in detail my first meeting with Jaruzelski. It was an event that everyone knew about; the atmosphere and reasons behind the meeting were no secret.

Jaruzelski wore a rather worried look. A confrontation with a real worker at the head of a big political movement was something unprecedented for him. The atmosphere in which we met could hardly be called cordial, but between the two of us, a current of understanding flowed that had been completely absent from my first meeting with Kania. With him, the meeting had been a battle from the start, particularly as I hadn't the slightest respect for Kania as a negotiating partner. I did have a certain respect for Jaruzelski, which wasn't exclusively connected with the uniform he was wearing. Even the tone of his conversation seemed different, a hundred miles away from Kania's wooden abstractions. We were talking about responsibility. My period as a corporal was a good starting point—Jaruzelski knew my file backward and forward and immediately listed all the reasons for which I had been promoted. We each said a little piece about responsibility, about the current difficulties and the necessity for creating a sound relationship between the authorities and Solidarity. I stressed to him that we would never go back now that Solidarity was here for good.

Our conversation lasted nearly an hour and it felt to me as if we had established a common language. It was a first step, and it seemed that Jaruzelski shared this conviction. But each of us no doubt understood things in his own way. For me this starting point was a compromise between our own goals and the interests of those in power, a reasonable middle road, acceptable to all and offering potential solutions. On the other side, it was no more than the hope of winning over an adversary.

If one looks at the recent history of Poland, one sees democratic leaders appearing from time to time and expressing popular aspirations, but after a certain period they let themselves be won over by the authorities. They are given a margin in which to maneuver and are allowed to act out their part. It wasn't impossible that Jaruzelski may have imagined me at some time or other in the Diet, in the role of speaker of that assembly. No doubt such ambitions could have been satisfied, but it was precisely there that our thinking was poles apart; it's my guess that he didn't follow my belief that the seeds we had sown in August 1980 would eventually bear fruit.

I am ambitious in my own way, but I never felt the slightest temptation to establish myself in the system and gain a place in the sun. I could have become president of the Central Council of the Trade Unions and then God-only-knows-what in the government itself, had I wanted to. They would have agreed to anything; it was an old recipe for keeping dissenters quiet. In 1970, they had already tried this approach on Baluka, and earlier, in 1956, on Gozdzik. And each time these people, troublesome to the government, reasoned in the same way: "After all, if I join them, if I operate inside, I can do something positive. I won't be the one to lose out."

In another, more confidential, meeting, the General promised me that a signal—to be agreed in advance—would be given a few days before if the government implemented any significant decision that would affect me. This promise, as with many others, was not kept.

The Bydgoszcz Affair

My meeting with Jaruzelski, placed in the context of events that took place only a few days later, showed how easily good intentions on both sides could be thwarted. If we succeed in mastering events, it is only within narrow limits.

From a broad perspective, what happened at Bydgoszcz was no

more than a routine incident. But the events at Bydgoszcz reflected the divisions, political confusion, and internal contradictions that marked the whole period. If real problems are neglected they reappear in unexpectedly dramatic form.

Behind these events lay the authorities' refusal to recognize an independent farmers' union. The farmers appealed to Solidarity, demanding quite justifiably that we should support them in the same way they had supported us. It was in the region of Bydgoszcz that pro-union activists—old militants who still remembered the activities of the prewar peasant self-management groups—were most active. The regional committee made a statement that henceforth everything deriving from what was called "the agro-alimentary complex" would come under its control.

Jan Rulewski, president of Solidarity for the Bydgoszcz region, then made contact with the district authorities in order to discuss the question at the next meeting of the district council. The demand for legalization of the independent farmers' union was to be the principal question on the agenda. Meanwhile the farmers had stopped work and occupied the headquarters of the local branch of the ZSL (United Peasants' Movement—a government-approved party). But when the council finally met, the session was unexpectedly suspended. The activists, led by Rulewski, protested against this decision and were supported by a number of the elected members. At this moment, the crisis occurred. The deputy district governor, who was presiding over the session, called in the police to expel the Solidarity activists from the council chamber, and Rulewski and two others were badly beaten up and had to be taken to the hospital.

Before the Bydgoszcz district council convened, I had been warned that there would be some provocation. It was obvious that the authorities intended to pick a quarrel with us and incite us to do something rash. The situation was serious and the presidium of Solidarity's National Commission was immediately summoned for the following evening.

In the north, meanwhile, the Warsaw Pact was maneuvering their forces. We were warned that martial law might be declared at any moment. We also knew that lists had been drawn up of activists who were under surveillance. And the confusion surrounding the Bydgoszcz incident didn't conform to the understand-

186

ing I had been given by Jaruzelski. It seemed absolutely incredible that those with whom I had been sitting at the negotiating table should have concealed such a scenario from me. Perhaps, within the government, there were other influential groups who thought they would settle accounts clandestinely, in their own way and fast—by force, even with a bloodbath if necessary.

We were not in a position to fight. I trusted in the wisdom of our people; I didn't imagine for a moment that we would ever get ourselves into that even with outside assistance. We weren't armed and we didn't want to fight. We would simply continue along the path we had chosen.

Andrzej Celinski

Walesa had called together the National Commission, knowing full well that we were facing the greatest conflict since August 1980. He expected very strong pressure in favor of launching a general strike and the only aim of his speech to the Commission was to postpone the strike date. He was aware that the present conflict threatened to end up as a general strike, but he was prepared to agree to it only if no other solution presented itself. Solidarity was once again faced with the challenge of "To be or not to be." Walesa sometimes goes through the motions of adopting someone else's position so as to keep a firmer grip on his own. At that time he was again preoccupied, his guard was up, he was like a fighter. He was once more the man who wins everybody's votes, once more the president of the trade union, steady and responsible.

But there were violent disagreements over Bydgoszcz leading to Walesa slamming the door and offending the National Commission. It was Lech who seemed to have won the argument, but the price he would have to pay was to refrain from any influence on the detailed decisions made in this affair. We moved on to the nomination of those who were going to Warsaw to negotiate and those who would be returning to Gdansk. As soon as Walesa was nominated as one of the negotiators, Jacek Kuron made a motion by which the negotiators would not have the power to sign any agreement that had not first been ratified by the Commission. I interpreted this gesture of Jacek's as a clear stand in favor of the general strike—and that was exactly what it was. Walesa grumbled but had to accept the conditions.

Konrad Maruszczyk

Last March we were teetering on the edge of a precipice. In my view, the other camp had already made its decision—the map showing the dispersal of armed forces over the whole country was explanation enough. Warnings were heard: Poland must be on its guard; it mustn't become a second Budapest; there must be no rerun of 1956! In Bydgoszcz, at the time of the incident, Lech had given Rulewski a clear warning: "Jasiu, don't let yourself be dragged into this, it's a trap, that much is obvious!" But Jasiu had replied: "I know what I'm doing!"

Although few people know it, the fact that Lech left the National Commission meeting, slamming the door behind him, resulted in a move away from a general strike in favor of an initial warning strike (the majority of those present had originally declared themselves in favor of immediately launching a general strike). Lech was a good judge of the stakes but few other people were as aware of the risks as he was, and of the danger of everything being compromised. Some people instinctively feel danger threatening them—themselves or the community they belong to. Lech is one of them. Hence the very cautious policy of the union leadership in March 1981 which, as it happened, was the only one possible at the time. March was generally recognized as the beginning of the end. This was what led Jan Olszewski to compare the situation to that which existed before the rising against the Russians in January 1863.

The turning point in March is a key event for understanding the trade union's history, just as the Gdansk Regional Committee's decision to reconsider Walesa's functions as the head of the movement explains his super-cautious position at the famous meeting of September 17 regarding the creation of a national trade union. At that meeting he took the view that to create a central organization without sufficient preparation and forethought would only result in internal dissensions. He had seen enough of them in his own region.

Without understanding the significance of this incident, one may find it difficult to understand Lech's behavior toward his colleagues at that time; just as, without understanding March 1981, it is impossible to understand the subsequent conflicts that were to erupt within the trade union itself.

Andrzej Celinski

The essential problem was Rulewski's ambiguous role in the Bydgoszcz incident. In the early days, there were some wild hypotheses, including one that cast him in the role of mole and put the whole responsibility for what had happened on to him. Certain facts appeared to justify such a hypothesis, however crazy it seemed.

Faced with a conflict that gravely undermined the country's political situation, the government was unable to produce the speedy solutions the population wished for. It needed to allow a certain period of time to elapse in order to find the right response. It was only then that it would have been permissible for us to draw conclusions from the government's actions and to act according to our analysis of the situation. No orders at all had been given: the general instructions were to wait until the situation stabilized, otherwise we would be acting in the dark.

And then the National Commission had to go and meet at Bydgoszcz, trying to do everything at once, without even rationally analyzing the situation in which the government was placed—to some extent its adversary, but also to some extent its partner—as if that was the least of its worries! Walesa was fully aware of all this. He was also aware that his own position, unlike the position of those around him (the members of the National Commission), was not dependent on the outcome of this particular set of circumstances. This had always been his trump card in the countless affairs he had had to deal with.

There was a moment in March 1981 when Walesa and Kuron were diametrically opposed in their opinions, though it never came to an open confrontation.

In my view, Walesa was convinced of one thing: that Poland is not really a sovereign country and that it is just a pipe dream to think that we could, by our own efforts, effect the slightest change in her status. Walesa never expressed himself on the subject and never employed this sort of language, but I think that his caution stems directly from this realization; it is the caution of a man always attentive to the voices dissuading Solidarity from rushing into things.

In Jacek Kuron's eyes, however, March 1981 was when Poland had to decide its fate and when the two camps had to mobilize all the forces at their disposal. This doesn't mean that Kuron necessarily expected a victory for Solidarity at that time. He merely stated—and time was to prove him right on this point—that progress was no longer possible, but that we had a chance now, however slight, to confront the government openly, and if we failed to seize this chance, it would be lost forever.

Walesa, on the other hand, tried by all the means in his power to avoid this confrontation. He felt that chances of modifying the system did exist and he hoped that, given time, we could redefine the ideas of the Communist government in our country.

Mieczyslaw Wachowski

We left Bydgoszcz for Warsaw in convoy. There were twelve cars conveying the regional presidents. We all drove with headlights on, in broad daylight. On the way, we passed columns of vehicles carrying Soviet Union license plates: the maneuvers were growing. We overtook horse-drawn carts transporting bundles of hay and I said to Marowiecki: "Look, Tadeusz, there's the straw for the cells they're getting ready for us. There are hard times ahead."

I recall Sila-Nowicki's memorable words when he later declared that the difference between March 1981 and December of the same year was that, after December, we were able to get in touch with some of the prisoners the following month, while after March, there was no reason to suppose that we would ever see them again. Incidentally, Rakowski put it bluntly to us in Warsaw when he said: "Do you think we extended the maneuvers just for fun? You must be joking! All this has gone on long enough."

A bitter period now began for all of us. We were still a long way from the goal we so wanted to reach, but the road seemed to be getting longer, so much that was unknown lay before us: we just had to keep plodding to the end of the tunnel. It was a gloomy prospect, all the harder to bear after the wonderful days of August 1980. Today, looking back, I nevertheless find that that period wasn't devoid of sense and even of a certain satisfaction. If the peasant doesn't work his soil, if the soldier doesn't carry his country's loam on the soles of his boots, if man's imagination doesn't bring him face-to-face with the ultimate threat, then we are left with nothing but empty theorizing and abstraction.

The End of the River

Where would the river end? Its current was strong now, it would have to be controlled. Intelligent action and some sort of plan were called for, to make use of its power and draw on its vast energy. But if, instead of imagination, there was only fear of the unknown, what then? The decision would be taken to dam the river! Was the idea to construct a dam that would retain the water and then make it possible to use its energy, or was it only to stop its course, and cause useless flooding? Today, looking back, we can say that when the river crashed into that great dam it divided: one part of the current went underground, another found its way around the obstacle and flowed out wherever it could. The rest remained under control, flowing through a whole system of sluices and conduits.

It was in the middle of 1981 that the government began deliberately organizing a "propaganda of chaos." Interminable lines built up outside the shops, which were virtually empty of merchandise. A journalist reported:

> In the autumn of 1981, the medical profession reported that the Poles were approaching critical protein deficiency. The system of ration cards had ended in failure. The administration, composed of the same men who had destroyed the Polish economy, demonstrated its incompetence by its failure to distribute existing food supplies. The ration cards turned out to be mere scraps of paper. The goods no longer reached their destinations.

> Solidarity was obliged to intervene as best it could in the work of putting the country back on its feet. But the economic reform was bogged down in paperwork. With regard to man-

agers, for example, there were endless arguments about whether they should be nominated or elected. Contrary to the notion of self-management, so essential to the spirit of reform, the government clung to nominations. It was the same for everything: not only economic but also political reasons prevented the starter of the economy from engaging, while Solidarity was accused of wanting to usurp the government's power.

The stream of accusations is all the more dangerous in that they flow from one single loudspeaker. Not having access to the media, Solidarity finds itself gagged. There is no authority in sight capable of reconciling the two camps; Cardinal Wyszynski is dead, the Pope is a long way away, Jaruzelski is not Pilsudski. So all eyes are turned toward Walesa.

He has emerged victorious from challenges from both sides of the negotiating table and is known for his talent in extricating himself from impossible situations. He has put out many fires, and fought several others, but for the masses in search of radical reforms, he seems too gentle, too conciliatory, too human. In every person, he tries to see the human being; he even believed in the good will of Deputy Premier Rakowski when the latter had already disappointed everybody else. "Well, he's got a bit worked up" was how he excused Rakowski's arrogance. At the time, this didn't go down well. Not only loudmouths at union meetings but self-satisfied intellectuals had begun to hold forth on the situation. They were of the opinion that we should charge, head down; in their eyes, Poland should have followed the example of Finland or Yugoslavia or found a third *modus vivendi* with Russia. Of course, they were aware of Poland's special position, that it lay "en route": we know that the western frontier of the Soviet Union is on the banks of the Elbe, rather than the Oder or the Bug. They said, that's why we watch the trains coming from the East, night and day, to see that nothing unpleasant happens to them. They kept talking about the "corridor": we'll grant them their bases and then the corridor, they said, forgetting that the corridor idea had already had fatal consequences for Poland in the past! They hadn't known that time, any more than they had experienced Stalinism; they didn't realize that they had grown up during a period when the forces of the militia were held at bay. With the pride that is typical of Poles they maintained on the contrary that: "We'll never see a scenario like the Hungarians or the Czechs saw."

It was in this frame of mind that, between September and October 1981, they held their first congress at Gdansk, in the Oliva sports complex. Although his vision of reality was so different from their own, Walesa was going to be chosen again— life had him marked out as one of her elect. He would get the majority of votes—even if, as they knew, his election was to involve some compromise with "internal democracy," the authorities' latest catchword.

On the eve of the Solidarity congress I realized that of the three main subjects—planning, represented in theory by our group of experts; organization, represented by the delegates who had come to Gdansk; and practical action—it was the third that would be judged the most important. The question was if and how we could reach a compromise with the government that would make it possible to fit Solidarity into the Polish political scene as an independent popular force and one not subordinate to the Party.

To know what concrete solutions were possible, one had to understand the practicalities. During the congress, the elections and the presentation of candidates for the presidency gave fresh proof of this: Rulewski's nomination may have had a noisy reception, but he was defeated nevertheless. The worker would have said to himself: "You spoke well, my man, but I'm sorry, I don't know you. It's the guy who's slaved away with us for the last ten years in the same workshop who knows what's what." And another: "He's as stupid as I am, so he'll not be trying any tricks; maybe I'll even be able to put one over on him!" "But take this clever fellow, do we know what *other* people he's been getting his ideas from? If they knew each other before, they'll probably do some crooked deal behind our backs." These were thought processes you had to know; you only knew them if you'd come up from the bottom, and they couldn't be learned anywhere else but on the job.

The problem was that the members of this assembly wanted to shine at all costs, to fly higher than their wings would carry them. Some of them really had something to say and said it well, but with many of them this simply wasn't the case. The fashion was for slogans, and they were trotted out at the slightest excuse.

To avoid dealing only with elections, I had proposed that the congress should take place in two stages. In the first stage, we would deal only with the distribution of functions; there would be no discussion; people wouldn't have the chance to draw attention to themselves and show off. We would just vote, as each candidate would have submitted beforehand a written curriculum vitae and service record, his program, the list of his supporters, and so on. In the second stage, people could discuss the program without the interference of any personal ambition of obtaining a place on the National Commission or the presidium, as these places would already have been filled. This would not prevent anyone getting a place on one of the various committees, but they would be judged according to other criteria, not as representatives of a particular group or region.

Well, believe it or not, my proposal was judged undemocratic, detrimental to our new movement!

As a result, the two stages of the congress were punctuated throughout with rowdy stage effects. The body of decisions and motions adopted had, in my view anyway, only a theoretical value, for only one thing was important now: to see if we could create in Poland a tripartite system involving government, church, and Solidarity. I tried to put forward this point of view during the debate and on several occasions I lost patience. Somebody even claimed to be shocked when I confessed not to know in detail the voluminous platform motion submitted to the congress members.

At the press conference concluding this long and stormy congress, I again put forward my idea of a triple agreement between the government, church, and Solidarity. It was during the final months of 1981 (the most tense and difficult) at a meeting of the "Big Three"—Jaruzelski, Glemp, and Walesa—that it would be officially proposed that Solidarity have not one vote in three but, at the most, one in *seven*. According to the blueprint for the Front for National Agreement, our large trade union was to have only one seat alongside a whole collection of other social organizations. The secretary of the Party Central Committee, Stefan Olszowski, an influential representative of the hard line, crushed my hopes for an agreement involving Solidarity when he said: "The Front for National Agreement is founded on a system of tripartite co-operation between the PZPR [Polish United Worker Party], the ZSL [United Peasants' Party] and the SD [Democratic Movement]. All social forces that recognize the socialist system and the Constitution of the People's Republic of Poland are invited to support this cooperation."

As the historian of this period, Jerzy Holzer observed that neither the church nor Solidarity were on this list as co-organizers of the Front; they could only confirm resolutions drawn up along the lines set out by the Party and its satellite groups.

A few days before the meeting of the Big Three, a violent campaign was launched against Solidarity, first at the plenum of the Party Central Committee, then, on the last day of October, at the opening of the session of the Diet. There General Jaruzelski spoke of the madness of strikes, the hate campaign launched against the country—against socialism and its natural allies. The Diet was informed that the government had tabled a bill in the assembly, aiming to endow itself with special powers in order to ensure the safety of its citizens and the interests of the country. If the strikes did not stop, if Solidarity did not submit to the law by calling for the abandonment of strike action, Jaruzelski threatened to take steps enabling this proposal to enter into immediate effect.

The meeting of the Big Three, announced for November 4, had good press abroad, and commentators saw it as opening up new possibilities for the future. Viewed from close quarters, the situation scarcely seemed to justify such an analysis. It is true, however, that certain leaks from leading circles within the Party created the impression that they had allotted two months to reach an agreement with Solidarity, but "such an agreement could only be reached within the framework of a structure or a body which would allow control to be exercised over the whole social scene."

It was a complex situation, difficult to analyze. The Americans, for their part, were laying down conditions indirectly, through bankers with financial interests in the Polish situation. Clearly, a declaration of martial law would not be viewed in a favorable light and financial aid would be granted only if Poland returned to normal conditions. It was understood that, under the circum-

195

stances, I was unable to visit the United States, as had been announced previously. After a triumphant welcome on the other side of the Atlantic, I was to have returned to the country as a prodigal son, bringing with me a large and solid credit, capable of rescuing the Polish economy. In fact, everything indicated that even if the welcome was splendid things were less likely to work out regarding the prospects for credit.

Local observers of the political game were of the opinion that if this meeting of the Big Three did take place, it would be only for the history books, so it could be said to have taken place once all the other possibilities had been exhausted. One of my collaborators describes the course of events as follows:

On the afternoon of November 4, Lech Walesa received a welcome from Cardinal Glemp. It would soon be time for the meeting with Wojciech Jaruzelski, who since October was not only minister of defense and premier but also first secretary of the Party. The journey from the Primate's residence in Miodowa Street to the government's headquarters was to be by car. But in the hall below there was a slight technical problem. Should Walesa get into the Primate's car? Some thought it would be tactless, others that it was no longer necessary to draw attention to a cooling of relations, which had been apparent to everyone for some months. In recent statements made by the church, in fact, everyone had been able to detect the tone of disapproval regarding Solidarity's "excessive politicization." But what is to be done in a country where everything you touch takes on a political slant? Admittedly, the Primate could not have been up to date with the course of the National Commission's debates, where people had gone so far as to contest the president of Solidarity's right to go and talk to Jaruzelski. ("The president of the trade union is a public figure and cannot speak as a private person. Let him explain his position to us in detail on every subject that concerns us! No one can go above our heads, above the National Commission! Walesa must not go alone!" Walesa's reply was: "In that case, I intend to summon a new Congress to elect a new President" and, speaking to Rulewski: "If my head doesn't fall by their hands, perhaps it will by yours, Jan.")

When he got out of the car behind Cardinal Glemp, Walesa seemed tense, in contrast to the General, who played the smiling host. He greeted them both and took them into a small private room. The doors shut behind them. Father Bronislaw Piasecki, the Primate's secretary, waited in the hall with Mieczyslaw Wachowski, Lech's assistant, and Wieslaw Gornicki, Jaruzelski's adviser, who sat down with a file under his arm. The meeting lasted a full hour. A light-hearted conversation about nothing in particular suddenly sprang up in the hall. But the moment the doors opened again and someone put his head in, Gornicki leaped out of his chair and handed over the file before coming back to sit at the table.

The text of the proposal setting out a line common to Solidarity and the government, which had been drawn up by Tadeusz Mazowiecki, wasn't even examined at this meeting. It made no difference that this proposal was the product of consultations with the Episcopate. Jaruzelski had fixed the agenda down to the last item. He renewed his final offer politely but firmly: join the Front for National Agreement on the basis of a "one in seven" vote. The welcome had been perfectly courteous, but there were no further advantages to be expected, apart from a possible future meeting.

Walesa wasn't happy. None of the journalists could get a word out of him. As is his habit, he went off on his own and ruminated over the meeting, looking for the positive points, trying to draw useful conclusions for the next meeting, organizing the facts in his mind, wondering about the future. It's only when his plans are obstructed that he livens up again and opens up to people.

Cardinal Glemp got ready to fly off to Rome and Walesa went back to Gdansk. The National Commission, meanwhile, had adopted a number of resolutions designed to form the basis of a possible social agreement. It accompanied these demands, which contained nothing new, with threats of action in conformity with the trade union statutes, including a general strike, if the demands were not met within three months. General Jaruzelski interpreted the tone of these resolutions as an attack on the spirit of the talks that had just taken place.

As soon as Walesa arrived in Gdansk, Tadeusz Fiszbach,

the district governor, Jerzy Kolodziejski, and Tadeusz Kuta, editor-in-chief of the local Party newspaper, met him in the parish of St. Brigid's, at Father Jankowski's. Acting on Jaruzelski's orders (or Barcikowski's), they urged Walesa to take rapid action to resolve this unfortunate disagreement. In their view, the trade union's president would thereby also be restoring his credibility. They argued that the resolutions taken by the National Commission gave a weapon to the Party's hard-liners, who claimed the talks with Solidarity no longer served any purpose and that recourse must be made to radical and definitive solutions.

This nocturnal meeting at the parish of St. Brigid took a dramatic turn when the representatives of the authorities made it understood that this would be one of their very last attempts to uphold any kind of agreement between the government and Solidarity. What they wanted was for Walesa to draft a statement to be co-signed by the presidium of the National Commission, modifying the tone of the Commission's resolutions. Caught between the hammer and the anvil, Walesa found himself confronted with an exceptionally difficult task: he was going to have to oppose the trade union's supreme body.

Cardinal Glemp, who had been informed before departing for Rome of the resolutions adopted by the National Commission, sent Walesa a telegram in which he thanked him "for his presence at the Warsaw talks." But the thrust of the telegram remained puzzling and, in the current situation, Walesa would no doubt have wished for less ambiguous support. The Gdansk authorities would also have welcomed such support. They obtained permission to make a telephone call to Rome. It was already past midnight and no one in Rome was answering. The printing of the Gdansk papers had been held up so that the desired communiqué could appear in their first editions. Day was beginning to dawn when the following text was finally agreed upon: "The presidium of the National Commission confirms that, in all negotiations with the State authorities, the National Commission is and will be agreeable to concessions and compromises justified for the supreme good of Polish society. Our trade union has always emphasized that it does not arrogate to itself the title of sole representative of the Polish population. Any interpretation of the resolutions recently passed by the National Commission that proves contrary to the two points set out above would violate the social agreements of Gdansk, Szczecin, and Jastrzebie and would infringe the statutes of our trade union, these statutes being consistent in their tenor with the Constitution of the Polish People's Republic."

It was the first time that Walesa had given so clear and forceful a warning to the hard-liners within his own party. It was the sign that he was prepared if necessary to part company with them in order to preserve a slight chance of dialogue.

The cold war the government had been waging was finally bearing fruit. Within the trade union, Walesa was accused of having compromised Solidarity's program, while the government blamed him for no longer being able to control the trade union and for having lost all credibility as a spokesman. What were the authorities proposing? Basically, they were demanding two things (which they had already expressed repeatedly): that he should exclude from Solidarity all those designated by them as extremists and that he should join Solidarity with the Front for National Agreement, according to the principles already laid down.

The meeting of the Big Three was a dead end, producing no results. That didn't mean that I turned a deaf ear to the government's arguments. Up to December 12, a halt was called to all strikes. The last one—the students' strike—was to end with a solemn mass at the sanctuary of Jasna Gora in Czestochowa. We informed the authorities of this and I also told them that the best solution to the problem of strikes would be to set up commissions to represent both sides: a general or regional strike would be called only after all possibilities of mediation had been exhausted. This would apply equally at the local level, even at the level of individual enterprises: no strike was to be called without prior mediation, except perhaps in the case of an open attack on the trade union itself.

Since the Solidarity Congress, I had also been involved in talks with all the groups which the authorities designated as "political," so as to eliminate what they considered the most important grounds for disputes.

The authorities proceeded to attack the appointment of trade union "advisers." Such attacks were quite unjustified: on many occasions our experts had put on the brakes and prevented the growth of radicalization, but they weren't accommodating enough for the authorities' liking. In the course of my talks I made proposals aimed at defining their status and the causes in which they could intervene as trade union representatives and those in which they would give their own views and exercise their responsibilities as private citizens.

I put forward a whole catalogue of similar proposals, of which the principal one, passed over in silence by the authorities, was to lead to a change in the functioning of the National Commission. In asking for a separate building to house the Commission it was my intention that its isolation from the regional bodies in Gdansk should allow it to devote more time to trade union problems, instead of feeling obliged to recite a litany of symbolic demands. It would have become a sort of think-tank rather than a tribune. Considerable time elapsed before the question was raised for discussion; it then turned out that such a decision was within the province of Deputy Premier Rakowski. The authorities' affirmative response allowing us to take over the Akwen Club, near the shipyard, only reached us on December 12, the eve of the declaration of martial law. It seems that somebody wanted to clear his conscience just at the moment when it no longer mattered either way.

The low-key reception of the December 13 coup may have been the result of modifications that had been made to the presidium of the National Commission during the congress. Thanks to these, the presidium no longer featured "personalities" who might have appeared politically prickly in the eyes of the government. I was reproached, incidentally, for having thus created a "rump Presidium," but in such difficult times of transition, this was no bad thing. The members were now able people—not strike leaders, but men nevertheless capable of hard work. The problem was that they weren't left any time to do it in.

I brought up all these problems in the very first hours of martial law, in Warsaw, on the occasion of my meeting with the military and with Ciosek, the minister of trade union affairs. But I felt that time was running out for me, too. Foreseeing that we had reached the end of this particular road, I began to think about two working hypotheses.

The first envisaged an agreement based on principles akin to those the government had put forward. With the experience we had already acquired, I thought that we could keep things going as long as we needed to and that we would be able to prevent a recurrence of what happened to the workers' councils after 1956 and to self-government after 1970. But one day I began thinking of what had become of all our proposals in the few months of Solidarity's official existence—of our proposed laws on trade unions, on workers' self-management, on censorship, of the whole series of demands of August 1980. These proposals had matured slowly but then, once we had finally succeeded in submitting them, they came back to us in such a mangled form, bearing so little resemblance to the original conception that, in any event, they were stripped of all effectiveness. Unprepared for these reforms, the government had taken fright and that was why it had cut them back, leaving us with nothing but the shreds of all our fine proposals. If we carried on like this, giving in to more and more self-censorship, allowing more and more of our projects and our ideas to be mutilated, we would end up conniving with the government and bring about our own destruction.

The second working hypothesis I examined took into account the possibility of imminent attack. In the event of such an attack, I would suggest to the trade union leaders and to the Primate that I give up my functions and retire, leaving the field open to those who thought there was still possibility for action. And once the authorities had launched their attack and made a clean sweep, I would salvage what was left and declare that, under my wing, Solidarity would continue to exist.

These were difficult questions. It may even seem improper to think in this way, but I had to face up to the situation. I couldn't subscribe to the first hypothesis, even if I'd had five chances of success in a hundred (which wasn't the case). And I was advised against the second. I then chose a third, which led to me making a speech at Radom. That famous speech, extracts of which—references to an "inevitable confrontation"—were avidly picked up by Polish radio and television as proof that Solidarity was inciting people to prepare for civil war!

The evening before the meeting of Solidarity's regional presidents at Radom, Ciosek paid me a visit at the Solec Hotel in Warsaw, where I was staying. He is a talkative man but on this occasion I had the impression that he had some hidden motive for prolonging our conversation. And so it turned out. When he was called to the telephone for a moment, Ciosek left a piece of paper on his chair with a simple handwritten note: *Keep Walesa in his hotel at all costs!*

After a time we learned that, while this conversation was taking place, a spectacular attack by special police units, supported by tanks and helicopters, had been launched on the Fire Service Officers' School. Several hundred students were striking there in protest against the authorities' decision to place this school, until then a civilian establishment, under the control of the minister of internal affairs. Anticipating that the government was preparing for a show of force there, I had intended to forestall this action by trying to end the strike quietly. But it had been decreed that it would not be Walesa who put an end to that strike.

I was convinced then that we were seeing the final preparations before martial law was declared and that we had just witnessed a spectacular dress rehearsal; the strike had been quelled by force and I had been kept out of circulation, so that the authorities could now proceed, unhindered, to a program of large-scale repression. Ciosek had only come to my hotel to keep me holed up there. He had left the piece of paper inadvertently—or perhaps he had even done it on purpose to dishearten or frighten me, making me realize that they had me in an iron grip.

It was then, at the very last moment, that I opted for the third and last hypothesis, traveling from Warsaw to Radom to attend the meeting with Solidarity's regional presidents. I deliberately used strong words on that occasion—words designed to prevent the disintegration of our trade union, which was already under attack. Those words have been quoted out of context and given a different weight by the authorities, but I used them nonetheless.

Martial law was now inevitable. The government had paved the way for it a long time back. It only remained to find some suitable pretext for declaring it. Whatever we did, they would soon declare martial law anyway, but they still needed to throw the responsibility back on us, or on me. At Radom, I became the most radical of the radicals, letting myself be carried away by the atmosphere in the hall. No doubt I wouldn't have been arrested in December if I hadn't made that speech (I learned later of a government directive, issued before the Radom meeting, to the effect that I was not to be arrested), but if I hadn't spoken as I did, I would have betrayed the delegates and rendered myself powerless in Solidarity's future: to look on, as some would have liked, with folded arms as the government did what it chose.

Instead I put down my head and plunged in blindly, against convictions I had stated earlier. I could have protested against the mood of the delegates, but in the last analysis I had no choice. In the eyes of the public, the blame would have fallen on me if the trade union movement was divided and weakened at such a critical time. And it would have been my fault if the most promising idea to inform Poland in more than half a century had been lost. If I had merely disbanded the meeting without speaking, many of the delegates would have gone to prison, as they did later during martial law, but then I would have been no more than the pale instigator of a lost cause—a promoter of discord, not solidarity.

Had we failed? I would have to answer "yes," if the only measure of success was our unwillingness or inability to fight force with armed force. We had, though, during those 500 days set in motion an alternative society, while the whole of Poland awakened from its long slumber. We were not the master of our own house; it was and is still ours, but we had returned to the pauper's role, while others in authority again took over. The people had tasted freedom—the cornerstone of Polish hopes had been laid—and now we had to bide our time.

Martial Law

On December 13, General Jaruzelski reappeared on the national scene in a completely new role. Martial law had been declared the previous night; thus the period of dialogue between union and government that had begun with the signing of the agreements negotiated at the Gdansk shipyard and elsewhere came to an end.

This state of martial law took no specific political form at first, but seemed rather like a large-scale military operation. Its full significance only became clear later on, and then it exceeded all expectations. Its consequences weren't just political: it unleashed a cataclysm that totally disrupted social and personal life and called into question the very idea of a national community.

Now that some years have passed, permitting us to evaluate the situation more objectively, it's probably correct to say that a movement like Solidarity was simply no match for the overwhelming measures undertaken by the government to bring Polish citizens to heel. It became increasingly obvious that we were in a state of civil war. The "dialogue for Poland" was over; the "war for Poland" had begun.

General Jaruzelski proved to be an astute and methodical director behind the scenes: events preceding the declaration of martial law had already helped prepare a climate of opinion regarding its inevitability. The days of hope and enthusiasm were over. The great surge of energy that had galvanized our society was doomed to fade away in frustration. The future looked grim.

The shops were virtually empty; the lines grew longer and longer. Never before had there been such a scarcity of the most basic consumer goods. It was as if the "Great Distributor" had gone on holiday until further notice, leaving his office locked and barred. Official propaganda hinted that responsibility for this state of affairs rested squarely with Solidarity, but according to the information I received, there were any number of warehouses full to overflowing with the basic necessities of life.

When people asked me about this, I'd reply: "Let's hold on, every month that goes by increases our advantage." But for the time being there was no longer any chance of a rapprochement, of reopening a dialogue with the authorities. And the very nature and existence of Solidarity depended on dialogue—that had been its strength.

Many of those in power favored using force, claiming that it was necessary to "apply pressure, throw the leaders of Solidarity in prison, break up their outfit, set them quarreling among themselves." These hard-liners were relatively well organized. The "liberals" in the Party and government, on the other hand, had lost ground. Those still on the fence sniffed something brewing in the air many months before martial law and began to take cover; they simply ran away.

While police in Warsaw were delivering summonses prepared at an emergency meeting of the State Council, Solidarity's National Commission was winding up two days of debate in Gdansk.

By midnight I still hadn't addressed the meeting, aside from explaining something during a recess to the journalists present. I had wanted to clarify the meaning of the word "confrontation," which I had used in a speech at Radom, and which had recently been misinterpreted by the official propaganda network: "When we speak of confrontation, we're thinking about the strength of our arguments. We do not have at our disposal, nor do we intend to use, physical force. We don't have any tanks, nor do we want any. Even though our words seem harsh, the message is one of nonviolence. Let the authorities consider our intentions instead of distorting what we say. Everything we have done confirms the integrity of our motives."

Shortly before this recess, at around six P.M., I'd telephoned the district governor to ask him about the concentration of troops observed in the vicinity of Gdansk, as well as the movements of the militia in Slupsk, Szczytno, and Szczecin. He told me he didn't know anything about troop movements. When he made inquiries, he was informed that there was a large-scale operation under way in the Tri-City sector, code-named "Walls." Officially, Operation Walls involved a thorough search of the vacant lots around the built-up areas and a sweep through the haunts of petty criminals—a simple police operation conducted by the authorities. Konrad Maruszczyk, my assistant in Gdansk, received the same answer later that night from Jerzy Andrzejewski, the commandant of the militia. Then Maruszczyk asked: "And what *walls* have been set aside for Solidarity?" There was no response.

Just before midnight a telegram was handed to me stating: "All communications by telephone and telex have been cut."

At that point I announced that the meeting was over. Five minutes later, the room was deserted. Snow was falling, gleaming in the yellowish glare from the lights along the path to the shipyard gate. On the way home the snow began to fall heavily. Everything was silent.

I knew that our movement had been stopped cold, for the time being. It was something I had to accept, like the rules of a game. When your opponent's turn comes around, you have to know how to fall back, to think things over calmly, to keep up your morale and summon your resources to face whatever comes next. Panic and disorganized struggle are worse than inactivity.

During the entire period of Solidarity's official existence, a main goal had been to gain time: one more week, one more month. That's how we finally arrived at the possibility of a settlement. But hadn't they wanted to crush our movement right from the start?

In August 1980, on the day when tension at the shipyard was at its height and we all expected a naval landing of troops at any moment (this was well before the signing of the agreement), the high-ranking security police official present in the yard told a journalist that he had been following politics since 1967, since this helped him understand where his own professional interests lay:

I'd prefer to keep strictly to my assignment. What people call "political diversion" is really only a matter of opinion. It con-

206

cerns the press, writers, and propaganda, not the security forces, but I'm nevertheless obliged to work in that area. Now I'm a Party member before all else, and I chose this profession in order to fight the real spies, the ones who create a real "diversion."

Then he began to draw a general picture of how things would develop in the short term, as he saw it:

Every political force in the country except one—the one in power—wants to see these agreements signed. The crunch will come *after* they've been signed. The factions that don't have the slightest need for a real democracy will use the agreements to further their own plans. They'll soon try to weaken morale to such a point that public opinion will demand a return to a strong authority figure, who will then appear in the guise of a sort of Polish De Gaulle.

We asked ourselves at the time who this Polish De Gaulle might be; we wondered even more when, shortly afterward, it was Kania who was named Party first secretary.

The Western journalist gave us the tape of his conversation with the police official, and we made a transcript of it. Many police and government scenarios of this type existed a full year before martial law, which clearly was not the invention of a solitary madman.

That night, our doorbell never stopped ringing. The first wave of visitors arrived at around one A.M., members of the Young Poland Movement who had come to announce that some of their friends had been arrested. They returned a while later to tell me what was happening in the city, and asked for my advice. I told them the same thing I'd already told my wife: that we had to wait patiently until morning, because it was difficult to evaluate the situation at that time. I also learned that my driver had been arrested; his wife came to see us, accompanied by a journalist on the weekly, *Solidarnosc.* Danuta consoled her as best she could. "Don't worry, Marzenka," she said, "they've arrested Lech so many times that nothing will ever surprise me again. But you see, we're still here, and nothing will happen to you either."

The declaration of martial law took the authorities in Gdansk by surprise as well. The military staff in charge of the operation that night had kept it an absolute secret. The district governor, Kolodziejski, was woken at the stroke of one, informed that the decree was already in effect, and then taken to the Party first secretary in Gdansk, Fiszbach. Both of them had had their telephone lines cut, just like the rest of the country, but in Fiszbach's apartment there was a direct line to the Party Central Committee that was still working. They called Warsaw and were able to speak first to Barcikowski, then to Rakowski, who confirmed that martial law was indeed in effect and told them that their first priority was to convince me to go unconditionally to Warsaw for negotiations. Those in Warsaw let it be understood that the decision had been made by General Jaruzelski, and that he was waiting to speak to me himself.

Fiszbach and Kolodziejski were driven to my house in Zaspa, where they found the apartment block on Pilotow Street surrounded by militiamen. The two government emissaries began by talking to us through the door; once inside the apartment, they delivered their message about going to Warsaw for the supposed negotiations with Jaruzelski.

I refused to consider their proposal until the authorities had first released all those who had been arrested. The two men went off to report to the Party Central Committee on their direct line. In the meantime, a "combat detachment" armed with crowbars appeared in front of the building demanding entrance, but they agreed to wait until Fiszbach and Kolodziejski returned. The two officials showed up at around three A.M., accompanied by the major commanding the "special" detail. When Kolodziejski told me that I'd be better off going to Warsaw of my own accord than being taken there by force, I realized that I had no choice. "It won't be for long," the district governor added. "And I'll gladly go with you if that'll help to convince you that you'll come back safe and sound."

"Why don't you go home instead, sir," I replied. "I have the feeling that you're going to be transferred at some point yourself. Martial law isn't something that's declared for forty-eight hours, or a month. This business is about as serious as it can get, and I think it's going to last a long time. I'll be ready in a moment, I'm just waiting for my wife to pack a few things for me."

Tadeusz Fiszbach must have been better informed about the situation; he said little, and suggested less. I had the impression the first secretary was almost petrified by the turn events had taken. I said good night to them: "I'll go alone, gentlemen. You go on home. You'll have your own problems to deal with."

I tend to notice people's attitudes, the way they speak, the general aspect of a given situation, and I remember everything people say, whereas my wife pays more attention to particular details that often turn out to be significant. Here are her recollections of that particular night in December:

Danuta

At three o'clock in the morning more people came to the door, and I got up to see who was there. Lech stayed in bed. It was Fiszbach and Kolodziejski. They wanted to speak to my husband, explaining that Mr. Jaruzelski would like to invite him to talk things over. Lech got angry and replied that it was too late for empty chatter like that, that we'd have no more of it. Then I spoke up. "Gentlemen, do you know that people are being arrested?" Fiszbach claimed that he didn't. Lech said: "That's right, I'll go and talk things over when everyone has been released!" Our two visitors went off to relay this condition to Warsaw.

Five minutes later, the doorbell rang again. I could see five policemen and three civilians through the peephole. They were carrying crowbars, the kind used to force open doors. They asked me to let them in, saying that they'd come to get my husband. I refused to open the door, so they waited outside for about an hour until the others returned. I let Fiszbach and the governor in, along with the policemen who were with them. Lech was already getting dressed. An officer stayed out in the hall with me while the others joined Lech in the kitchen. He kept calm so as not to frighten me. I was pregnant at the time. All they told me was that Lech had to leave to take part in some negotiations. It was five-thirty when he went downstairs to the car.

The two officials came back again at around nine o'clock to tell me that Lech was already in Warsaw, that he had a meeting with Ciosek (minister of trade union affairs) and would meet Jaruzelski later in the day. They offered to help me. They both seemed nervous and upset; Fiszbach even forgot his hat, which he'd left in the kitchen. Kolodziejski was wearing one brown sock and one black one. They looked quite shaken by what had happened, and it was obvious that they hadn't been informed in advance. I remember thinking that my husband had always gotten along well with them, even when things had been difficult.

On Sunday, at around six o'clock, I was able to speak to Lech from the governor's house. "They've really done it, and it could last a year," he told me. "Are they going to keep you that long?" I asked him. "I don't know. But martial law—that's going to last at least a year."

What was the reaction in foreign capitals? From what I heard later, the declaration of martial law took governments around the world entirely by surprise. It's hard to believe that in an age of spy satellites and super-sophisticated information systems, a lightning move that paralyzes a nation of millions of people in Europe can be planned and carried out in complete secrecy. And yet that's what happened.

Theoretically, the operation had been a purely internal one, which didn't prevent Soviet troops from being held in readiness just in case Polish resistance turned out to be violent. Some people wondered if a bloody uprising wasn't inevitable now. This was the situation at the Gdansk Shipyard during those critical days, as reported by Jan Mur in *Dziennik internowanego* (*Journal of a Prisoner*), an underground work published in Paris:

> On December 13 the radio broadcast a number of official statements; starting at noon, the TV did the same. The announcers read the communiqué from the Council of State, the declaration of martial law, and all its attendant provisions, including curfew, suspension of the right to travel, shutdown of all telephone and telex communications, suppression of freedom of expression, suspended publication of all newspapers and magazines, reduction in radio and television programming, suspension of classes in schools and universities, forced contribution of funds to the army, militarization of numerous

businesses, service in the civil defense, suspension of all student organization activities, freezing of bank accounts.

This went on all day long. People began to understand what had happened. They realized they'd been reduced to nothing in their own country, and that those who had declared war on the nation could do whatever they pleased with them.

A large crowd had gathered in front of the local union headquarters. A young man raised the Solidarity flag on the roof. Two men with the movement emblem on their jacket lapels and armbands answered every question with: "We don't know anything, keep moving along." At the main entrance the crowd reminded us of August 1980. Loudspeakers broadcast an announcement from inside the building: "We expect the militia to arrive—please do not remain in front of the entrance. Women and children should go home." People were already beginning to whisper: *Wrona, wrona,* the Polish word for "crow," a takeoff on the acronym WRON (Military Council for National Salvation)—the organization used to legitimize Jaruzelski's regime. A few days later, an old tune from the German occupation would be on people's lips, with an updated refrain: "It was on the 13th of this dreadful month / That the crow hatched out of its red shell . . ."

The inhabitants of the Tri-City area had received a terrible shock, but it was nothing compared to the blow delivered to the activists of Solidarity. No one was expecting anything like this. They began to ask themselves: "Shouldn't we have prepared people for this eventuality? Are the leaders of the movement at fault here?"

It's true that the union had worked out a specific plan, but it applied only in the event that the Diet voted to endow the government with special powers. Our plan was envisaged only as a response to a legal action by the Diet that would openly threaten our rights as citizens and workers, not an underhanded betrayal. We'd assumed that if this kind of thing happened, it would be the work of the Diet, not of the army and militia. We thought we'd be faced with an openly promulgated law, not news bulletins and proclamations posted on walls.

There was no time to lose. We set up a provisional office of the local strike committee at the shipyard. Everyone was tense and upset, and we received word of a heavy concentration of militiamen nearby. Unable to reach the members of the national strike committee, we decided to organize ourselves on our own as best we could.

A buffet of tea and sandwiches was set up for the committee in a ground-floor room. The crowd waited outside despite the freezing cold. More than a thousand people whistled every time they saw a militia vehicle pass the shipyard. We'd already been through this sort of war of nerves in August 1980, and it didn't worry us for the moment. The only difference was that Lech wasn't with us.

We learned that a meeting at six that evening was planned for members of the national, local, and shipyard strike committees; about a hundred of us were waiting when the strike leaders showed up. The crowd was particularly moved when Danuta Walesa and Father Jankowski arrived. The strike chairman passed the microphone to Jankowski, who told us he had talked to Lech, who was being held in Warsaw. "He asked you to wait for his decision," the priest said. "He'll be speaking to government representatives either this evening or tomorrow morning."

Then a man stood up and shouted: "Why wait? Does the union have rules and regulations, or not? It does! Have the leaders of Solidarity been arrested? They have! So there's only one answer to all this—a general strike!"

Mrs. Walesa took the floor. "I've spoken to Lech, too. His morale is good, as always, and he's not giving in. He's with you in spirit. He asks you not to make any rash decisions."

Someone yelled: "Walesa isn't the union all by himself! We have to act according to our own statutes!"

The dock worker standing next to him went red with rage: "You say Walesa isn't the union?"

It looked as if there was going to be a fight, but Mrs. Walesa intervened. "You've got to calm down! Lech will talk to them in Warsaw, and you should think about what he asked you to do. August 1980 is gone for good. This time there could be bloodshed, do you realize that? I'm speaking as a woman, as your wives and mothers would speak to you. We have to avoid a real tragedy!"

212

Someone else shouted out: "There's only one answer to violence and anarchy—strike!"

Father Jankowski tried once more to convince everyone in the room to postpone any decision for the time being. He was interrupted several times, and the crowd shouted its displeasure. Finally he gave up. After speaking briefly to the members of the national strike committee, he left with Mrs. Walesa, saying that he'd be back when he had any news.

After they'd gone, someone proposed a vote for a general strike, but people no longer even wanted to hear the word "vote"—the decision had already been made. The national strike committee was authorized to make any decision it cared to, and everyone wanted immediate action.

The shipyard workers decided to spend the night in the yard, while the others returned to their homes. There were representatives of more than a dozen commercial enterprises with us who had come out in favor of a general strike; as soon as the meeting was over, they had to slip out one at a time, taking advantage of the huge crowd to avoid being arrested.

We'd agreed that on the following day all the workers at sites that hadn't been militarized would launch a strike and occupy their own premises, the way the Italian workers do. All those plants in the Tri-City area were to fly the red and white flag in protest against the imposition of martial law and the arrest of Solidarity's leaders and advisers.

The messengers set off to get the word out, and people started to leave the room. Now we had to decide what we'd do if the militia invaded the shipyard during the night. After some discussion, we decided on passive resistance: "Our greatest strength is precisely our weakness—our living bodies and empty hands confronting tanks and nightsticks." We adjourned the meeting by singing the national anthem.

At around seven o'clock there was still a large crowd in front of the yard; red and white flags and flowers were beginning to pile up. Gdansk was once more solidly behind its workers, but the present situation was so different from those days in August 1980. Now the overwhelming feeling was one of sadness and uncertainty—and one man was sorely missed.

The inexperience and indecision of certain strike leaders was only too obvious. How could they possibly control all those nervous, angry men gathered inside the shipyard? There were probably about a hundred and fifty of us, while about ten times that number were massed in front of the gate. Their sad and worried faces said it all; they didn't believe the workers' protests would once more carry the day.

It was getting close to curfew time. Shadows came and went along the walls of buildings near the shipyard as small groups of militiamen slipped inside to warm up. Police vehicles continued their rounds.

We went off to spend the night in a workshop, lying down on benches or on the floor, as close as possible to the radiators. The freezing temperatures reminded us that August was long past, and that it was a black night in December for all of us.

Sometime after midnight, a messenger from the second gate brought us the bad news: the militia had entered the shipyard. They'd arrested eight of the young men guarding the entrance, torn down the flags and flowers, and flushed out a few more hapless workers within the yard itself. We immediately went up to the first floor, where we remained undisturbed until dawn.

At around six A.M., we went outside to find the front gate stripped of its decorations and standing wide open. Workers were beginning to arrive; we looked at each other in some confusion.

"Well, are we on strike?"

"Of course! It's a general strike!"

More and more people gathered around us.

"If we're on strike, we have to do it right!" one worker insisted. "Shut the gate again, give me the flags!"

The workers handed out the red and white banners they'd had the foresight to bring with them. Questions were flying thick and fast: "Where's the information bureau? Who's leading the strike? What are our demands?"

We had a hard time trying to answer all their questions, but we could tell the workers one thing: a general strike had been called, and it would last until Lech, the Presidium of the National Commission, and everyone else who'd been arrested, without exception, had been allowed to join us in the shipyard.

I was in Warsaw when all this was going on. The militia had driven me from my house to the airport, where a plane was waiting. At dawn we were in Chylice, in the suburbs of the capital, at the villa belonging to Lukaszewicz, the former secretary of the Party Central Committee.

The initial meetings were simply a preamble to my internment. Minister Stanislaw Ciosek was there, along with several generals whose names I didn't know. Their attitude seemed to be one of apologetic embarrassment: "We had no choice" or "You know what it's like."

When I've had troubles in the past that delayed my plans I've tried to deal with them in a spirit of forbearance; it doesn't make much difference whether one reaches one's goal a year early or a few years late when involved with a movement that promises to change the basic social order.

Imprisonment cuts one off from daily life, from all responsibility, especially the need to act. Prison and I were already old friends. During Solidarity's heyday, when things were happening at a hectic rate, I used to joke sometimes that what I really wanted was forty-eight hours in jail to sleep my fill and recharge my batteries. That's how I saw my internment to start with: as a chance to rest and sleep—a defensive mechanism against the constant, overwhelming fatigue and tension that had gripped me ever since Solidarity's legal existence.

I was in a state of semi-stupor when the guard told me that Deputy Premier Rakowski had arrived to speak to me. Not being fully awake, I thought I heard the guard say "Makowski." That name meant nothing to me, so I growled: "Throw him downstairs, I refuse to talk to him!" I don't know whether they repeated my exact words to Mieczyslaw Rakowski, but I do remember waking up fully and hearing: "Mr. Walesa, Rakowski was just furious when he left. He slammed the door so hard it almost jumped off its hinges!"

In this case, fate was on my side, for after proving to me that I had no choice in the matter, reeling off all his arguments, wearing me down, and saddling me with I don't know how many responsibilities, Rakowski would surely have come out of the interview with the upper hand.

After this incident they changed their minds about allowing my driver, Mieczyslaw Wachowski, to keep me company as a sort of aide-de-camp. They'd already released him from Strzeblinek Prison after holding him for only ten hours; he was allowed to remain at liberty and later was able to help my wife in a semi-official capacity.

I began my period of internment, which was to last one year, in the villa in Chylice. The inevitable staff officer was always stationed just outside my door; kitchen personnel prepared all our meals downstairs. Two days after my arrival, I was allowed to receive a visit from two representatives of the episcopate. Danuta was allowed to see me on the third day.

Danuta

I was able to visit my husband on Wednesday. Frankly, he seemed rather pleased to be locked up; he told me he was resting. I was upset and discouraged, but he said that we had to be dignified about it all, because even in a place like that, we still had the upper hand: we, not they, were making history. He also told me that on the first day of his internment the authorities had urged him to make a television appearance to reassure people, but that he'd refused.

When they moved him to Otwock and I was told that I could visit him there, I heard a rumor that I might be kidnapped on the way, so I brought my children along with me. I was surprised to find that Lech had a shortwave radio on which he could listen to the Polish-language broadcasts from the West. He was constantly listening to Radio Free Europe, the Voice of America, the BBC, whatever he could get, and he drove the guards so crazy that after a while they announced that the radio was broken. I can understand how they felt, because I know how loud he plays the radio. It makes such a racket your head feels as if it's about to explode. One of the guards complained that it gave him migraines. Lech sat at the radio all day long, fiddling with the knob.

The tone of the meetings I had with Ciosek was ambiguous from the start, and it remained that way for some time. The authorities maintained that without me the trade union didn't exist, but at the same time they suggested ways in which Solidarity could continue—under certain conditions. The official line presented by Ciosek all along boiled down to one demand: We had to expel all members classified as political enemies by the authorities. The list of such "enemies," originally only a few members of KOR who had joined us when we began our strike in August 1980, now included all those who had anything to do with running Solidarity. The martial law propaganda harped on this insistently. At the very top of the list were all the advisers and experts of the movement.

Throughout these initial meetings, they never told me what my status was. As far as I knew, I hadn't been officially charged. They seemed to be treating me as an important political personage whom they were constrained to keep in isolation because of the difficulties resulting from the imposition of martial law.

Shortly afterward when I was transferred to Otwock, an isolated villa where Wladyslaw Gomulka himself had once been forced to live under surveillance, I took that as a good sign; it was from that villa, in fact, that Gomulka had staged his triumphant comeback in October 1956.

Meanwhile, I heard that the military had been brought in to deal with the dramatic situation in Silesia, where miners were occupying the pits at the Wujek mine. The authorities deliberately rejected the suggestion I'd made after my arrest and renewed a few days later: that they allow the Wujek miners to return to the surface. The police opened fire on them on December 16, killing several. The new leaders needed this bloodshed to prove to themselves and to the public that they wouldn't back down. My suggestions and proposals had been woefully off the mark. And they didn't hesitate to point this out to me: "Mr. Walesa, you'll never make a good politician. Do you know why? Because you're afraid of bloodshed." I couldn't deny it.

The idea of keeping the trade union going under one form or another was a bargaining point throughout my preliminary talks with Ciosek. Obviously, Solidarity would only continue to function under severe restrictions. The authorities had been harassing me constantly since early 1981 in an attempt to force the expulsion of certain people from the movement, and I had already talked this over with the people in question. I told them that sooner or later I'd be faced with only one option: "Listen, Solidarity can

217

continue to operate, but you've got to drop this guy, and that one, and these others." Of course there was no guarantee that we weren't being deceived, and that we wouldn't end up with nothing to show for our sacrifices but shame and discouragement, for Solidarity and for myself as its leader. I could never abandon anyone like that. I'm quite capable of settling a score with someone, of throwing him out myself, but I could never allow the government to get rid of him, simply because he'd worked with me once. My official visitors would run down the list of names, saying: "This one can stay, that one's out, he's a traitor." I'd answer: "Gentlemen, show me some proof, let me talk to him, and then we'll see." They were reduced to saying to me: "You're a politician, after all, but not a very good one, because you don't know how to sacrifice the little things in order to save the important ones."

Then I'd reply: "That's not the way I understand sacrifice. I can't ask someone to make a sacrifice if he doesn't understand why. That's not how I see politics."

"That's just what we've been saying all along—you're no politician. Our assignment is a waste of time!"

The "assignment" continued, however, despite repeated announcements that it was over. Set in the heart of a forest, Gomulka's former villa proved to be ill-suited to the needs of my large family. When the children arrived with Danuta, they felt trapped in rooms intended as a holiday home for sedate comrades. When the authorities moved me to the Branicki Palace in Otwock it was probably with the idea of settling me there with my family for two years or so, all expenses paid. The children would have everything they needed including private tutoring. The Branicki Palace is an architectural treasure, as photos appearing in Western newspapers at the time clearly showed. Surrounded by a moat, guarded on the outside by the army and on the inside by the security forces, it was an inaccessible fortress in answer to rumors that were circulating about attempts to rescue me. I never did completely give up the idea of escaping even though they let me know the watchdogs roamed the grounds at night.

The rooms in which I was interned were closed off from the rest of the palace so that the curators and custodians could continue their restoration work. I tried to make contact with them several times by throwing first a key, then my wedding ring, through a window overlooking a leafy corner of the garden. In the afternoons, after work on the grounds had ceased for the day, I was allowed to go fishing. A photo appeared in Western newspapers showing me looking well-fed, sitting bundled up in a parka at the edge of the moat, fishing peacefully. This picture contrasted sharply with the idea most people had of my internment, and it wasn't the only misunderstanding of its kind. Walesa carried along on the shoulders of shipyard workers, Walesa addressing a crowd at the stadium, Walesa surrounded by his advisers: all these well-known images showed me constantly at the center of a crowd. Many people, including my wife, thought that my current isolation would be a crushing burden, even harder for me to bear than being incarcerated with other inmates in brutal prison conditions.

It was my faith, together with an unshakable belief that Solidarity would win out in the end, that helped me through this period. And I should admit that I've always been a loner at heart. Whatever I do, I do on my own, even though talking to other people and listening to their views is important to me, as is learning what I can in situations where I'm just one among many.

I certainly had more than enough to think about, and turned my thoughts to the future, as well as the recent past, what "might have been." For the first time in years, I really had time to think.

Of course, *they* came frequently to explain their side of things: why the movement had failed, and so forth. I didn't reply to them as the leader of Solidarity, but gave them my personal point of view. I told them Solidarity could only be represented by the trade union leadership, our Presidium, and a certain number of key advisers, and why consultation with the entire membership of the National Commission was also important.

One or another of these conditions constantly figured in my casual proposals to the authorities, who seemed to lean toward a convocation of the Presidium as an option. They probably felt that the Solidarity Presidium would be more likely to come to terms with the new state of affairs than the National Commission, which might display a spirit of resistance undimmed by martial law. Neither I nor the authorities could be sure what direction the National Commission might take. Of course I pushed hard for the convocation of the entire National Commission once I had finally decided that any compromise was impossible so long as martial law was in effect. I still hoped that after about three months or so, when things had cooled down a little, the authorities would realize how disruptive and costly martial law was proving to the fabric of society and that they would relax their grip, adopting a more reasonable approach.

Ciosek continued to visit me briefly once a week to gauge what kind of a mood I was in. On January 26, about six weeks after the declaration of martial law, they gave me the writ of internment to sign: I refused. My response was a hastily written note passed over the wall at Otwock and published by *Le Monde*:

> I have not signed the original writ, which was presented to me on January 26, 1982. They're using a process of elimination. I wouldn't be surprised if they start spreading ridiculous lies about me—all prepared well in advance, of course, complete with fake witnesses. They've tried to deceive public opinion at home and abroad by claiming that I haven't been interned, when the writ in question was drawn up as early as December 12. Please publicize this simple fact, because it's a perfect example of their treachery and continuing dishonesty. There must be no retreat! No one should be expelled from the movement, because that would be giving in to their methods.

Despite the imposition of martial law, the church continued to play the role of mediator. Although in complete sympathy with the ideals of Solidarity, the Roman Catholic hierarchy in Poland avoided all overtly political actions and pronouncements, for which the authorities were grateful. In return, I was allowed to meet with certain priests and bishops, among whom were Father Alojzy Orszulik, a spokesman for the Polish episcopate; Father Henryk Jankowski, my friend, counselor, and priest from Gdansk; and Father Potocki from Przemysl. Their visits, along with those of my family, were a relief from isolation and the constant surveillance of my captors.

Between Western shortwave broadcasts, which distilled the reports of Western journalists on the scene in Poland, and the news brought by my visitors, I was able to form a fairly clear picture of the situation. Under cover of martial law, the authorities were bent not only on taking back from Solidarity and the Polish people everything that they had won, but also on cheating them out of any advantages to be sought in an eventual compromise. From our point of view, the situation was desperate. Martial law had finally given the authorities what they'd always wanted: naked power, in its purest form, through the use of armed force.

Now that I was their prisoner, they took a certain interest in coming to talk to me and to observe me. They finally had me alone, without those hated advisers who demanded respect for our position, employing a kind of "moral blackmail" against them; alone, without those stubborn union representatives; alone, without the support of crowds gathered outside the Gdansk shipyard and in the streets of Poland. Alone, for the authorities to study: the mystery laid bare.

Our first exchanges were courteous, holding out the distinct possibility of further negotiations, although no specific proposals were offered from either side. It was actually I who tried to get things started by sounding them out, risking a series of suggestions, always coming up with new ones.

That first game lasted only a few days, after which the government and the military, busy coping with the practical problems of martial law, left the job of saving appearances to Ciosek, the minister of trade union affairs. Later they handed me over to experts in the security police who were told to "condition" me: in other words, to wear me down, once and for all.

In the eyes of the authorities, this was the most rational way of dealing with the "Walesa problem." Another way was to let the church have relatively easy access to their prisoner, and the church delegated Father Alojzy Orszulik as their intermediary with the military authorities in these matters. Trained in the priesthood during the time of the formidable Cardinal Wyszynski's ascendancy, Father Orszulik had become a great pragmatist. A man with a strong personality, he is not easily influenced, and displays not only a firm sense of moral responsibility, but also a deep respect for customary formalities, conducting business through the proper channels.

My first meetings with Father Orszulik were tense and uneasy. I must have seemed restless at first, bursting with ideas he considered unrealistic. I was unable to accept the ready-made situations being forced upon me, and in my rage and despair I shouted at him arrogantly: "They'll come to me on their knees!" The priest disapproved of my lack of Christian humility, and it took us some time to get used to each other.

A week after his first visit, Father Orszulik arrived to see me with some important news: as a result of the recent events in Poland, the Polish bishops had sent messengers to the Vatican, and a papal envoy was on his way to Warsaw. During a meeting with Barcikowski, the secretary of the Party Central Committee, and Czyrek, the foreign secretary, the envoy had obtained certain promises which were then relayed to the Pope: Solidarity would be allowed to continue its activities according to its own statutes, but further negotiations on other points would be necessary; there would be no more political prisoners or trials; and all those who wished to leave the country would be allowed to do so. The bishops' representatives then proposed that I be transferred to neutral ground so that I might meet with Solidarity's advisers and the leaders of the National Commission who had been interned. Choszczowka, the former residence of Cardinal Wyszynski, was suggested. I had only to promise not to take advantage of the situation by attempting to escape. The episcopate had also offered itself as an intermediary in negotiations between the leaders of Solidarity and the government, but without any intention of participating directly in the negotiations themselves.

This information seemed flagrantly contradictory to recent events touched off by martial law. Miners who had attempted to defend the independent trade union had been murdered at the Wujek mine in Silesia. It was my duty to protest forcefully against such atrocities and to receive some satisfaction before any negotiations took place; otherwise they would serve only as an alibi for those officials who had sent the militia to attack the miners.

If we hang on another two weeks without compromising our position, "we'll have won." That was what I said at the time, and it was said, in part, so that those who were eavesdropping on our conversation would overhear me. At the time the Polish state was in disarray, and for all I knew the authorities might have feared violence. Yet deep down, I knew that the Polish people would never take up arms against the government: it's not our way. At this time the Primate appealed from the pulpit for negotiations to be opened; I agreed with him and when asked clearly stated my support for the church's position, but the authorities disagreed. They felt that they had to defeat the people by force, to teach them that force could and would be used whenever they so desired.

I realized that the idea of having the trade union's advisers attend preliminary negotiations was realistic; I insisted on the participation of Bronislaw Geremek and Tadeusz Mazowiecki, my close allies in Solidarity. The church, however, had been swayed by the insistent propaganda against these two men in particular and hinted strongly that it would be better to select lesser-known figures, men who hadn't been arrested and weren't likely to antagonize the authorities. I gave in on this point.

In the course of our conversations, I abandoned all my initial conditions, one by one, finally aligning myself with the church's position, but that didn't produce any tangible results either. That must have been their plan from the beginning: to use the church simply for the sake of appearances.

Later on, I often wondered why the church, with all its experience, agreed to take part in such an empty charade, and I came to understand that therein lay its wisdom. Accepting the rules of the game imposed upon it, the church plays for its own stakes in order to exist as an unaligned force within the society, even though this may not look like much at first. This was the policy of Stefan Wyszynski, a policy followed by the church in Poland since the end of the war: taking suspect promises and agreements at their face value and building on these to become a moral force the state had to recognize. I realized that the church was taking the same approach in dealing with the situation under martial law.

On Christmas Day, with my wife and Father Jankowski at my side, I received a letter from the Holy Father, along with a copy of the Pope's appeal to General Jaruzelski:

Mr. Lech Walesa
President of the National Commission of Solidarity
103 Grunwaldzka Street
20-244 Gdansk-Wrzeszcz, Poland

Dear Sir,

I enclose my appeal to the Premier, General Wojciech Jaruzelski, regarding the recent tragic events in our country. I wish to assure you that in these difficult times, I am heart and soul with you and your family and with all those who suffer. I commend you to Him who descended from Heaven and was born of the Virgin Mary for us and our redemption.

The Vatican, 18 December 1981
John Paul II

Mr. Prime Minister
People's Republic of Poland
General Wojciech Jaruzelski
Warsaw

Recent events in Poland since the declaration of martial law on December 13 have resulted in death and injury to our fellow countrymen, and I am moved to address this urgent and heart-felt appeal to you, a prayer for an end to the shedding of Polish blood.

During the last two centuries, the Polish nation has endured great wrongs, and much blood has been spilled in the struggle for power over our Fatherland. Our history cries out against more bloodshed, and we must not allow this tragedy to continue to weigh so heavily on the conscience of the nation. I therefore appeal to you, General, to return to the methods of peaceful dialogue that have characterized efforts at social renewal since August 1980. Even though this may be a difficult step, it is not an impossible one.

The welfare of the entire nation depends upon it. People throughout the world, all those who rightly see the cause of Peace furthered by respect for the rights of Man, are waiting for this return to nonviolent means. All humanity's desire for peace argues for an end to the state of martial law in Poland.

The Church is the spokesman for this wish. Soon it will be Christmas, when generation after generation of Poland's sons and daughters have been drawn together by Holy Communion. Every effort must be made so that our compatriots will not be forced to spend this Christmas under the shadow of repression and death.

I appeal to your conscience, General, and to the conscience of all those who must decide this question.

The Vatican, 18 December 1981
John Paul II

About ten days later, after Bishop Kraszewski and Father Orszulik had celebrated mass, we began talking about problems of a moral nature. Bishop Kraszewski launched into a kind of meditation on the realities of life under martial law, the responsibility borne by those who speak out, and the ability to remain silent. I maintained that the West would apply economic sanctions in an effort to force the General to open a dialogue with the opposition (which is what did in fact happen), but we all agreed that the Polish people themselves would be the hardest hit by an interruption in Western aid. Then the conversation returned to the need to resolve the crisis in our society. I argued that since I was being kept incommunicado, I was not able to exert any influence over Solidarity members, and that certain radical elements might evolve into an explosive and uncontrollable underground movement. It was therefore imperative that I be set free so that I could take up the reins again and prevent the situation from deteriorating beyond repair.

I repeated my argument three days later at our next meeting in Gomulka's villa in Otwock, but to no avail. The bishops had been unable to win over the military, even though I had promised— provided that I was moved to neutral territory in the custody of the church and allowed to confer with our advisers—to try to exert a positive influence, specifically by attempting to defuse a new and ominous strike in the Piast mine in Silesia.

The stumbling block was our disagreement over the relative importance of certain mistakes made by the union. The authorities maintained that the internal struggles of the Party and errors committed by Solidarity were equally to blame for the economic and political crises in which we now found ourselves. I couldn't accept this position, even though I admitted that some of our leaders had foolishly underestimated the real strength of those in power. Exactly which "civil war" General Jaruzelski was supposed to be protecting Poland from remained unclear. Evidence pointed to a rift within the Party, which was continuing to worsen, and if that was the case, why was the union the only target under attack? Why was the "zero option" being forced on Solidarity alone? On the contrary, it was obvious that martial law was a screen for the authorities' true objective: the liquidation of Solidarity, and of the aspirations it had shared with the Polish people. The government had simply chosen the most expeditious method to justify itself.

On New Year's Day, I gave Father Orszulik a statement which was to be delivered to Barcikowski, who was to pass it on to Jaruzelski the following day. Here is the gist of what I wrote:

> I'm not about to cut my own throat. I have no intention of inciting a riot or organizing more strikes. I want to help find a way out of the paralyzing effects of the general strike, because I realize that society can only be weakened by continued stress and shock. I ask you to release the jailed members of the National Commission and allow me to meet with them, even if this meeting must be sequestered from all outside contact. I would like to remind the National Commission of my intention to request the resignation of several among them; if they refuse, it is also my intention to put the issue to a vote among the workers. We should be realistic about our situation, taking into account all our assets and options, starting from the principle that our movement does not aim to eradicate socialism. The authorities are well aware that although I used the language of violence at Radom, this was a tactical move on my part, one aimed at allowing me to control the growing threat of radicalism within Solidarity's leadership. It is clear to me that the period of martial law, even if it lasts a year, could be profitably used to resolve our differences through peaceful discussions. I also consider martial law to be preferable to any outside intervention. The situation has not yet slipped past the point of no return. We can still repair the damage, but only on condition that we do it ourselves.

A few days later, the ideas we had been discussing were presented to me, through Father Orszulik, in the form of a memorandum sent to Barcikowski by the ecclesiastical authorities, along with "Proposals for Negotiation," a document drawn up by a group of Solidarity experts still at liberty and in close contact with the episcopate. The church was to be informed on January 13 of the authorities' decision on the possibility of negotiations. If the response was positive, our advisers were to deliver a document signed by me to the members of the Presidium of the National Commission and help to prepare them for such a meeting, to take place at Fiszor.

Finally, I suggested that the government should present its own proposals for negotiations for our side to study, after which work groups could be established composed of representatives of the government and Solidarity, whose task would be to piece together the terms leading to a social contract.

Following receipt of the document the authorities forbade Father Orszulik to visit me until further notice. I didn't see him again until March. The government wasn't pleased with the Catholic hierarchy's response to the imposition of martial law, which in turn led them to reject the church's offer to mediate between the authorities and Solidarity.

It was at this time that I was formally charged and notified that my internment was officially sanctioned. At last I knew exactly where I stood.

Father Orszulik was finally allowed to visit me again on March 7, in Otwock Wielki, the eighteenth-century palace where the last partition of Poland was signed. It was in that historic setting that I reaffirmed my belief that Solidarity was too great and important an idea to fail, but that if the authorities insisted on dismantling the movement's structure they would have to do it entirely on their own. As for the government's proposals for the creation of new unions, I suggested that they could install Ciosek, their own minister of trade union affairs, as union president. At least then everyone would understand what they were up to.

Father Orszulik did not visit me again for another two months.

Because Solidarity wasn't banned outright when martial law was declared, it looked at first as though we might come to some sort of an agreement; Danuta helped keep up my confidence, as she had done in the earlier days of my union activities. I also drew on my inner resources, "spying on life," as I used to say, treating each new situation as an adventure to be lived, a mystery to be solved.

For the moment, the turn of events had simply taken political decisions out of my hands.

Just when martial law and official propaganda seemed to be wearing thin, the Plock region in Poland was devastated by serious spring floods. The Vistula overflowed its banks, isolating thousands of people. A massive rescue operation was mounted with the aid of the army, which gave the authorities an opportunity to do something positive. The loss of life was horrendous and the property damage extensive, and when the arrival of medical services and supplies was hampered by the interruption of telephone communications, the people rioted. So much for a reconciliation. Demonstrations and violent confrontations between militia and citizens followed. Not enough was being done to help, and the situation was made worse by official indecisiveness and incompetence. Underground broadsides barked disapproval: the population was finding the voice to defend itself. The authorities had made the mistake of moving too slowly—in all respects—after the declaration of martial law. And the longer they waited, the closer they crept to the point of no return. Now they were terrified we were going to overwhelm them.

Ciosek came to see me toward the end of my stay in Otwock. I wasn't in the mood to talk; discussions seemed futile at that point.

"I've been here for quite a while," I grumbled. "I know the whole palace by heart. The royal palace in Warsaw has just been restored, so what are we waiting for? Shall we take over Warsaw?"

The minister wasn't amused. Two days later I was transferred to a state-owned hunting lodge heavily guarded by the army and surrounded by Arlamow's dense forest, near the eastern border of Poland.

Despite my doubts and misgivings over what had happened since the declaration of martial law, I still considered myself Solidarity's leader. At the beginning of June 1982, I managed to smuggle to the West a mandate that allowed the trade union to be represented at an important meeting of the International Labor Organization. The delegate selected was Bogdan Cywinski, assistant editor of the weekly *Solidarnosc*, who was living abroad at that time. This authorization—signed, sealed, and delivered despite the three barbed-wire fences and strict security of Arlamow—caused a certain chill in Ciosek's attitude toward me.

I'd previously had a good relationship with Rakowski, the only member of the group in power to have had any real dealings with me, but by now he was launching fierce attacks against me. The other side had made things plain: I was *with* them, or *against* them. They stopped at nothing in their disgusting propaganda. I won't name names, because the people involved still occupy positions of great responsibility. What I can say is that they harassed me in any number of ways, before always demanding a simple answer: yes or no.

On October 4, Ciosek presented me with a memo on the free unions that would have resulted in the death of Solidarity and an invitation to attend its funeral by accepting an important position in PRON (Patriotic Movement for National Renewal) or in the government's advisory council in charge of union affairs. If I said yes to either offer, I was a free man. "The key to your release is in your own hands," I was told.

"I'll wait for martial law to be lifted," I replied. "I didn't ask to be brought here but I won't beg for permission to leave. In two years, PRON will have become what the Front of National Unity used to be"—as one organization after another was discredited, the authorities simply changed its name; I also argued that by suppressing free unions and destroying what was left of the people's will to work, the country would soon plunge into an irreversible economic depression. "After I'm released," I replied, "I'd rather go back to being a simple electrician in some shipyard, and if you won't permit that, then I could work for Father Jankowski."

For the time being, I was taking the longest vacation of my life. I occasionally ate with my guards, who always asked if their presence bothered me. We never had much to say to one another, and we ended up by not saying anything. But I often switched plates with them. "Here, take this serving," I'd say to one of them. "If they want to poison somebody, I'd rather it be you." They'd offer me several different dishes, to see which one I liked best, and then they'd keep serving it to me until I couldn't stand the sight of it. I was very fond of liver, so they gave it to me every day, in addition to a number of other dishes. It was the same with fish, especially eel. There was a refrigerator stuffed with food just in case I wanted a snack between meals, and talk about champagne, that, too, was readily available. I was the king in exile.

At the start I had a radio on which I could get almost any shortwave frequency, but after a while they adjusted it to eliminate shortwave reception. Having nothing but time to kill I tinkered with it until I finally managed to pick up Radio Free Europe on longwave. The next morning when I went downstairs for breakfast, they fiddled with the radio again. Later I'd get it right; this continued for some time until one of the perplexed guards asked me how I managed to get programs from abroad on a longwave set. I wasn't sure myself, I just tinkered. Then one day a miniature transistor radio was smuggled in to me; from then on I could listen to my programs (usually in bed) with an earphone. I still have that radio. When the guards' television set broke down, they'd come up to my room and ask if they could watch my TV; I never refused. And while they watched their program, I'd be lying on my bed, secretly listening to the radio. Even today, I'm not sure whether they knew about that transistor radio.

I occasionally listened to tapes Danuta smuggled in, tapes of events like the 1982 May Day demonstration in Gdansk. It was good to hear all those spontaneous expressions of personal liberty from people who hadn't let martial law get them down.

Danuta was now the family torchbearer. I often heard her on the radio, taking a stand on different topics. She was one of those thousands of women left to manage their families on their own while their husbands were interned or imprisoned. She shared their distress and spoke in their name about the Polish people's two great preoccupations: the state of the family and the fate of the nation. The authorities didn't touch her. Our daughter Maria-Wiktoria was born while I was at Arlamow. Danuta continued to give interviews by radio throughout the world, and she met with representatives of the Polish church, the Vatican, and various Western embassies. She was magnificent. I often thought that she was far more effective than I ever was.

In the fall of 1982, a series of interviews with Danuta was published independently under the title "The People Alone Have the Power," in which Danuta answered questions about my internment and other subjects.

230

First Interview, late September 1982 (extracts)

Lech Walesa's wife looked depressed as she came into the room; her first words were: "I've got too many responsibilities." We reminded her of her reputation for courage and confidence in the face of adversity.

"I prefer to expect the worst," she replied. "If things go well, I'm happy, but in general, I expect the worst."

"Have you taken Lech any information?"

"I've never smuggled anything in writing, because Lech was against it. He said that if they found anything on me, they could use it as a pretext to make trouble. Once I did take him a tape recording of the May Day demonstrations, and he listened to it, but the guards heard it, too, so after that they frisked me and confiscated other tapes."

"What does your husband think about the propaganda campaign that's been unleashed against the union?"

"He doesn't talk to me about that. He doesn't tell me what he really thinks about these things. I think the isolation is beginning to affect his nerves."

"Is he no longer optimistic?"

"He's never lost faith in the future, and he still maintains the belief that Solidarity will succeed."

"The facts seem to be against him—the trade union could be outlawed at any moment by the authorities."

"Yes, Lech has just been told that. When I was visiting him two weeks ago, he was worrying about what would happen then."

"The Military Council for National Salvation [WRON] intends to prevent all the leaders of Solidarity from participating in the new unions. When Solidarity has been outlawed and Lech is no longer its president, what then?"

"Who knows what these new unions will be like? From what I hear, no one has any intention of joining them. You see, the authorities have to be careful they don't make life absolutely impossible. What will happen if all our leaders are thrown into prison? Do the authorities think they can govern just by washing their hands of them? That they can simply set up new unions? Who would join them?"

"Is Lech afraid he'll wind up in a real prison permanently?"
"I've never spoken to him about that."
"What do you find most distressing?"
"At one point, I thought the worst was already behind us. As if I were starting to get used to it, but now I feel—I don't know how to say it—I feel as if I'm not going to make it. When you listen to people, they can't agree on anything, they're at odds with one another."

"Have you thought about what will happen when Lech comes home?"
"I often think about it, but I can't imagine what it will be like. Sometimes I'm afraid that we won't understand each other anymore, even though I visit him every three weeks. I leave on Monday and get back on Friday, and the trip takes one day each way, so that gives me only three days. I worry that things may have changed between us. We've never been apart for so long, but I'd never thought we could ever become strangers to each other."
"Does your husband miss you very much?"
"Oh yes, I think so, and just when we're beginning to feel comfortable with each other every three weeks, I have to leave. It's awful!"

"What do you think of the different ways in which people are protesting under martial law?"
"My husband used to tell me that it's the duty of every member of Solidarity to defend his rights. I agree completely. Those who founded it should never give up. But each situation demands different tactics, of course."
"Have you talked to Lech about this?"
"Yes. He feels people have to carry on fighting, but he never says how, he never says what individual people should or shouldn't do."
"Do you think Lech is right to keep quiet?"
"He's behaving very wisely, because he's a long way away,

cut off from everything. If he were to say 'Do this or that,' it just wouldn't work now."

"Is Lech disappointed about what's happening?"

"Sometimes he thinks people aren't trying hard enough, or that what they're doing should be done differently, that they should act more decisively, more positively."

"Do you trust the authorities?"

"No, they can make all the promises they want, I don't trust them one bit. It's only the people who can get us anywhere. I'm confident the Polish people will find the solution to our problems, but that doesn't stop me worrying. Today a woman told me that she had nothing at all to do with the movement, that she was fed up with the whole thing, that her little girl didn't have any shoes and that they had to spread their butter so thinly on their bread that they couldn't even taste it. You hear a lot of complaints like that, and I realize I'm in a precarious position—if things turn out okay, I'll be fine, but if they turn out badly, then I'm in real trouble."

"Does Lech feel responsible for what's happened?"

"No, not at all."

"Does he reproach any of his colleagues, his advisers in Solidarity?"

"He doesn't blame anyone for anything. He thinks that what happened was bound to happen."

Third Interview, late October 1982 (extracts)

"Your recent visit to your husband in Arlamow seems to have been particularly upsetting."

"I went to visit him on Monday, October 18. I left Arlamow on Friday the 22nd. The person who usually drove me back was supposed to drop me off at the priest's house in Przemysl. The car was late arriving, and this time my usual escort had an official driver with him. Two of my children were with him. I had the feeling then that they were going to search me. When we arrived in Przemysl they took us to the police station instead of to the priest's house, and when the driver stopped the car I told him he must have taken a wrong turn somewhere. 'For the moment,' he said, 'this is where you're going.' 'I know why you've brought me here,' I answered, 'and I'm not getting out of the car. Or rather, I'll get out and take the children with me; we'll walk the rest of the way.' I wasn't expecting him to use force. 'Don't be stupid,' he said, trying to bar my way. I managed to get out of the car with Anna and Magda, but I couldn't get away fast enough. The girls started to cry and I couldn't just leave them there. The other man held my wrist and kept telling me to follow him; in the meantime the driver had gone inside.

"I really don't remember how I got to the door of the police station; I only know that I could hear my daughters crying [they were somewhere behind me], while that man was dragging me along or perhaps even carrying me with the help of somebody else. I found myself standing inside the building, with the children's cries ringing in my ears. 'Let me go,' I told them, 'I have to get my little girls home.' The first man held on to me while another one led my children in by the hand. They were taken up to the second floor, and I followed them.

" 'We're going in here,' the man told me. Lots of people were coming out of the adjoining offices. I tried to argue with him, but he wouldn't let me speak. Little Anna was standing in front of me, and suddenly the man pushed me so hard he knocked Anna down. When someone reproached him for being so rough with the child, he started yelling and pushed me into an office where two women and a man were waiting for us. I was almost out of my mind with fear by this time.

" 'Shut your mouth, you bitch!' he yelled at me.

" 'Shut your own! And who do you think you're talking to! Haven't I any rights?'

"The other three tried to calm me down. The man started telling me how they were authorized to do this and that, and I told them that didn't mean anything to me. 'Either treat me like a human being and tell me what my rights are, or admit that I haven't any!'

"Then the man who had shoved me into the office, Captain Bobinski was his name, left the room, and the other man told me that I didn't have any rights, although that didn't stop him from explaining at length about their authorization to detain me. Bobinski returned and asked me several times if I'd been informed why they were holding me. The other man seemed to hesitate, as if he wanted the captain to take over, but he finally turned to me and demanded that I hand over any messages and everything in writing that I had on me.

" 'I'm not carrying anything of that sort.'

" 'Then we'll have to search you.'

"The two men left the room and the women searched me. They looked everywhere, all through my things, poking into every fold in the shirts and even checking through my husband's dirty laundry.

" 'Why's the lady looking everywhere?' Magda asked.

"I was going to explain to her, but the woman stopped me. She didn't want me to say something I shouldn't have. So I told my daughter that the lady was doing it because she thought her daddy was a nice man, and that seemed to reassure the woman.

" 'I thought you were going to say something stupid. You should never explain things to children, they don't understand.'

"She didn't realize that children understand perfectly well. I had a little piece of paper on me showing a crow wearing a cap with the red star and the hammer and sickle. The caption read: 'To be continued.' The policewoman read it, and I told her: 'There'll certainly be another chapter!' All she said was, 'The sooner the better.'

"They searched my daughters, too, without taking their clothes off. That's when Bobinski came back and insisted that they be searched again. They started with Magda, taking off her shoes, which have orthopedic soles. They wanted to take them apart.

" 'You mustn't take them apart,' said Magda, 'they're supposed to be like that.'

"Then I asked them not to destroy my child's shoes because I didn't have another pair for her to wear. That's when they started undressing her, which made her cry. I took her in my arms and told Bobinski that I hoped the same thing would happen to his daughter one day.

" 'My daughter is six years old and they were going to kill her!' he replied.

"So that was it. The authorities had convinced those who worked for them that Solidarity was going to assassinate their children.

"The search lasted two hours, and they confiscated a train ticket, photos, religious pictures, a copy of the newspaper *Slowo Powszechne*, and two checks, one for twenty dollars, the other for five dollars. They even kept my driver's license.

" 'You have no right to take away my money or my license,' I protested.

" 'We're going to write down the numbers of these checks,' the man replied. 'We know your husband has two and a half million dollars in various foreign bank accounts!'

"He kept spouting his nonsense, but there was no point in explaining to him how little money we had. Others had complained that Lech had a million dollars, had sold out, and worse. We were used to hearing such stories.

"The captain had calmed down once he'd got what he wanted; in fact, he seemed quite pleased with himself. Up till then he'd behaved like a brute, and at one point I'd even thought he was going to strike me. He'd been absolutely dancing with rage. Now he said he was going to make an official report on how I'd insulted him; I replied that I wanted to lodge an official complaint about police brutality. When I left I told him it didn't matter how fancy his uniform was, he was still a filthy pig.

"This man had tried to win my confidence during earlier car trips together, and then he'd behaved like a madman when I wouldn't snap to and obey his orders. It had never occurred to him that anyone might stand up to him. He thought that under martial law I would just keep quiet and act like a little lamb. After that, I fully realized a human being deprived of his or her rights is no better than an animal ready for slaughter.

"At one point, the captain had said that almost two years of *our* regime was more than enough, so I shot back: 'And what about you, how many years have we had you on our backs? And you're still there; do you think you can hang on much longer?' That put him in an awful mood. I think he was embarrassed, even shamed that I had spoken to him like that in front of his colleagues."

The brutality of the security police toward Danuta shows just how powerless people were at the hands of the authorities. Although our political leaders were careful not to overstep certain limits, the security forces felt bound by no such constraints. They knew they were indispensable to those in power, and they didn't care what impression they gave us of those whose dirty work they were doing.

The authorities had finally given up trying to get anything out of me at Arlamow, since it was now clear to them that what they considered interesting proposals had no interest for me. I was careful not to be disdainful, however, because I knew that there was only a narrow margin between the game we were playing and a much more savage one. The game being played was nonetheless exhausting: no one ever put all his cards on the table, and the constant bluffing kept us from ever reaching the moment of truth.

Whatever else my captors said or did, the generals, at least, promised something concrete. And the offers they made had their temptations even though General Jaruzelski struck a familiar chord with his Polish uniforms and rallying cries from the "good old days," the interwar years whose nationalism was not without an undertone of menace.

They'd banked on persuading me to go along with them by creating the proper settings, together with the promise of high-level meetings. But all I said was, "No. What's important here isn't me," I'd tell them, "but the movement itself. We can't let the people lose hope. They must be shown that everything is honest and aboveboard, that important issues and problems won't be brushed aside. We can't betray the ideals of August 1980."

I wasn't worried about my popularity in the movement because I was certain that we'd come out of this difficult conflict more united than before. If I'd weakened at this point, someone else would surely have tried to "save" Solidarity by splitting off his own faction to follow a different political line. That's why we had set up the Presidium at the first Solidarity Congress; in principle none of its members would ever be able to split up the union. "Death before dishonor," a noble sentiment, but that's the way I looked at it. When anyone tried to grab the spotlight during my internment, the response was always the same: "Only with Walesa." We in Solidarity would settle our own accounts with those who had given tangible proof of treachery—as some few did—or political incompetence. *We* would do it, no one else.

During the year of my internment a Temporary Coordinating Committee (TKK) was established as a decision-making body operating independently of Solidarity's president. This underground organization took charge of channeling the resistance activities of the Polish people, whose hopes were reflected in many of its decisions.

The TKK appealed for a massive demonstration on November 11, 1982, to mark the 64th anniversary of Polish independence after the First World War. I doubted that such a move would succeed on a large scale, and was afraid that the only tangible result would be another round of arrests and preventive detention for key union members. I feared that Solidarity would run the risk of exhausting its reserves and lose influence with the general population. Another important point was that flagging support for a massive demonstration at this time might encourage the growth of radical groups, which could only lead to a bloodbath. That kind of tragedy wouldn't solve anything and would only make things worse for all of us. It was no accident that events tied in with commemorative demonstrations and the committee's decisions were bypassing me more and more in my remote prison in Arlamow.

I decided to risk taking the initiative, and wrote the following letter to General Jaruzelski.

Arlamow, November 8, 1982

General Wojciech Jaruzelski
Warsaw

It seems to me that the moment has come to take a good look at our problems and to reach some kind of understanding. Enough time has passed for it to be widely known now where we stand and what our options are. I propose that we meet for a serious discussion on these matters which concern us all, and I'm sure that with goodwill on both sides, we can come to an agreement.

Corporal Lech Walesa

The newspapers published the text of this letter the next day, along with the following comment:

As a result of Lech Walesa's letter and his proposal for a "serious discussion of matters that concern us all," Czeslaw Kiszczak, a member of WRON, the Military Council of National Salvation, met him at Arlamow. At the end of this meeting, the minister of internal affairs ordered the commandant of the Gdansk militia to release Lech Walesa from internment.

The reason for my letter was simple. When I learned that the Temporary Coordinating Committee had called for mass demonstrations on November 11, I felt certain, as I said earlier, that they were making a major mistake. I also felt more and more cut off, especially when the priest whom I was expecting to visit me in Arlamow hadn't arrived and neither had my wife. I didn't know what was going on. News of my recent decision to begin a hunger strike hadn't got out. I overheard scraps of conversation among the guards, who were clearly worried about forthcoming political demonstrations. Their fears about the safety of their families increased. The tension was palpable, even in Arlamow. "It's going to be bad, really bad," one said. "I left my wife out in the country, and I don't know how my kid's going to get home from school, because that's the street they'll be using for the demonstration."

From what I'd heard, there was also the alarming prospect that they would send the army in. That's when I wrote the letter—to forestall the demonstration. And that's where I let myself be had, right down the line, because the letter was published *after* the demonstration had been snuffed out; it didn't have the intended effect.

I'd given some thought to how I was going to sign the letter. If I signed as president of Solidarity, the letter wouldn't be published, but if I didn't mention the union, people would say that I'd betrayed them. I wanted the letter to be a proposal, not a plea. I decided to sign it "Corporal." Of course I realized that some people might think it was some kind of joke, but I went ahead anyway. This is how Jan Mur described the situation in his underground manuscript that was later published in Paris. He evokes the general atmosphere in Gdansk when I was released from internment—the confusion, the anxiety, the expectation:

Wednesday, November 10

The underground called for an eight-hour strike to reaffirm the unanimity of the union's position and the continuing support of the population, but why did they choose a gesture that would force a head-on confrontation with the authorities? The latter had plenty of time to marshal their forces, and it was no contest at all. They were just waiting for a chance to teach us a lesson, and we would have been pulverized. Yesterday the situation was still fluid, and it was hard to tell which way things would go, but this morning confirmed the need to abandon this lethal tactic, which has claimed so many brave and valuable lives. Their sacrifice has not been in vain: all those now in prison, interned, and lying in the cemetery have strengthened our social conscience with their courage and determination. As of this morning, however, something has changed. I'm already convinced this strike will not succeed.

I went to the shipyard around noon, where I saw from the street that someone had written SOLIDARITY in chalk on the black background of the LENIN SHIPYARD sign over the hull workshop. You could hear men working inside, and one of the cranes was operating: there was no sign of any tension. The militia's combat unit had the shipyard under siege: tanks, guns, and armored cars had taken up positions at the end of Lagiewniki Street, where they watched, and waited. They were on the square in front of the Gdansk Theatre, and scattered more or less everywhere throughout the city. The hours passed, but there was no sign of trouble. The Polish people had apparently decided that today was not the day. By three in the afternoon it was clear that there wouldn't be any major street demonstrations. The armored cars going up Grunwaldzka Street were lost in the crowd. Even though the strike scheduled for today hasn't materialized, I still have the impression that the people have won this round. Their opponents came out armed to the teeth and took aim at the rabbit.

The shipyard workers went home, talking among themselves about the morning maneuvers of WRON. They were critical of

240

what they considered to be a flagrant waste of paper; in the morning everyone who entered the shipyard had been handed an extract from the declaration of martial law, the text detailing those penalties risked by anyone failing to comply with the rules enforced in a militarized industry. For the last few days, the authorities have been using the foremen to threaten people with dismissals and prosecution. A few of the more well-known agitators were given several days off—and told not to set foot in the shipyard. Fully armed militiamen patrolled through the crowd, who remained utterly indifferent. The underground's appeal for a strike has gone unanswered. Does this mean that they've lost touch with the pulse of Polish society? Or that Poles have turned away from the classic forms of protest, now blocked by the authorities, and are seeking other ways to reach their goals? It's too early to say.

According to intercepted communications on the militia's radio frequency, a hundred and twenty-nine people have been arrested, of whom fifty were released within twenty-four hours.

Thursday, November 11

I got home late tonight. I was able to avoid the patrols and identity checks. I was at the basilica, where there were about five thousand people, less than had been hoped for. Monsignor Stanislaw Bogdanowicz announced that Lech Walesa had been freed, and the news was greeted with prolonged applause.

Today has been eventful: news from Moscow, the WRON communiqué convoking the Diet on December 13 (probably to announce the lifting of martial law), and right after that the television news of Lech's handwritten letter to General Jaruzelski, signed "Corporal Lech Walesa." Has Lech chosen the correct approach? It seems to me that he's the only one who has been able to retain a certain objectivity about himself and the state of martial law. In his own way, after a difficult period of soul searching, he's come to grips with reality. This letter certainly opens the way to new talks. It's dated November 8, two days before the strike was due to begin. It looks as though Walesa doubted that the strike would succeed, and wrote the letter to try and head it off. But how do the leaders of the underground come off in all this? Does Walesa's letter put some distance between himself and their decision, or does it manage to salvage an idea whose timing he knew was doomed to failure? In any case, by writing this letter, the president of Solidarity has played an important card, and the WRON must make the next move. Their entire staff is probably racking their brains to come up with some way of discrediting Lech's initiative. Will he manage to avoid being manipulated by them? Was he right to trust his own instinct?

Monday, November 15

We waited three whole days for him near his apartment at Zaspa; he arrived during the night. Several thousand people greeted him, and he addressed them from the window of his apartment nineteen times in a row, until he lost his voice. The crowd delivered its verdict on their leader's latest initiative by promoting him, orally, to "General."

That's how the people perceive his role. How does he himself see it? What will happen to him if the authorities deny him a role in the efforts toward accommodation? Especially since they've resolved that there'll be no more agreements like those of August 1980. Their propaganda has been claiming that traditional pacts between the government and the people have always been the root cause of weakness in the Polish state. They're not constantly harping on that aspect of our history for nothing. Would it be possible to reintroduce the proposals of August 1980 in a new form? And what if Walesa is now merely considered a "private citizen"? When he was president of the union, he learned how to speak for us, how to deal with the authorities on equal terms when they came to meet him in Gdansk. After his internment, will he still have the strength to rise to the occasion? The authorities have put on a show of force and demonstrated that Walesa is not a law unto himself. We ourselves have had to submit to circumstances beyond our control. Many people have been confused by propaganda generated by pseudo-democratic-Catholic writers following the government's line. WRON oppresses the people with decree after decree, claiming all the while that their obedience will be rewarded. All these threats and promises must be weighed against the ideals of August 1980 and against the person of

Lech Walesa himself. The president of Solidarity was strong because he spoke the language of truth. Today, in limbo under martial law, at the mercy of the militia, in a situation where no one has the right to speak the truth, will he be able to find a way to continue the dialogue? Or is the moment for dialogue now past in Poland? And if so, for how long?

Everything rests for the moment on the shoulders of this man, who comes once more to the window, under the anxious gaze of his wife, who is only too familiar with the humiliations of daily life under martial law. Lech shouts one more time: "We'll win!" And we look up at him with hope, but filled with bitter thoughts.

Private Citizen

After eleven months of silence a press conference took place on November 16, 1982. It was an opportunity for Western journalists to test me. Like a team of doctors who have gathered around a patient's bedside, they were most concerned with their subject's "overall condition." Had Walesa come out of his imprisonment in a state of shock and physically altered, or was he the same man he was when he went in? They were interested in finding out if I had turned into a political time bomb, a kamikaze who, seeing no other means at his disposal, was capable of taking action that could only be called suicidal—and by this I mean a call for a general strike. The consequences of such an uprising would have been impossible to calculate. Paradoxically, I had the impression that my earlier interview with the minister of internal affairs, General Kiszczak, had as its only aim just such a "test."

From the press conference:

Mr. Lech Walesa, here you are again at home, but the question is the same as ever: What does the future hold for you, and for Solidarnosc?

I arrived home only late last night. If I am to remain true to the spirit of August 1980 and committed to victory—I must first study the political situation carefully, and then find out how things look to the man on the street. I'll need to find what roads are open to us—and to me. I would like to proceed in a reasonable manner, taking care not to aggravate the conflict.

Please do not bombard me with questions that I am in no position to answer today. I need to make sure I am not compromising myself or others. All I want to do during this first month is to be with my family, then to observe what is going on, and, finally, to get back into the swing of things.

There is still one thing you—and we—should know: What importance do you give to the fact that Solidarnosc *no longer officially exists?*

Though things have changed, the spirit of Solidarity continues to exist. To keep it alive we must avoid violent insurrection. There is another road to victory, a road that has been much traveled by others in our century. It is the road of nonviolence.

Was your release subject to any conditions?

I did not commit myself to anything, I did not sign anything, nor did I agree orally to any implicit contract. I examined all the propositions that were put to me in the light of the 1980 accords, and I have no intention of discarding that frame of reference.

In that case, why did they release you and not anyone else?

You know, I'm surprised myself. In my published letter to the premier, I was making a proposition, but I wasn't asking for special treatment. I was convinced I'd be the last to get out. That is why my position, as I see it today, is that of a man who finds himself obliged to walk a tightrope over a prison yard. I intend to make my way right to the other end.

Did they give you any assurances as to when martial law and the state of emergency would be lifted or when the other internees would be released?

I had no idea of what's really been going on. Even if someone had come to me with a proposition, I would not have been able to accept it. I was alone. As our trade union is democratic, I, as its president, had no right to modify its earlier decisions.

Could you give us a rough idea what you said in your television interview? What could it have contained that kept it from being broadcast at the time originally announced?

I don't know the answer. We're talking about a very long interview—perhaps it could not fit into the time slot allotted to it.

Do you see yourself having contact in the future with General Jaruzelski or Primate Glemp, among other people?

Certainly, I plan to explore all the channels open to me.

Has either proposed such a meeting?

Not yet. I know nothing of their plans. I would welcome it after I have had a chance to reacquaint myself with the current situation—this will enable me to avoid costly mistakes.

What were you doing between the time of your release on Friday evening and your arrival here yesterday [Sunday] evening?

I was taken by plane to Otwock, where I spent the night. I wasn't feeling well. Perhaps they interrupted the journey out of consideration for my health. There may be other reasons of which I am not aware.

Did they give you a chance to tell your wife you were coming?

No, they didn't. My release papers were signed only yesterday. I did not receive the papers until I arrived here—and they mention the date and the time. I was in total isolation until yesterday when they brought me here.

So in fact you were in detention until yesterday?

That's right, until yesterday.

Do you consider yourself a private citizen now, or do you still consider yourself president of the free trade unions?

I was democratically elected to office. As far as I'm concerned, nothing has changed.

What conclusions should we draw from the fact that you signed your letter "Corporal Lech Walesa"?

I'm not sure. Certainly there are conclusions to be drawn, but today it is up to each of us to draw his own.

Did you meet with any church or government representatives between the time of your release and your return home yesterday?

No, the only people I saw were the ones who were authorized to see me.

Between the time you sent your letter and your arrival here in Gdansk, had you been in contact with any government officials apart from the prison authorities?

I received visits from General Kiszczak and Colonel Kutz, and then yesterday from state attorneys who gave me a lecture on the law. Do not forget the date on which my letter was sent: it was November 8, before the commemoration ceremonies [on the 11th]. There was nothing accidental about this.

What are your plans for the future?

Obviously, there is a lot of catching up to do. I will spend time with my wife and children, to get to know them again. And after that, I'll lend my ear to my country and listen to what it has to say.

How do you hope to accomplish this? By talking to people?

Certainly I plan to talk to people, but it won't stop there. I have a good nose for a story, and an ear for martial music.

What do you make of your reception?

I am gratified that people have kept faith with me. They in turn can count on my keeping faith with them, for I am one of them.

At one point when you were still in prison there was a rumor that you had changed your ideas about what forms the struggle could take, and in particular that you were no longer so adverse to the idea of violence. Is this true?

I have never advocated the "knockout" approach to victory, or claimed that victory could be achieved through recourse to violence. For me, victory means making many friends—people who understand each other. This is the kind of victory I value the most highly, and that I hope to bring about. I have done a lot of thinking over the past eleven months and I believe I have uncovered several roads that could lead to victory—victory that satisfies the conditions of both parties, so that everyone profits from it.

Could you tell us how you propose to bring about such a victory?

Sir, if you are a student of life you already know that it is a mistake ever to try to anticipate results—situations change and no one has the right to impose anything on anyone. Each person must convince himself of the merits of what he is doing, both as a member of a group and as an individual. I may have thousands of ideas, it could be that all are unrealistic. I return to my opening remarks: I need a month—a week at the very least—to examine the situation, to see how we can even approach a national settlement, not just an agreement on paper but one that yields tangible results.

You have already been asked about the eventual lifting of the state of emergency and the release of other internees. Let me phrase the question in another way, is—?

I know what they're going through and I shall do everything I can to ensure that each of them regains his freedom. Realistically speaking, this will happen of its own accord if we take care not to act in such a way as to bring about an increase in the number

247

of detainees and prisoners. I weep for them and my heart aches for them. I am with them and I shall remain so right up until the moment when we can all meet again over coffee right here in my home.

Do you expect martial law and the state of emergency to continue much longer?

I'm not the one who can call it off.

As far as the underground is concerned—people like Bujak, for example—don't you feel just a bit as if you're on the other side of the barricades?

Our trade union is democratic. It is regulated by its statutes. Each member had the right to express his views, and each had a say in its decisions. My own ideas on this subject have not changed and they will never change. Am I alone in this? I don't know. But I do know that I, along with everyone else, am bound to respect its statutes.

What is your opinion of the people who were not arrested, and who are now in hiding, and continuing their activities in secret? What is your position on them?

You can find your answer expressed in our ideals of August 1980.

Let us return to the matter of restrictions. Under what restrictions are you living at present?

None whatsoever. I repeat: during the entire time I was in detention, I only drafted one document—a letter to the General— and this other one which I signed on my release. In other words I signed two, and only two documents, I did not commit myself to anything, I did not renounce anything—in short, my release was unconditional.

Have you been instructed by government representatives as to what you are no longer permitted to do?

Of course! As I have already said, we had a long talk, lasting from eleven o'clock until half past two, during which time we discussed the law, the penal code, the decree bringing into effect the state of emergency, and so on.

And what was the outcome of this conversation? Are there certain things that you are not permitted to do?

The law is the law, and since I went outside the law, they spent time going over it with me and explaining it. I know that you would like to know much more about this, but try to understand that I have absolutely no intention of evading your questions or of hiding my fear. All I want to do is act reasonably. I am determined to remain faithful to the goals we set. I do not wish to act blindly.

Mr. Walesa, do you think that the organization that goes by the name of TKK [Temporary Coordinating Committee] will continue to exist, and if so, will it answer to you?

I have already spoken on this subject. I remain faithful to our cause, and he who is faithful remains so forever.

You once said that the Pope's visit was partly responsible for the birth of Solidarnosc. *What effect do you foresee him having when he comes for his next visit, which is planned for June 1983?*

I have never wasted much time building castles in the sky, and I am not going to start now—I am a realist, pure and simple.

Jan Mur (extracts from *Journal of a Prisoner*)

Sunday, November 21

At half past twelve, during mass at St. Brigid's, the parish church of the Gdansk shipyard, there was an unusual ceremony: the consecration of the emblem of the shipyard, the *Solidarnosc* flag. This emblem, which was created in 1980, has clearly become a symbol of the utmost importance. Those participating in the ceremony were fully aware of this. Almost ten thousand people had packed into the church and the square in front, where the crowd was enormous. There was a rumor that Lech Walesa would be present at the consecration, news that was said to have been announced by the rector, Father Henryk Jankowski. This would be Walesa's first appearance in public—up until now he hadn't left his home.

Western television teams, press correspondents, and reporters had all taken their places inside the church. The moment the ceremony was due to begin, someone came to say Lech wouldn't be coming. We took that with a grain of salt, thinking that Lech wouldn't wish to disappoint all those people who were waiting to see him—especially since the celebration was so closely related to his own efforts.

Holy Mass was celebrated by Kazimierz Kluz, the suffragan

bishop of Gdansk, and by two other priests who stood on either side of him, the Dominican Father Slawomir Sloma from Gdansk, and Father Jan Gorny from Olsztyn. When the time came for the introit, both Father Jankowski and Monsignor Kluz gave the response to the assembly. Their words of welcome to Walesa, physically absent but present in spirit, were received with thunderous applause of a kind rarely heard in Polish churches. The news went around that Walesa had gone to mass in a small church still under construction, in his parish of Zaspa. Despite his absence, this mass had all the qualities of a solemn celebration of a kind both patriotic and religious. At the end, after the presentation of the flag bearing the emblem of the Gdansk shipyard—a crowned eagle with the inscription Solidarity embroidered in gold—the congregation sang the hymn "God save Poland." Ten thousand hands were raised in the sign of a "V." It was the emotional high point, and the air seemed to sing with hope. Someone next to me said in a loud voice: "They won't break our country's spirit!" The words of the prayer "God, set our country free" resounded above our heads, dramatically summing up the ideals of an organization over which the government had already said funeral rites.

Nothing had been lost, nothing had been buried. The song was greeted with applause. A banner was displayed bearing the Solidarity inscription. Someone shouted out "Long live General Walesa!" and the whole crowd began to shout it and then they clapped. At this point Father Jankowski reminded the congregation of the liturgical nature of the gathering and invited them to leave in peace.

People didn't want to leave. They were radiant. They seemed to be waiting for something, as if strengthened by some inner knowledge.

Not far away, in the neighboring parish of St. Nicholas (which is run by the Dominicans), quite a different service was taking place. Father Jacek Salij, the well-known Catholic journalist, was speaking there about civic courage in a situation like our own, and of our moral obligations to hold our own against the authorities' systematic attempts to undermine us.

I will long cherish the memory of that Sunday celebration at St. Brigid's. But leaving aside our emotional response for the moment, what should we have made of Lech's absence on that occasion?

By the evening, I was already convinced that he'd made the right decision in not coming. Chance played no part in it; on the contrary, he'd thought out his position carefully. By avoiding drama and sensationalism, he was saving his inner strength for the true test that he knew would come later. Walesa thus gave us irrefutable proof that he was, as ever, in good fighting form, because it could not have been easy for him to stay away from St. Brigid's. This was the second time (his press conference being the first) he'd defied expectations and shied away from fine speeches, calmly putting his views on record.

People had been told I was going to make a speech a couple of days before December 16. This speech was my way of holding to my promise to visit the monument every year on that day. Though I won't always be able to be there in person, I shall always be there in spirit. The purpose of the December speech, which was recorded on cassette, was to describe my plans and share with others my vision of the future since my release. The text follows:

We promised to meet and so here we are, together once again, although the conditions under which we're meeting are not quite as we imagined. We've received another blow, and we've still not reached our goal.

This is why we must say it again today: we are still fighting the workers' cause, and victory *will* be ours.

What can I say to you as president of a large trade union which no longer exists in theory?

I'll tell you what I can say: the union exists in our hearts, it exists even in the hearts of those who have denied it. You, too, you must feel that.

It's our tragedy that we have failed to put our ideas into practice as we had hoped. Once again, we have failed to make our country live up to our hopes and our people's potential. There are many who feel they've been deceived. The workers most of all, but also the young, who were hoping for better living conditions. Perhaps we wanted too much too soon.

But we must keep on hoping. I'm confident that the seeds we

have sown have gone deep. We're not the same people we were in August. We know what our aims are, even if to achieve them we'll need more time, and other means.

Many people have given their lives in defense of our ideals, in defense of Solidarity and its honor. We must never forget this. Those of us who are still alive are accountable to those who fell while defending our cause. We must find ways and means of achieving our goals.

We have come under heavy criticism, but history will judge us by our acts and sweep away the slander.

There's one question to be answered: "What do we do now?" How do we go on after all we've been through since August 1980? Many people come to me asking: "What does the future hold? What future is there for our cause, for the people, for those who are no longer in our midst, who couldn't accompany us further?"

I give you a broad answer first: we must remain faithful, faithful to our original ideas. The great Pole, Pope John Paul II, spoke about this, and he had us all in mind when he said: "Don't forget the need for spiritual revival, for freedom and moral dignity."

How are his words to be understood in the context of our program? How should we translate them into action? We ought to be able to find the answer ourselves. We have immense reserves: our minds, and a boundless human energy that will be looking for ways to apply itself—and will succeed.

Do I need to tell you just what is possible, and where the truth lies? All those who took part in the events of August 1980—and it's important to remember that we are still taking part in them— must use all the tools at our disposal, and we must use them in an open democratic fashion, so that our trade unions, artistic associations, and other institutions can be improved from within, and profit from the lessons we have learned through experience.

As a worker, I'm for progress and against any initiative that would involve further losses to our economy. If things are not working as they should, if people are paralyzed, if the economy itself becomes paralyzed, then we must act. We will lead the re-forms.

In the past, the union saw fit to tackle many problems that were not technically within its sphere of activities, but had to do with the larger implications of the social movement we had started. The time has come for this powerful social movement, this great river that has drawn into its currents the unresolved problems from so many shores, to subdivide into several streams. And each of these streams will follow their separate courses toward the sea.

The trade union we fought so hard to establish will be the first stream. As far as unions are concerned, I'm still in favor of pluralism, but I'd also like to see the return of statutory activity in defense of workers' interests.

The second stream will be the stream of worker-managed enterprises, governed by principles of economic logic. Each of us must know how to be master in his own house, and also at the factory and in the university, in a newspaper office, a cooperative, neighborhood, or a city! The independent artistic associations and all organizations responsible for nurturing new ideas make up the third stream. It will be up to them to pool the resources of scientists, men of letters, dramatists, and filmmakers; they won't allow us to be muzzled or undermined. They want to see the country well served by its intellectuals.

The fourth stream will be made up of independent institutions and associations in which young people will work to ensure autonomy and freedom of expression for the new generation. We cannot allow our young people to live by the same old lies. We must not teach them that the only way to get ahead in life is through scheming and duplicity. The fate of Poland depends on this perhaps more than on anything else.

We also have to find ways of coordinating these different activities. No single one of them could function properly without the others. None is expendable either, although we must accept that there will be many mistakes, many changes to be made along the way. I'm ready to give everything I've got to such a program. Our cause is not directed against any person or persons. We are not trying to overthrow the government, we accept the political facts and the imperatives of history. It is under those conditions that we hope to serve our country.

I uphold the ideals we expressed in August 1980. I uphold our Polish workers' cause, both as a Pole and as a worker.

I ask those of you who are waiting for the fulfillment of your hopes to go home in peace. Think about what I have said. And then perhaps we can begin to move in the directions I have suggested—making sure meanwhile that we don't add to the losses we've already suffered.

This speech captures the style of our preoccupations at the time: we were living in circumstances that didn't allow us to progress beyond moral abstractions. All other roads were blocked; the government was conducting an all-out effort to undo our work. It had just abolished the Student Union, the Polish Journalists Association, the Actors' Association, and all our independent trade unions—in other words, Solidarity. Next to go would be the Artists Union, then the Writers Union.

This was the start of my long walk across the tightrope. I found myself facing a number of dilemmas. Should I take steps to be rehired at the shipyard, or should I take advantage of my relative freedom and try to generate activity by traveling around the country? Should I rejoin the activists who had taken Solidarity underground, or distance myself from them?

I discussed these questions openly with the circle of close associates who had once again rallied to my side. I hadn't tried to call together a team of people, the team had simply formed itself. It turned out to be an interesting mixture of people, reflecting a wide variety of experiences and ideas. There were the old advisers from the Warsaw circle, as well as representatives of the Young Poland Movement, teachers and researchers from the University of Gdansk and from the Gdansk Technical University, plus a group of journalists with a wide variety of special interests. Many came from the banned daily and weekly papers and the underground press; all were excellent publicists. So I had at my fingertips experienced reporters, old Party hands, the Catholic press, even first-rate television directors. And if that isn't a multimedia consortium, I don't know what is.

We turned my home into our headquarters, organizing ourselves in much the same way as we do today—although there have been a few small changes. We made the sitting room into the secretariat. It was run by Bozena Rybicka, the fragile-looking woman with the will of iron, whose madonnalike face reminded us of the mass celebrated in the shipyard during the 1980 strike. Happily, she got along perfectly well with Danuta, which was no small consideration as the office had to fit inside our small apartment.

Bozena started to keep my action journal in 1983. She made sure all my interviews were taped and transcribed. They are now in my archives and it is thanks to them that I am able to reconstruct many forgotten details from this period when meetings, trips, visits, interviews, and problems were again piling up one on top of another.

I remember being stopped on the road outside Slupsk, early in the morning of March 22, 1983. At the entrance to the town three vehicles belonging to the militia were parked in the way of our VW van, which I was driving at the time. As usual we had been followed all the way from my home at 17 Pilotow Street by a special car (on this occasion it was a Fiat carrying four civilians). I had picked up the coded communications between them and the militia's headquarters on my shortwave radio. It was clear that it was no accident when we were stopped outside Slupsk.

I was traveling to a trial involving Solidarity activists. Six people were accused of having pursued trade union activity after the declaration of martial law, and were due to appear before the Koszalin military tribunal, which had moved to Slupsk for the occasion. Among them was the vice-president of Solidarity's regional directorate in Slupsk, Krzysztof Szeglowski. This was to be my third journey to a trial involving members of our trade union. I had also attended the trial of Anna Walentynowicz at Grudziadz, as well as the trial of a group of internees at Elblag.

We were made to wait half an hour, and then the road was finally cleared. The occupants of one of the cars directed us to the courthouse.

A crowd had gathered around the building and they cheered enthusiastically when we arrived and began asking for autographs. Inside I was greeted by the young president of the tribunal who explained that he had nothing to do with the roadblock, and that he saw no reason why we shouldn't be able to observe the trial. He provided us with passes giving us access to the courtroom. And a few minutes later the trial began.

During this period, I made a number of trips like this one. It was difficult not to think back to the days before August 1980, even if things had changed. The trials now took various forms. There were the trials like the one at Elblag, for example, where they convicted Solidarity members without even bothering to establish guilt or provide a shred of evidence. A group of prisoners at the Kwidzyn camp had been badly beaten by prison guards: the prisoners were convicted, despite expert appraisals and medical certificates showing they were victims.

The "bad blood" was increasing and the gulf was again widening between the authorities and the people. This was duly noted by Stefan Bratkowski, the former president of the now-dissolved Polish Journalists Association, who was still active in the underground press circuit. His view was that the government was tying itself up in knots. It had no choice but to proceed along the road it had chosen, but this road led nowhere. Tempers were mounting, making the thought of any future reconciliation almost inconceivable. And so the deadly trap, which certain farsighted state and Party functionaries had predicted, was closing. The General himself was caught in it: he missed one opportunity after another and was obliged to abandon his plan to call an end to martial law, first in December, then in the spring of 1983. Events conspired to contradict everything he said. It was as if the facts had paralyzed him, leaving him without free will.

Because I was constantly under surveillance at that time, I was obliged to plan my every move in advance. Every step I took was scrutinized by several pairs of vigilant eyes. I also had to take into account the fact that everything I did would be seen and judged in public.

It's this kind of tension that makes the burden of leadership a heavy one. The results can be disastrous in an emergency when you suddenly discover that you're just not strong enough to do what you have to do, that your good intentions exceed mental and physical resources. Every time we made any plans, we also had to ask ourselves: was I in good enough shape to do it? Would I be able to cope in the next emergency?

I tried to plan each step as carefully as if I were climbing an alpine peak. Even so, events arose that forced me to make abrupt changes in strategy, to interfere with other people's plans—and these people had cards to play that were as legitimate as mine.

This is what happened in April 1983, when I was invited to attend a meeting of the underground TKK, the Temporary Co-ordinating Committee of Solidarity. This meeting was a vital one for the people who had been working in defiance of martial law for almost a year and a half. But my presence at the meeting would undermine the strategy that had been so carefully prepared for me by my staff. Our objective all along had been to force the government to act, implement change, and initiate its own projects. The last thing we wanted to do was provide it with simple excuses. Now they could say: See? even the leader of the Solidarity movement accepts its underground status; the government could destroy the entire movement in no time at all thanks to the new powers it has been given under martial law and here he is willing to take that risk. I decided to go to this meeting nevertheless, because the time had come to reconcile the two tendencies inside our movement. Both the public and the underground activities were absolutely necessary. It was important, therefore, to strengthen the underground, support those who were working in it, conquer the fear that people had of the slightest contact with these activists lurking in the shadows, brush aside the accusations leveled against them by the propaganda machine, and thus attract new recruits. There were many people who were willing to join the underground on condition that I recognize their activities as legitimate. I also decided to go so that I could hear what they had to say, and so that I could present my own views. And I wanted it to be clear to everyone afterward that I *had* been with them.

We were left with a few technical problems, the most pressing of which was how to give my secret-police bodyguards the slip and also keep them off the trail of my colleagues in the underground.

We took all necessary precautions. When the first invitation to the meeting arrived, we left it unanswered. It was not until we had confirmation that the information and the second invitation came from an absolutely trustworthy source that I answered the invitation.

It was April 9, 1983, a Saturday. All day we had been busy with "Operation Smokescreen." I had walked around the house talking at length in a loud voice about the trip I was planning to Warsaw. I often went to Warsaw to see my church contacts and

257

meet with my advisers. The usual thing was for my Gdansk body-guards to pass me over to other cars stationed along the way. This time, too, they had probably radioed ahead to ask the authorities of other districts to assist in the surveillance of our party farther along the route.

I had been instructed that the underground would make contact with us on the Warsaw road, near a place called Karczemki. So our problem was how to give our bodyguards and escorts the slip before we got to Karczemki. When we left the house, they were nowhere to be seen. Mietek Wachowski, my driver, was at the wheel. The car with my bodyguards in it appeared on the viaduct near Zaspa. We were able to lose them by going around the traffic circle, then the cloverleaf below, at top speed. The usual way to go to Warsaw is to take the viaduct over the crossroads; what we did was go underneath. We made a number of detours and even-tually found the exit for Warsaw. As we sped along to our des-tination, our bodyguards were busy searching for us in the city. We were alone.

We passed the place that had been designated as the point of transfer for Karczemki, and drove as far as Cedry Wielkie. There wasn't a soul to be seen. We then went back the way we'd come and parked on the side of the road. A man emerged from behind a tree and said the password. A bit farther down the road was a Fiat, which then took me the rest of the way.

I must say here that I was impressed by the efficiency of the people who organized the meeting. It brought together everyone in the underground, with the exception of Zbyszek Bujak. He had had serious problems after walking into an ambush set up for him in Warsaw, though he had escaped without being recognized; it was crucially important for him to stay in hiding and not expose himself again to the risk of capture. As he had become a legendary figure in our underground, he had to take good care of himself.

The importance of this three-day meeting was primarily sym-bolic; nothing could disguise the fact that we couldn't swap roles. Each of us had to stay in his place, where he was most needed, and where events had placed him. They told me about the network that linked the various branches of underground Solidarity and they also described their activities. The underground had at its disposal an impressive array of tools and methods, an operation

258

tuned with the precision of a fine piece of audio equipment. At this stage in our long-term strategy, the underground was important because it was living proof that we existed, a guarantee that we would continue to exist—even if, like all underground movements, it had no control over its own ultimate fate. And as with any underground organization, its members had to change roles in the light of day, without forgetting the discipline necessary for clandestine operations.

When the meeting with the TKK was over, I was taken back into the center of Elblag. I was wearing a woolen hat, which I'd pulled down over my ears, and glasses that someone had given me, so that I could go incognito. When I saw my reflection in the rearview mirror I saw someone who resembled a mole. I hailed a taxi and said: "We're going to Gdansk." I kept quiet the entire way. An hour later I was home. I didn't have my keys so I rang the doorbell. I saw Danuta peering at me through the peephole. Then I heard her voice saying: "Who do you wish to see?"

In my pocket was the joint communiqué announcing that I'd met with the underground. We had agreed that I should make the text public and that the TKK would then confirm it indirectly in the independent and underground press. The text was dry, purely informative: only three sentences. Nevertheless I was expecting a certain backlash from the government.

The following Tuesday morning, the telephone didn't stop ringing. As I was trying to catch up on sleep after my three-day meeting with the TKK, the communiqué was transmitted first by Danuta, and then by my associates. Everyone who had come into contact with this brief communiqué was later to be called in for lengthy questioning and subjected to different kinds of harassment. Many were stopped under the slightest pretext, deprived of papers, stripped of driver's licenses and so on—even their families were threatened. This went on for several months.

During his weekly press conference, Jerzy Urban, the voice of the government, provided me with an excellent ploy which I was able to put to good use when later interrogated at militia headquarters. Here Urban fell into his own trap because he had previously taken the line that I was no longer president of Solidarity and emphasized over and over that I was nothing more than a private citizen. He was forced to maintain this line when foreign and domestic journalists asked him about the importance of my meeting with the TKK. He couldn't admit that this meeting was of any social importance. He could only regard it as a private conversation. Since that was the way he saw it, that was the version I stuck to when I was taken in for questioning.

From the Action Journal, April 13, 1983

14:10: Visit from security officials and a militiaman in uniform; they want Lech to accompany them to their headquarters where everything will be explained. An argument in the doorway. Lech doesn't want to go without a proper summons. The security official says that in that case he'll have to resort to force. In the end, Lech agrees to go. The militiaman stays behind: he posts himself outside the door. In a loud voice, Danuta expresses her low opinion of officials.

15:35: Mrs. Walesa rings up Andrzejewski, the commandant of the militia. She asks for news of Lech. The answer: "The commandant will be back in half an hour." Danuta rings up the district attorney to ask about Lech's arrest. The attorney isn't in his office, and there's no one else there who can answer her questions. The secretary knows nothing. Danuta describes the circumstances of the arrest. She's told to ring back in a few minutes.

Father Jankowski has arrived and he's speaking to correspondents on the telephone.

16:00: Danka rings up General Andrzejewski. It's he who answers. Danuta describes the circumstances of Lech's arrest, stressing that the officials didn't introduce themselves and so on. She asks when Lech will be returning. Andrzejewski replies that in his view Danuta should also have gone to be interviewed. Danuta refuses to agree to this. She senses that she's being intimidated, even blackmailed. She inquires as to the purpose of the interview, Andrzejewski tells Danuta that it would be in her own best interest if she went. She's not convinced. Andrzejewski doesn't wish to reveal the purpose of the interview. There ensues an argument about legal points: does the militia have the right to interrogate anyone they wish? Danuta says that it's enough if her husband is there. Could he explain why it would be in her best interest to agree to this interview? In any case, she's in no position to answer a summons today, due to her state of health. She asks when Lech will be returning. No answer. In what capacity would she be interrogated? Andrzejewski doesn't want to say; he repeats his suggestion that she should agree to an interview.

Lech is released early the following morning.

Monday, April 18, 1983

8:00: Lech leaves for Warsaw with Father Jankowski and Jozef Duryasz to take flowers to the Warsaw Ghetto monument and the cemetery. Inform journalists after they're gone.

This trip we took to commemorate the anniversary of the Warsaw Ghetto uprising is a perfect example of how Solidarity not only looked to the future, but also felt bound by its obligations with regard to the past. In Poland today, anti-Semitism is no longer the issue it once was, but that doesn't mean we can overlook the major part it played in our past. Even if it seems to have little bearing on current events, we are duty-bound to bear witness to the fate of those who, especially under the Nazis, were no longer even fighting for their lives, but merely for a dignified death. This is why I took with me to Warsaw a short note to Dr. Marek Edelman, delegate to the Solidarity Congress and sole surviving Jewish leader from the Warsaw Ghetto uprising of 1943.

To Dr. Marek Edelman

Dear friend,

Although our paths in life have been so very different, we have already met as representatives of the same cause, the human cause: in the one life we have been given to live, we have committed ourselves to express a common truth and a common belief, and to act according to the dictates of our conscience—with our heads held high, in the manner befitting true men.

I have tried to imagine the tragic days of the Warsaw Ghetto uprising when you yourself faced your most difficult ordeal. I respect you deeply for the part you played as leader of that life-and-death struggle. I am also deeply respectful of your last public declaration, in which you stated so very clearly that you weren't fighting just for lives, but for the right to live in peace and dignity.

Despite the differences in our backgrounds, we find ourselves together once again, as men and citizens guided by a solid and unshakable determination to act within the framework of this organization: an organization that was created by the workers of Poland so that they could live decent and honest lives. So that they could live their lives according to religious beliefs and the natural rights of man.

It is these aspirations that have brought Solidarity into being. We are still traveling together toward those same goals, fighting to win for man his rightful place on this earth and thereby in Poland itself.

When my small team of associates and I decided to call a press conference for April 20 in spite of the fact that we were virtually under siege, what we were hoping to do was break the government's stranglehold by throwing a direct punch, to borrow a term from the boxing ring. I wanted to make it understood that I was determined to pursue an open and public strategy and that I was not going to allow myself to be delegated to the role of a suspect who could be taken in for questioning at the drop of a hat, who could always be found guilty of something. We had also decided to invite both the press and local television teams to the press conference, just as we had always done in the days of Solidarity's official existence. Our aim was to break down the psychological barrier created by attacks on me in the media. The editorial staff of the coastal publications were visibly shocked to have been called to a press conference in such an offhand way. Even on the other end of the telephone line, we could sense their stupefaction—the silence was so long we had to make sure we hadn't been cut off.

Western correspondents had built their own obsessions around Solidarity: most wanted to see in it a subversive underground organization that was committed to bringing about an all-out war of resistance against the state. They were interested in reporting only the sensational news—items about the repressive measures against me or Solidarity, and anything connected with our defense. It was as if they thought we were pawns in an international plot. And, in fact, the real or imaginary plots against my life (there have been three) do raise questions of this sort: were they linked, for example, with the apparent plots that figured so prominently in the attempt on the life of Pope John Paul II by Ali Agca. Western journalists also tended to follow the lead of the government spokesman, Jerzy Urban, who seemed to say something about me each week at his press conference. Urban would serve the ball; minutes later the telephone would ring at my home. The whole world, it was said, would want to know my response to whatever it was Urban had just said. What we wanted to do, however, was to speak independently and in our own time about subjects of our own choosing, instead of being forced to respond to government accusations and insinuations without having time to collect our thoughts.

Much had changed since I sat as a child in our little Popowo house with my stepfather listening to the Polish programs on Western radio stations; it was thanks to these shortwave broadcasts that I was able to discover the other side, the hidden face of Poland. And now here I was, one of the centers of attention for the Western mass media! Thanks to them I could speak out without having to worry if I would be deprived overnight of the right to do so. And I could speak out knowing that people were still listening to me— played back by Western shortwave radio—even though Solidarity had been officially shut down. Newspapers, radio, and television were all important to me. Western radio and news agencies gave my beleaguered compatriots access to sources of information other than the official and censored one; together with the underground press, they brought something that was otherwise lacking in Poland: a breath of fresh air.

I didn't close my door to Polish journalists, even if, after press "verification," it left only those on editorial staffs who had declared themselves fierce critics of the "period of anarchy created by Solidarity." Yet in five years, to March of 1987, I can remember only three occasions on which Polish journalists came into our apartment. The Walesa affair was stamped "censored"—you could write about him, but only if you criticized him. You couldn't go to him for comments or suggestions. That left only the Western reporters.

I have always enjoyed talking to the press, although contact has its own built-in limitations. One learns that the important thing is to convey a style, give a sense of where you stand and what you plan to do, and liven things up from time to time with a bit of humor and make use of metaphors and proverbs. It's not the same with specialists or diplomats or trade union activists; with them, you speak in concrete terms.

It's clear that a diplomat represents first and foremost the interests of his own government, his own country. So you must always bear in mind that a diplomat isn't in the least interested in the fact that in this particular country, no Pole has ever been able to come to an agreement with any other Pole. This topic might be of interest to the general public, and it's one that dominates the media's attention. But the diplomat only wants to know what his country's stakes are; what benefit it can derive from a given situation. It's in this context that I would like to discuss one of the central problems of the period of martial law, the effects of which we are still feeling today: the West's economic sanctions against the government headed by General Jaruzelski. Although I refused to speak to journalists on this matter, I couldn't get off the same way with foreign diplomats.

This business with sanctions is best summarized by the old homily about hunters who walk into their own traps, but that's too simple. Ever since the August 1980 strike, there had been general agreement that people would make sacrifices in order to bring about much-needed changes in the way their lives were structured and gain the civil liberties that should be an integral part of one's life. We were saying: we're prepared to work for peanuts, provided that there's hope for something better in the future. This was still the case in December 1981, when, in response to the declaration of martial law, the West generally responded with economic sanctions. Almost everyone in Poland saw this move as a clear gesture of support for us, and as one of censure against the government. Of course, the sanctions affected everyone's standard of living, but we all hoped that the government would be sufficiently alarmed by the low standard of living, or anxious enough about economic disarray or social discontent, that it would look for other solutions, such as a compromise with Solidarity. In a country that was clamoring for reforms and in which the majority had been deprived of the opportunity to influence the social and economic order, we couldn't guarantee that Western aid or extended bank credit would be used advisedly or efficiently, or that it would be possible to repay the debt in the future. Credits would not bring about good results in the short term, and they might end up being a burden in the future; so it seemed to me that certain things had to happen before we could take on new debts. What we had to do was bring about the social changes that Solidarity was calling for.

The government, on the other hand, interpreted what I said as follows: Walesa has seen fit to make pronouncements on economic sanctions, and he says that the worse they are, the better it is.

Just before the end of April 1983, I finally received my summons to appear for work in the shipyard. It would be my third appearance at the scene where Solidarity began.

I was taken on as a level-9 electrician. They assigned me to a team that was small but made up of an interesting cross section of people including a trusted foreman, an activist from the trade union, a member of the Party, and one or two other salaried employees. My job was to repair the electric carts that had been said to "wheel in the revolution" in 1970 and that had served as stands during the August 1980 strike. I was working in a small workshop, almost completely cut off from the rest of the shipyard, to which I nevertheless still felt very close.

On my first day back, it took me at least two hours to get home. In the square, in front of the second entrance, across from the monument to the 1970 shipyard workers, I had to shake thousands of hands and sign hundreds of autographs. I felt tremendously happy, I felt as if by returning to work, I had finally set my feet on solid ground. All my friends assured me that we had done things right.

In the beginning, I used to go to the canteen for my break, and people would sit down and start asking me questions. The officials who kept tabs on me always overheard these conversations and the workers involved soon found themselves in difficulty. I quickly came to the conclusion that these casual meetings couldn't continue. I couldn't carry on sitting around when the entire world was expecting me to *do* something, especially when we were being spied on constantly. I therefore decided the best thing to do would be to conduct my public activities well away from my place of work, using my home, primarily, as my base, as I had done until returning to the shipyard. I began to eat my lunch in the workshop, and the security forces stopped the harassment; they just watched me instead. In the shipyard, we got into the habit of communicating without speaking or even meeting; if the shipyard was to take up its former role, we would have to make do with a new type of contact. Thanks to the underground press, the meetings that took place outside the yard, including the foreign radio broadcasts, everything I did and wanted reported from then on became public knowledge.

My workday became a great deal longer. I got up at five in the morning. Danuta would jump out of bed at the same time and make a good breakfast. I would pack a thermos of tea or coffee and a few sandwiches into my bag and then race downstairs. "Grandpa" Henryk Mazul arrived on his motorbike at dawn. This wonderful old seaman from Wilno, a boatswain by trade, had been my closest companion since August 1980. He was the kind of friend who asked for nothing in return save friendship. Like the air I breathed he was always at my side, no matter what the weather, never out for himself, never selfishly calculating. We were practically the same flesh and blood, and he was like a protective older brother. Four security officials would always be waiting outside the building for me, usually standing next to their car. Sometimes I would catch them dozing, and I would go up to the car, rap on the roof, and shout: "Wake up! Time to get going!" It was a never-ending game of hide-and-seek, and they had become indifferent to the actual outcome. Once I even persuaded them to help me start my car on a cold morning.

After work, I usually had a string of appointments to keep. Sometimes these were social, but more often than not they were of a public nature: discussions with diplomats, interviews, contacts with trade unionists (domestic and foreign), meetings with our advisers. The irreplaceable Father Henryk Jankowski would play host on most occasions, often at St. Brigid's church, and from time to time so did Monsignor Stanislaw Bogdanowicz, at the nearby basilica of Notre Dame. It was difficult to predict when I'd get home, but it was usually sometime after four in the afternoon. Then, following a short rest, I'd be ready for the second half of the day, devoted to planning our strategy for the days to come, with advisers preparing statements, receiving other visitors.

May Day 1983 was approaching. I had decided I would spend it at home. To be more precise, I was planning to spend the day on my balcony, from which I intended to address all the people coming into Zaspa from other parts of the city for the day. The indomitable Danuta could always be counted on to rise to such an occasion. She had already experienced what it is like to be in contact with large crowds of people after my arrest; and more recently at Maria-Wiktoria's baptism, when forty thousand poured into our neighborhood to mark the occasion. With the exception of May Day the previous year, this baptism—which took place toward the end of my stay at Arlamow—was the most major public demonstration during the entire period of martial law. Danuta was as fascinated by this contact with the crowds as I was; she used to run to the window or out onto the balcony, and lean out to speak to them, or to shout insults at the militia when they attacked. At times like this she'd no longer be the mother with seven children: she was a charismatic revolutionary.

On May Day there were several pitched battles with the militia. When the squads marched up to the buildings to attack demonstrators in the crowd, our neighbors threw jam jars, flowerpots, old household utensils, and scalding water out of their windows. It looked like a siege from the Middle Ages. Bands of children took part in the confrontations and learned to receive their share of tear gas. For several years afterward, one of the favorite games of the Zaspa children was to reenact the 1983 May Day drama. They would divide into two teams and stage mock battles, Pilotow Street against Startowa Street. Two of the most ardent activists among them were my own sons, Slawek and Przemek. My frequently calm approach and constant talk of nonviolent methods enraged them; the idea of moderation meant nothing to them. And so they found an outlet for their frustrations in the form of organized juvenile war games. That worried me somewhat with regard to the future.

If every May Day was a test of our endurance, it was also a barometer which enabled me to measure public support and morale. In 1984 the celebration took the form of a May Day parade on a route parallel to the official one but moving in the opposite direction. As planned, at a crossroad we made an about-face and joined the column on the official route. Despite a number of attacks by the militia, we succeeded in taking the Solidarity procession right up to the grandstand where the officials and their guests were sitting. Stopping in front of them, I raised my hand and gave the "V for Victory" sign.

In 1986, the Gdansk authorities decided to do away once and for all with the now-embarrassing May Day holiday. The army and the militia shut down everything along the route which only the official procession was to take through Gdansk. But by then we had already moved into a new danger zone: the Saturday before May Day a tragedy occurred to remind us all of our possible extinction, the explosion of the central reactor at Chernobyl. A deadly cloud moved across Poland from the Ukraine in the southeast, contaminating fruits and vegetables, livestock, and, possibly, people. Confronted by this sudden emergency, the government responded in a way that could only be described as pigheaded: it simply ignored the danger. The Chernobyl accident and the greater fears it represented left a profound impression on me. When this kind of thing happens, you cannot help but look at yourself, your family, especially the children, and wonder what kind of world we are living in. You ask yourself if your children will even be able to give birth to healthy children. We are one big family—a world family—and we share a common fate. Must we go on fighting and at the same time live with the prospect of nuclear disaster? Isn't the nonviolent struggle the only answer for the future—our only option?

We were living with a new awareness now. The Chernobyl accident forced us to think about nuclear politics, and as immersed as we were in Solidarity's struggle, we realized that we were also involved in a larger confrontation with the world's military-minded politicians over our future.

But I'm getting ahead of myself. In April and May of 1983 we had to bolster our organization, to find out if we could move

Solidarity along aboveground. We met with leading activists from the regional committee in Warsaw to formulate a plan for a common platform with all the other trade unions that had been dissolved during martial law. I should make it clear that we had more or less ignored the existence of many of these other free unions during Solidarity's official period: they had gone about their own business in our shadow. But with the passage of time and the declaration of martial law, it turned out that they, too, had been hard hit by the government's repressive measures aimed at wiping out the independent trade union movement. We were in almost total agreement on important issues, particularly on the key point: opposition to the government's zero option. There was a part to be played by each in a renewed independent trade union movement, and that was the platform that emerged from our meeting.

This Warsaw initiative was received with some suspicion in Gdansk. People asked if "the others" mightn't be trying to assume a central organizing role. This obsession with the movement's center—any center—had long afflicted Poland, and Solidarity broke new ground in saying that, no, there was no need for every initiative to come from one center, that it wasn't a bad thing to have more than one active center expressing different points of view. This was the very basis of our movement. When Solidarity was first created, most people agreed how important it was that our movement had its headquarters outside the capital, because this meant it was sheltered from the direct, almost physical pressure that the government brought to bear on most organizations located there. Even so, the old, deep-seated Polish mistrust began smoldering.

Warsaw took care of all the arrangements, conducted the discussions, prepared the documents, and arranged the appointments. A date was fixed for the meeting that was to include representatives of all the Polish trade union organizations. My action journal contains a complete account of the meeting. Here are some extracts:

On Friday, May 6, 1983, Lech took the streetcar to the shipyard. He rarely did this—only when his plans for later in the day precluded using his easily recognizable white Volkswagen van. The day before, he had asked us what our plans were for Saturday and Sunday, and if we might be interested in a quick trip to Warsaw.

269

"Is something interesting happening there?" we asked.

"You might meet some people," he replied.

Mietek Wachowski's Peugeot drew up in front of the third entrance to the shipyard at half past two in the afternoon. Lech Kaczynski and Jacek Merkel were already in the car. Aram Rybicki and Adam Kinaszewski were in the second car, a Fiat that Walesa had used for official union business when he was president. Walesa got into the Peugeot and we drove off in the direction of Warsaw, having agreed in advance to stop halfway at a roadside inn. The two cars arrived in Olsztynek, where we made our planned stop for a rest and a meal. There's an inn there comprising several houses. We chose the one at the farthest end of the road. The restaurant was less than half full. The waitresses didn't take long to figure out who the man with the dark brown mustache was, and they started whispering in the corner. We were all in an excellent mood when we sat down at our table. Lech picked up the menu and said that the meal was on him: "Eat something substantial; who knows how long it'll be before our next meal," he said jokingly, and he ordered himself an enormous knuckle of ham.

As it turned out, it was no joke, even if we laughed at the time. Looking through the curtains we saw a militia radio car pass by. It flashed its signal to indicate it was turning into the restaurant car park. We nevertheless finished our meal without being disturbed. But the moment we were on our way again Walesa's car was stopped. The driver of the Fiat parked on the curb and waited to see what would happen next. A little later, the Peugeot passed by. It, too, was pulled over, and all the passengers had to show their papers. Nothing more. We went through the same verification process outside Warsaw as night was falling. At a traffic circle, the militiaman directing the traffic stopped the Fiat, signaling it to pull up on the pavement. The Peugeot, meanwhile, had disappeared in the flow of traffic. The militiaman asked the driver for his license, examined it at length, and then said: "You can't be serious! This car belongs to Walesa?"

"Yes, it does," the driver responded. "He's just arrived in Warsaw."

"That's good!" the militiaman said, apparently delighted. He seemed to be sincere.

"What's the problem?"

"Your license plate isn't very clear, but since you're from Gdansk go on, get back on the road!"

We later parked the Fiat in a lot near Krucza Street, not far from the apartment belonging to Sila-Nowicki, where there was to be a preliminary meeting. The Peugeot was in the courtyard. A young man was stationed in front of the elevator and looked carefully at everyone's face as each of us entered. We were met by the daughter of the host and taken into a room where the others were already assembled: Lech, Kaczynski, Merkel, Wachowski, Rybicki, Kinaszewski, and Stanislaw Rusinek, from the regional committee in Masovia.

Cake and coffee were served in the large room that was used as Sila-Nowicki's law office. Wachowski went over to the window that looked out over the street, and lifted to his ear a small transistor that was tuned to the band used by the militia and the emergency services.

"We don't have much time," he said to the rest of us in the room. "They've blocked off the roads in every direction and they're calling several special brigades into the area."

Rusinek, who was sitting at the table, presented the document that was the result of several weeks of discussions between representatives of all the trade unions active before December 13, 1981—the free trade unions, the various trade union branches, the Polish Teachers Union, and Solidarity. We all read the contents and then looked them over a second time. Rusinek crouched next to Walesa. His muscles were tense as he waited for Lech's reaction.

"What do you think?" Lech asked.

One of us said: "The text is fairly ordinary, although the idea behind it is good. But what do we stand to gain from this? To use a military term, it's not a case of widening the front but simply of crowding it. So is it really necessary? That's probably what the official line will be, in any case."

"I don't think there's any need to make a decision now, especially since we're under pressure. I'd recommend postponing signing this document," Rybicki said. It was his habit to advise against rushing into things.

But Walesa continued to examine the piece of paper. Rusinek became impatient.

"Unless the document's signed today, I'm withdrawing from the entire business," he said emphatically. "There are important people involved in this, people who have had to make their own difficult decisions. They're waiting for you only a few streets away from here."

This exchange was interrupted a moment later by the arrival of our host, Wladyslaw Sila-Nowicki, with Jan Olszewski. They joined our group around the table.

"Everything looks as if it's been carefully thought out," Sila-Nowicki declared. "The letter is addressed to the Diet. Its intentions are clear." He was resorting to his usual gentle persuasion, directing his words at Lech. Olszewski also came down in support of the letter.

"I'd like to hear what everyone has to say about this. My Gdansk group has the right to express its opinions, too," said Lech, thus postponing further the moment of decision.

"There are people waiting for us, and we've already made our own representations—we must go," urged Rusinek, "even if there are objections."

"Okay, so it's decided. We're signing," Lech replied. "Only those of you who really must should come with me. I mean Jacek Merkel and Lech Kaczynski. The rest of you, wait for me here."

Rusinek made the first move, slipping a copy of the document into his briefcase.

"We'll take my little Fiat. It's parked on a street near here. With a bit of luck, we'll make it there," he said.

The front door slammed. Sila-Nowicki sat down at his desk, which was covered with deeds and open files. He was trying to look as if he were in the midst of reading one of them when the bell began ringing insistently. A moment later a gray-haired man of about fifty leaped into the room. Behind him was another man dressed in civilian clothes. Behind him came two or three more. One of them shouted: "No one move! This is a special team from the ministry of internal affairs."

The oldest of the group, his face crimson with anger, began feverishly searching the first one of us he could lay his hands on, shouting: "Where is Bujak?" We didn't move—it seemed as if we were in a detective movie; we were afraid of making any gesture that might provoke these overwrought men. His rudely shouted question, so insane in the circumstances, loosened our tongues.

"But we came from Gdansk to Warsaw with the militia trailing us all the way, you must know that," said one of the men from the coastal region.

"Colonel, we know each other, don't we?" said Sila-Nowicki.

"We know each other extremely well, sir," replied the gray-haired man.

"So what are you doing here, and why are you so worked up? I really must complain," Sila-Nowicki said.

In the meantime, another man, who was standing next to the table, ran his fingers over the tablecloth. Reaching underneath he pulled out a copy of the letter that someone had shoved there when the doorbell rang.

"Look, it's no secret, it's addressed to the Polish Diet," Sila-Nowicki said.

"We'll take care of that later. First we're going to make a full search. And we're taking everyone in."

The colonel had pulled himself together. His bearing and appearance were now under control, only his wild eyes continued to betray his feelings.

A quarter of an hour later the Gdansk men were reassembled, this time at Mostowski Palace, headquarters of the security forces. They were ushered into one room: first Wachowski, then Kaczynski, Kinaszewski, Merkel, Rybicki, the journalist Tadeusz Mazowiecki, Professor Geremek, and other signatories of the letter to the Diet. It was really an extraordinary situation: in one little room in the middle of the night, it was now about midnight, they had reunited most of the representatives of the Polish trade union movement before December 13, 1981, when the deputy prime minister's "zero option" was declared. The only one who wasn't there was Lech.

The authorities had already conducted searches at everyone's house. Professor Geremek was especially upset because they had confiscated some important material he needed for a scientific study in progress. An hour later, Sila-Nowicki's stiff figure appeared in the corridor, preceded by a young man in blue jeans and leather jacket (unmistakably obtained from one of the hard-currency shops and popular with the young). He was carrying a bundle of files tied up with string, which we recognized from having seen it on his desk.

According to Kaczynski and Merkel, who had gone off with Lech in the Fiat, they had had no trouble getting to the apartment where the others were waiting. When they went into the building, Walesa was the first to go up the stairs. Then Kaczynski, Merkel, and Rusinek. A few steps behind them came the security officials, who stopped at the door. After a brief exchange of greetings inside, everyone signed the letter, each signatory keeping a copy. The security men allowed Walesa to go past when he came out with his Gdansk associates, but they had different plans for the others. They burst into the apartment, confiscated all the copies of the letter, searched the place and arrested everyone there, except for the host's wife—women are apparently excluded from "zero option" operations.

Walesa and his group got back into the Fiat and drove off to the secretariat of the Polish episcopate. Just before they arrived, Merkel heard the following dispatch on his police radio: "Stop the car, we're taking them in." And that's exactly what they did. They took Walesa to Mostowski Palace separately, and after a brief stop in the courtyard, they left for Gdansk. In the morning, Lech found himself in front of the door to his own apartment.

Meanwhile, at the Mostowski Palace, one after the other, the detainees were taken into an isolated room to be interrogated; a few were subjected to body searches.

During the rest of May my associates and I were subjected to a series of shock treatments. The atmosphere was becoming more and more oppressive and it was difficult to see clearly through the fog of events.

Everyone, inside and out, it seemed, was trying to understand what was going on in Poland. I had already given hundreds of interviews which had furnished me with many opportunities to express my ideas on the subject. However, certain basic questions kept cropping up. Here are a few of them, along with my answers:

Question: If you decide to compromise the movement by joining the Patriotic Movement for National Renewal [PRON] your popularity will probably suffer. If you don't agree to a compromise, on the other hand, you'll be cut off, and have no power to negotiate directly with the government or, even more serious, no power to make contact with it. How do you plan to resolve this problem?

Walesa: We in Solidarity were not the ones who started PRON. Instead, we began independent trade unions with the country's approval, and that's what matters to us.

Question: Certain Party and government representatives say they had no choice but to respond with the sword. Some of them believe that if Solidarity had been more realistic and the society more stable, the authorities would not have acted. What is your opinion?

Walesa: They want us to come to an agreement on our knees. Poles know better than most how uncomfortable this position can be. But we're not trying to rush solutions simply for the pleasure of being tough; we don't want future generations to be brought up on suicide slogans. One chapter of history has closed; the appeal I'm making now is to carry on resisting until we've solved some of our problems and created a better world for future generations to live in. We need something more than just a change in the ruling elite. Poles only have to look at the map to know that we cannot rebuild our new house alone, and the new should serve the entire world.

Despite general speculations (to which I had to respond in my interviews to the press), I never doubted that the Pope's visit in 1983 would help us enormously. I had said so many times to dispel people's doubts. A year earlier, during the period of martial law, in response to steps taken by the Polish episcopate, the security forces had drafted a document entitled "A memo concerning the dangers to be anticipated in the event of a visit by the Pope to Poland in August 1982." They drew up a list of weighty arguments: the presumed existence of three hundred and fifty terrorist groups; the illegal and widespread possession of arms, munitions, and high explosives. We recognized the tune. Just before May 1, 1983, the government stated bluntly that May Day demonstrations that were being organized might jeopardize the Pope's visit. At the time, I was in close contact with Cardinal Glemp, the Primate, whom I found understanding (I won't hide the fact that certain ecclesiastical bodies had their own doubts). I also took into account the opinions of the TKK, whose authority was unchallenged at this time. I didn't want our people to be blackmailed into silencing their true wishes, so I decided that the best thing to do was to apply to them for judgment; Cardinal Glemp agreed with me on this point.

We made our position public at a press conference, where we reminded the authorities of our minimum conditions: trade union pluralism, an opportunity to set up workers' self-management committees, the reintroduction of basic individual liberties, and a total revamping of the national media. The answer from the people was clear.

The May Day celebrations didn't lead, in the end, to the cancellation of the Pope's visit. Gdansk wasn't informed in advance of his route, and nothing had been done about my meeting with him. I had complete confidence in him and was ready to go along with whatever decision he made; yet the country's morale didn't depend solely on our respective feelings and intentions.

The propaganda machine, on the other hand, was waging a fierce campaign to undermine the resolve of the Polish people, and it was willing to go to any lengths to achieve this. During this period, I was the target of countless attacks in the press and on television. Coming in the midst of this heated campaign, the Pope's decision to meet me couldn't help but challenge all the accusations that had been leveled against me. He might even have to confront the propaganda machine head-on and refute the attacks directly. I think that the authorities were perfectly aware of the weight the Pope's decision would carry.

I hadn't even begun to calculate all this when the time came for me to submit my application for an audience, in keeping with Vatican protocol. If I did apply, it was because from the very first day we went on strike three years earlier, I had felt a profound spiritual communion with the Holy Father. In deciding to strike we had undertaken a moral commitment to pursue our aims in accordance with the teachings of the church: it was by putting its teachings into practice that we would achieve those aims. After considerable soul searching, I finally decided to request an audience.

276

I thought back to October 1978, to that day when we received the moving news that a Pole had just been elected Pope. When he paid his first visit to his country in 1979, we couldn't help feeling that we had been chosen by the rest of the world, as if the world had finally noticed us, finally elected us. During this visit we stood shoulder to shoulder, several million of us experiencing the same joy. And as members of the Free Trade Union of Gdansk got ready to leave together in my dilapidated old car—Anna Walentynowicz, Bogdan Borusewicz, and a few others—the car broke down. Because I wasn't able to obtain additional leave (I'd been working at the ZREMB for less than a month), the others left without me. Anna told me how she had caught a glimpse of the Pope from a distance in Gniezno, a city in the region known as the cradle of Poland. I didn't think I would be able to join up with the pilgrimage on Sunday because enormous traffic jams were predicted. I couldn't see clearly what use my presence would be in the midst of those crowds of pilgrims, and that was how I missed out on an extraordinary, possibly unrepeatable, moment.

In the end I didn't miss out, for in January 1981, I went as one of Solidarity's delegates to the Vatican, where I was received by the Pope. And two and a half years later, on May 14, 1983, under different circumstances, I addressed a letter to the Pope, from which I quote: "We refuse to live in the past, to founder in misery and regret. Our faces are turned toward our country's future. It is in the name of my country, Holy Father, that I permit myself to ask you for an audience."

If I prefer not to reproduce here in its entirety my request for an audience, it's because I consider the matter to be above all a private and spiritual one. Let's just say that in referring to certain national problems, I wanted to stress our open-mindedness about the future, because the propaganda machine took every possible opportunity to portray me as a man desperately clinging to the memory of August 1980, which was ancient history as far as the government was concerned. They tried to portray me as a man too inflexible to define new objectives or find a new role for himself in the conditions created by the declaration of martial law. I felt that, in certain parts of the church hierarchy, there was a similar tendency to relegate me to the "Solidarity museum," where I was both head curator and principal attraction.

In the days before the Pope's visit the leaders of Solidarity were under close surveillance, virtually kept in isolation. There was even a phony trial brought against members of KOR, and I was brought before a magistrate for alleged tax evasion. The government went so far as to claim that a meeting between the Pope and myself would be a menace to state security.

The day before the Pope arrived all obstacles disappeared when I received a telephone call from the commandant of the district militia: I was to see the Pope!

What I remember most of our meeting was the atmosphere of openness and simplicity—his words were like an invitation to remove the daily mask one wears to cope with life.

One curious thing struck me during that meeting. I suddenly noticed the Pope's large feet, and I watched how he walked. Surprisingly, his steps were steady, measured, and confident. They seemed to give me back my strength.

On August 13, the eve of the third anniversary of the August strike, at the presbytery of St. Brigid's—home of my friend Father Jankowski—I made the acquaintance of a young priest from Warsaw, Jerzy Popieluszko. He was wearing jeans and a white polo shirt, with a pack of Marlboros sticking out of his breast pocket. I embraced him and then introduced my associates.

The next day, this youthful-looking priest had undergone a complete transformation. He was wearing the robe that the shipyard workers had presented as a gift to their parish and was preaching to a church that was full to bursting. We listened to his sermon, spoken in clear and simple language. His moral stance was uncompromising: "If we lack freedom, it's because we submit to falsehood. It's because we don't expose it, don't dispute it each and every day. We don't try to rectify it. We remain silent, pretending to accept it. That's how we come to live in falsehood."

He didn't speak for long, but he asked a great deal of his audience. He was asking them to take concrete steps to effect change. It wasn't enough to come here and listen to him, and then go home, or to work, and keep silent. He didn't stand on ceremony: he gave this silence its true name.

At the end, he said something I've never been able to forget. The people who'd been keeping him under surveillance for quite some time by then and who, these last weeks, were sticking to him like leeches (they'd come all the way to Gdansk) would also do well to recall his words. Father Popieluszko said: "As Christ says in the Gospel, fear not, fear not those who kill the body, they can do no more than that."

Two weeks later, the shipyard was buzzing with the news that the deputy premier, Rakowski, was coming to conduct an open meeting with the employees. I was asked if I intended to take part in it. They were planning to hold the meeting in the famous hall of the Health and Safety Office, the very same hall that had served as headquarters for the strike committee and the Presidium of the Inter-enterprise Strike Committee and where we had signed the 1980 August Agreements. This new meeting couldn't have taken place anywhere else. Rakowski needed the best facilities available. The meeting was to be televised. The Party secretary in my workshop asked me if I was going to take part in the meeting; if so, he asked if I'd mind not mingling with the crowd that would be waiting for me in front of the hall, but enter the hall with him through a side door.

At the meeting, the Party secretary was seated on my left, while someone from the new, government-sponsored union was on my right. This seating suited me fine; no one would be able to say that I'd encouraged the men to protest, because I was in no position to. They didn't need encouragement in any case: they received Rakowski with hissing and shouting. He rallied quickly, just as an actor might in a film, took off his jacket and rolled up his sleeves, as if he was getting ready for a boxing match. That was enough to provoke the audience, which was probably what he was after anyway. By coming to speak in the historic hall, he wanted to recapture history. He was trying to appropriate the slogans of our movement for himself. What that amounted to is a perfect example of political plagiarism, or in other words, falsehood pure and simple.

The speech that Rakowski made to the shipyard workers rang hollow. He accused me of setting my followers against him and held me responsible for the hissing and booing with which he'd been received. He tried to give a point-by-point explanation of how the sixteen months of Solidarity's official existence had been nothing more than a period of strike disturbances, "betrayals, and

279

anarchy." It was the same old song we'd been hearing for two and a half years.

The last thing I wanted to do was to let the meeting disintegrate into a shouting match. I took it upon myself to remind him that it was thanks to us and to the events of August 1980 that he and his cronies had been able to seize power from Gierek, and that all we had got in return for our good services were tanks and truncheons. But I didn't want to dwell in the past, so I urged him to sit with us around a table and talk, and invited him to come with us to leave a few flowers in front of the monument in memory of the shipyard workers who fell in 1970. His only reply was to make a joke about my honorary doctorate.

It was the first time I had made an officially sanctioned public appearance, or rather, an appearance sanctioned by Mr. Rakowski. He needed to have me seated next to him for the television cameras. My short speech, even though it was cut by the censors, was nevertheless able to give viewers an idea of what had transpired at the shipyard. The very fact that this duel had taken place between us was significant in itself and sparked off a number of discussions.

According to the very first polls conducted by the Center for Public Opinion Studies and by the center that measured television audiences, the deputy premier's performance had been well received. But this impression was modified by independent surveys from Warsaw, and from other big cities as well as the provinces, which tended to indicate that the moral victory was mine.

As paradoxical as it may at first seem, you can argue that, by participating in this meeting at the shipyard and giving a "tough-minded" speech, Rakowski had taken a step similar to the one I had taken in December 1981, when I went to Radom to mingle with the members of the most radical section in Solidarity. He wanted to show that he was capable of throwing his weight around, despite complaints people had made about his liberal sympathies. But all he'd succeeded in doing was to compromise his reputation: while the hard-liners in the Central Committee continued to attack him, he now also found himself in trouble with some of his close allies.

In my opinion—and in the opinion of the general public—the Rakowski contingent's main failing was its inability to overcome internal weaknesses and openly take up the challenge expressed by Solidarity. Instead of looking to Poland's future, instead of joining forces with us and drawing upon this enormous reservoir of human energy which Solidarity had pooled, they contented themselves instead with a competition for the vacancies in the top echelons of government after the Gierek regime. In so doing they missed a once in a lifetime opportunity and, by declaring martial law, they merely succeeded in paralyzing the country and creating a situation in which there were no winners.

This was the price the liberal wing of the Party had to pay for failing to play its rightful role in our country's history. And this was why I said to Mieczyslaw Rakowski at the 1983 meeting in the Gdansk shipyard: "You've moved to the top by clambering over our backs; the least you can do is to acknowledge it!"

The fall of 1983 was fast approaching and, as always, I took advantage of this time of year to reacquaint myself with the natural world. Whenever I had some free time, I would leave Gdansk with Henryk Mazul and go to Kaszuby, which I had come to love and which now took the place of the region where I was born, the countryside around Popowo.

It's a beautiful part of Poland known, not without good reason, as the "Kaszubian Switzerland." The countryside is dotted with numerous lakes. Grandpa Mazul gathered wild mushrooms while I fished at the side of the lake or splashed around in the water in my waders, or, occasionally, took out a small boat.

I needed fresh air. In Gdansk I'd become the target for an entire propaganda team. It was at about this time that I began to be deluged with anonymous letters, all written by the same hand, all slipped into identical envelopes. One day I received seventy-five of them, and the following day a hundred. Then I noticed a trailer for a television program entitled "Money" that was scheduled for the following day. It contained extracts from a conversation that was alleged to have taken place between me and my brother Stanislaw during my internment at Arlamow. It concerned the implementation of a plan to recover a sum of almost a million dollars that I was supposed to have accumulated in the West thanks to winning various awards.

It was clear what the authorities were trying to do. By surrounding the Walesa family with a "wall of money," they hoped to cut me off from the millions of Poles who were faced with the rigors of a tough working life.

On the day after I was released from Arlamow, long before this program went on the air, the authorities tried to show the program to a group of representatives from the episcopate; an effort had also been made to send a tape to the Holy See through the inter- mediary of the permanent Polish mission to the Vatican. Other copies were circulating throughout the country and were used by government groups as part of their propaganda campaign against Solidarity. My copy was picked up by supporters while I was under wraps. Putting the program on the air was a way of bringing in the heavy artillery.

The day after the program was shown on television, I was at an international soccer match between Juventus and Lechia-Gdansk, which was played in Gdansk, where I received an indication of the public's response. Forty thousand people greeted me by shouting over and over again: "Solidarity!" and "Lech Walesa!"; the militia had to disperse rowdy youths whose gravest crime was to wave flags bearing the Solidarity emblem. So much for the smear cam- paign.

It was a week later, on Wednesday, October 5, 1983, that it was announced that I had been awarded the Nobel Peace Prize.

The Nobel Prize

After winning the Nobel Prize, I was obliged to put myself at the disposal of a number of reporters who were busy marking the occasion with their "latest updates." It seems reasonable now to avail myself of some of their on-the-scene reports:

> It was two o'clock in the morning when Lech and Danuta were awakened from a deep sleep by the telephone ringing. It was Krzysztof Wyszkowski on the line; he sounded overjoyed: "Lech! You've won the Nobel Prize!"
>
> "Yeah, yeah . . ." Lech growled, still half asleep, and then he put the receiver back.
>
> At about eight o'clock, Maciek was awakened by the tele- phone's shrill ring.

"This is Father Jankowski. Tell Lech not to go out picking mushrooms. The people we were expecting are already there. He should have a quiet cup of coffee at home and wait for them."

Maciek, who was still asleep, passed the message on to Slawek, who passed it on in an even more garbled form.

Moments later, a procession of vehicles stopped in front of the house; at the front was Lech in his white Volkswagen van and behind it were eight taxis and other vehicles with Warsaw license plates.

Slawek went up to the van and said: "Listen, Lech, Father Jankowski just rang. He says that someone just arrived and that you were supposed to go home."

"Come on, get in, we're going looking for mushrooms."

At about ten o'clock, the procession arrived in the village of Kaszuby, a hundred and twenty miles outside Gdansk. Sitting in the van with Lech, who was at the wheel, were Mr. Paczek, from the house next door to the Walesas, and his wife, Eugenia (who is a translator), along with a woman friend; Kazik (Danuta's cousin); the inevitable Henryk Mazul; and Slawek Rybicki. In the other vehicles were the representatives of the official Polish press agencies along with some Norwegian journalists. All of them parked in front of the farm belonging to Grandpa Mazul's friends.

In the yard, the journalists swarmed around Lech. Only the German correspondent stayed behind by his car to listen to the radio. A few minutes later, he cried out: "The Nobel Prize, the Nobel Prize!" Slawek was the only one to hear him. He rushed toward Lech. "Lech," he said, "the German just said you won the Nobel Prize!"

Lech brushed him aside. He still refused to believe it. A few minutes later, they were back on the road. At half past ten, the horns began to beep.

"This time you really did win the Nobel Prize!" somebody said.

"I refuse to believe it until I've heard it with my own ears," Lech replied.

Toward eleven o'clock, in the midst of a clearing, near the forest warden's house, there was a brief press conference. Lech

283

announced that he still didn't believe the news, but that if it was true, he'd donate all his prize money to the agricultural development fund.

At eleven o'clock on the dot, everyone stopped and listened, bent over the radio. And suddenly, the news came. A German station announced that the Nobel Peace Prize was awarded this year to Lech Walesa. Mr. Paczek, Kazik, and Slawek lifted Lech up by his arms and legs and threw him into the air a few times. "Grandpa" Mazul stood back, watching to make sure they didn't mishandle the president!

Lech was tense. He was happy and smiling, but still tense. They did the return journey in silence. The back of the van was full of empty boxes that had been intended for the mushrooms. Walesa and Mazul's expedition had been forgotten.

At four o'clock in the afternoon, as they were going through Zukowo, Radio Warsaw broadcast the first Polish Press Agency announcement of the prize.

"They haven't had time to finalize their commentaries," smiled Lech.

There was tremendous excitement in the streets of Gdansk. When people saw Lech's car, they stopped to wave at him.

With every passing minute, Walesa was becoming more withdrawn.

He arrived home at about half past five. Everyone already knew in Gdansk. As he drove through the streets, people waved at him enthusiastically and made the "V for Victory" sign. Father Jankowski was waiting for Lech on the road, up by the little private gardens. He was nervous: people had been arriving since noon, and already there was a large crowd, and more than a few militia. Danuta didn't have a moment's rest; foreign journalists were telephoning one after the other.

"We must think fast, decide what to do with the prize."

The people who had gone along with Lech on his mushroom-picking expedition burst out laughing. Walesa replied: "It's already been decided!"

People carried Lech from his car to the front of his house. There were congratulations, applause, and wishes for a long life. People were shouting: "Lech! Lech! Walesa! Walesa!" and

"Solidarity! Solidarity!" There were flowers, happy faces, and lots of friends, all of them invigorated by the news.

Walesa went into his apartment. A moment later he reappeared at his window with, next to him, his wife, children, sister, and friends. He was wearing a pullover and the work trousers he'd put on for the mushroom-picking expedition. He spoke in a hoarse voice, coughing slightly from time to time, and there were moments when he lost his voice altogether. But he was calm, very much his own master. This is what he said:

"I see this as a prize for us all, as a reward to each of us who wished to attain the truth by following the course of nonviolence and common understanding. I believe that if foreigners can understand us—people who may be even more intelligent than we are, certainly the state of their economics and their standard of living would indicate this is so [laughter, applause]—then sooner or later we will be recognized by authorities in our own country. I still believe the day will come when we will sit down together at the same table and come to an understanding about what is best for Poland, because whether we like it or not, we have no choice but to come to an understanding; there is no other solution. I hope that the Nobel Prize will help us achieve this goal. As for the material side of our common prize, although I haven't asked for your opinion, I hope you will approve of my decision to present the money to the Polish episcopate, which will pass it on to the agricultural development fund. We all have to eat; agriculture is still what counts most today.

"Now I would like to eat my dinner and enjoy some champagne with my family and friends to celebrate this happy news."

But the crowd refused to budge. People wanted to stay where they were, in this happy trance in which, for a moment, everything seemed possible, and anything could be said. They wanted to stay on this piece of earth which seemed to be a nation unto itself, protected by a world authority of the Nobel Peace Prize, as militiamen and security agents wandered around like lost souls, not knowing where to put their faces.

People kept arriving from Warsaw, from Elblag, from all over. They jostled on the stairs, mingling with television teams in an attempt to reach the apartment and give Lech and Danuta flowers and greeting cards for the family, to ask for autographs, or even just to catch a glimpse of him.

Walesa knew what was going on. He came back to the window several times. He was exhausted but still kept going back to talk to people for a few minutes at a time, until late at night. In the apartment plans were being made for the following day, arrangements for the press conference that was to be held at Father Jankowski's home.

From a few short interviews:

Question: Did the prize surprise you? Will it change your life?

Walesa: I've never worked for prizes and I never expected to receive any. I've always worked like everyone else—in response to certain inner needs. I'm as ready to receive prizes as I am to be thrown into prison, not that I'm ungrateful for this honor; it's just that neither the one nor the other could ever divert me from the course I've set myself.

Question: Do you think you deserve the prize?

Walesa: I see this prize as intended above all for the Polish workers, whom I simply represent. It's a prize for the determination they've shown and the efforts they've made to bring about change in the name of truth and justice. It's also intended for the entire Polish people, because this country's workers don't operate in a vacuum, isolated from the rest of the nation. There were *no* social groups that weren't involved in drawing up our demands and our program—in Solidarity.

Question: Don't you think that this prize has a political dimension to it, and that it was given to you in order to accredit the wave of anti-Soviet feeling in the West?

Walesa: I'm not a politician, you'll have to ask the Prize committee that question, although I think they've already said in their announcement what they intended to say.

Question: During the past few months, and particularly after the meeting with Rakowski at the shipyard, you've been given an increasingly bad press. Do you think they've got more tricks up their sleeve, or do you think they'll ignore you now, despite the fact that you've won the Nobel Prize?

Walesa: I'm not the first to be the target of a smear campaign.

I was put into prison for doing the exact same thing that has won me the prize. The important thing is to know yourself what you intend to do. Too many people have faith in me for me to worry about the repercussions of an official propaganda campaign. But at the same time it's important not to go too far and lose all respect for the people with whom you're trying to conduct a dialogue.

Question: You've chosen the course of nonviolence. Isn't this a form of weakness, of your inability to achieve freedom or independence by any other means?

Walesa: It's the course chosen by the majority of Poles, and the majority of people worldwide. And it's probably thanks to nonviolence that I am where I am now. I'm a man who believes in dialogue and agreement. I strongly believe that the twenty-first century will not be a century of violence. We've already tried and tested every form of violence, and not once in the entire course of human history has anything good or lasting come from it.

Question: How will the prize help you personally?

Walesa: It's given me new strength. It's convinced me that my efforts haven't gone unnoticed, that they've been understood in Poland, and abroad.

Danuta

I was very pleased that he won this prize, but there were always—and there still are—so many people around him that I didn't have a chance to tell him.

It's not for me to say why they decided to give him the prize, or to say if their reasons are legitimate. It's for others to say, for outside observers to decide. Certainly, for a Pole to have received such an honor is a wonderful thing. What more could we hope for? Time will tell whether he deserved it or not. All I know is that he'll never change. This prize won't change him one bit; there's not a living soul who could change him. I know that he'll carry on doing what he's been doing, preaching the same ideas, ideas he's been committed to ever since Solidarity started.

We've never wanted fame or glory. We've tried to react simply to this honor, tried to show ourselves to be worthy of it; we realize that we're in the hands of destiny. Lech didn't work for reward. He never imagined that one day he'd be honored by such a prize. He's a straightforward man, honest through and through. He does what he believes to be right.

It's a great honor for the family. It's like a one-way ticket to history . . . perhaps one day the children will read a few lines about it in an encyclopedia. But will that really be any good to them? They're still too young for this moment. They don't really understand what it means. On the other hand, they do know that their father is always busy and that each day that God gives them, they see precious little of him. Perhaps fate will be unkind to us. Perhaps everything Lech has gained, he will lose through his children, because, absorbed by public life, he's had so little time to give them. I often wonder about this and want to talk to him about it. I'm a traditionalist. I want to have a model family, perfect in all respects. I want the children to be well brought up, and I want a husband who gives more time and attention to his family than Lech can. I'm afraid for us, and for our children. Only time will tell if this honor has really done us any good. In the meantime, my greatest joy is knowing that this prize has washed away all the mud that they've been flinging at us.

I suggested that I be represented in Oslo by my wife and by my eldest son, Bogdan. When the time came, they would go to Norway with a representative of the Polish episcopate, who would be there to receive the prize money. I was hoping that Tadeusz Mazowiecki would give the keynote speech in my name, although there was always a chance that he might not be granted an exit visa. My doubts proved to be well founded when he failed to obtain one in time. But from the start we had made a contingency plan for the speech to be delivered by Bogdan Cywinski, Mazowiecki's assistant on the editorial board of *Solidarnosc*, who had been living in Switzerland since the start of martial law.

Reacting to the objections already put forward by the propaganda machine—according to Jerzy Urban, the government spokesman, the prize was "an award given to Polish citizens acting against the interests of their country"—and in order to head off any future attacks, I let it be known that I wished to avoid any possible trouble that could arise from my being awarded a prize which I held in such great esteem. I would so much have liked all

Poles, regardless of their political affiliations, to join with me in celebrating the receipt of this prize.

We had had long discussions about what I should say in the Oslo speech. We all agreed that I should speak in the name of Solidarity about the aspirations of the Polish people and the universal significance of the Polish experience. But we also wished to make use of this exceptional opportunity to show that a dialogue between Poles was possible when it came to the overall interests of our country. And so I was to ask in my speech that Poland be given aid. It would be spelled out word for word: "It is both a necessary and a worthwhile cause to grant aid to Poland. . . ."

At the beginning of December, during a press conference conducted in the presence of a Polish television team, I made a direct reference to the West's attitude toward Poland by drawing attention to the speech I was preparing for the ceremony. I made a clear distinction between the economic "restrictions" meant only as a gesture of disapproval of martial law as instituted by General Jaruzelski's government, and the question of effective economic aid to Poland, which was in my opinion an altogether different matter, as this type of assistance was vital to us:

"I am in favor of real foreign aid, which is vital to my country, where living conditions are deteriorating daily. It is clear to everyone that there will be no improvement until a new boost is given to our dying economy or, to put it differently, until new and important commitments are signed in the name of the Polish people. The basic condition of any grant of economic aid is that the donor will retain the right to influence and control the way in which the money is used, in order to ensure that we don't once more swamp our country with debts by any irresponsible action. It is both a necessary and a worthwhile cause to grant aid to Poland, and one that would enable us to use our own resources to pull our country's economy together, and to fulfill the commitments we have undertaken as a member of the family of civilized countries."

In the meantime, Danuta was preparing for her departure in her own way. She spent a lot of time in "consultation" regarding the correct form of attire for a Polish woman, wife of the prize winner, who was to receive the Nobel Prize in my name and, in a sense, in the name of all Polish women.

I asked her to be careful what she said during the press conference she would have to give while abroad, and I warned her about the pressure people would undoubtedly be putting on her. After we said good-bye at Warsaw Airport, I watched her every move and listened to her every word. When I was asked how well I thought my wife had acquitted herself during the first hours of her stay in Norway, I replied: "Three plus" (an average mark), hoping that this comment would be passed on to her, warning her to show more restraint.

In the end, everything went extremely well and Danuta handled the situation perfectly.

Danuta

Monday, December 12

All the newspapers in Norway, Europe, and America are filled today with reports about Solidarity, Lech Walesa, and myself. I won't pretend it wasn't nice to read that I had "represented my husband and my country with dignity" or that I had been a true ambassadress for our country!

Everything went perfectly. If Lech had come, I don't know how it would have turned out. In any event, there was much talk of Poland in Oslo, and there were a lot of people speaking Polish. A good many of our countrymen had come from Denmark, Germany, Sweden, France, and England. And then the Norwegians "elected" me! I even heard someone say that if he had a wife like Lech's, he would win the Nobel Prize too! What does one say to something like that?

I hardly had time to glance at the newspapers, because at nine thirty-five I left on an SAS flight for Copenhagen, where I transferred to a flight for Warsaw. Lech was waiting for Bogdan and me at Okecie Airport, along with Father Jankowski and the Norwegian ambassador, Kare Daehlen. There wasn't a very large crowd, the militia had set up barricades everywhere, and there were patrols stopping everyone going toward the airport. And then there were the special squads in combat gear, with their covered trucks and their dogs. My God, what a different world! Behind this hedge of uniforms were several hundred people who had come to express their support for the prize winner and for those of us who were returning to Poland with the medal that they helped to win.

We stopped off at the episcopate, where we had a quiet meal. The Sisters examined the Nobel medal with interest. Lech had a new plan; he had decided that, after a brief rest, we should go straight to Czestochowa, to the sanctuary of Jasna Gora, and leave the gold medal and the certificate there.

The journey from Warsaw to Czestochowa took place without incident. We arrived late in the evening.

Tuesday, December 13

At five in the morning, we went up with Father Jankowski to attend mass in the chapel. He had agreed to look after the certificate and the medal. After breakfast, Lech had another interview with the scientists and inventors who were having a reunion of their own at Czestochowa.

We set off again for Gdansk at about nine o'clock. No sooner had we left Czestochowa than we were stopped by the militia. This happened thirteen times in the course of our journey! I carefully noted down the times of all the stops in my travel notes: 9:00, 9:10, 9:30, 9:50, 10:10, 10:20, 10:35, 10:55, 11:20, 11:55, 15:47, 17:20 (I didn't have the strength to write down the last one). It wasn't enough for them to stop us either—they kept us waiting for an hour outside Lodz, after which they took us to their headquarters and searched us. They were looking for something without apparently knowing exactly what. We couldn't quite believe that they were looking for the medal and the Nobel Peace Prize certificate! Finding nothing, they confiscated the little tape recorder and the radio set on which Lech tuned into and then taped conversations between the various patrols and their headquarters. But though they pilfered the radio and the tape recorder, they didn't find the tape.

Finally toward half past seven in the evening, and after twelve hours on the road, we arrived home. That was when someone mentioned that our itinerary from Okecie to Gdansk via Jasna Gora traced a "V for Victory." We used the same sign to greet the people who had been waiting so patiently for us outside our apartment.

In Gdansk, on the morning of December 10, I put on my best suit and went to the parish of St. Brigid. Father Jankowski had given pride of place to the radio set, thanks to which we were going to be able to follow the Nobel ceremony. One of my assistants turned the knob; the sound came and went and we could only catch little snatches. We'd been told that we wouldn't understand much! Persen, the correspondent for the major Swedish newspaper, ran back to his car and returned with a specially equipped Japanese radio set. All we had to do then was find the frequency for the station that was broadcasting in Polish, and finally the words rang out loud and clear.

I was overcome by emotion. My heart melted when I heard Danuta's voice coming to me from so far away.

> At a time when my country didn't even appear on the map of Europe, Henryk Sienkiewicz, in accepting the Nobel Prize for Literature in 1905, spoke the following words: "She was pronounced dead, but there is proof that she lives; she has been called incapable of thought or work, and here is proof that she is capable of action; she has been declared conquered, and here is proof that she is victorious."
>
> Today few are pronouncing Poland dead. But these words take on a new meaning.
>
> I would like to express my gratitude to the illustrious representatives of the people of Norway, for providing proof that we still live, and proof that our ideals are strong, by awarding the Nobel Peace Prize to the president of Solidarity.

I can still remember the music that was playing, and the joyful melodious voice of the journalist commenting on the atmosphere of the Nobel ceremony. It was one of the most beautiful moments of my life. Father Jankowski offered us all champagne, and afterwards, Grandpa Mazul and I went home together in the car. The motor purred softly as we slowly drove across Gdansk.

We talked about the recent past and the immediate future. Since my release from Arlamow, the nonviolent course had proved to be a more treacherous one than it had originally seemed. It was lined with temptations. There was still unrest in the city and we had to diffuse it. I could just as easily decide to go underground now as set up shop in a church and devote myself to philanthropic activities.

"It's fantastic that you came back to the shipyard and that we've made it this far today," one of the others said.

I replied: "I agree, and to have ended up receiving the Nobel Prize. We should see it as the result of the course of action we chose in our first committee. That was good work. Now we've got great reserves to draw upon. Our wings have caught the wind and we can fly as far as we want to. We must take care not to ruin what we've achieved."

We had turned into the main road linking the Tri-City; Grunwaldzka Avenue was on the right and we were heading for Zaspa, which was fully visible from up on the viaduct. That day, it looked better to me than it usually did. It was as if the drab grayness of the identical cement buildings had lifted. I was happy, and I felt as if I was forging ahead toward new challenges. This moment was also a breathing space, a time of reckoning, a milestone on life's journey.

My Country

Dilemmas

There were three days to go before the anniversary of the 1970 strike. I realized that having been so recently awarded the Nobel Prize, I couldn't afford to risk losing the goodwill I had thus gained by involving myself in a demonstration that could easily turn violent. The anniversary of the August Agreements had flopped; troops didn't let anyone past the cordons except me. I had to walk alone across the empty square with my bouquet of flowers, until my path was blocked by a patrol of militiamen in combat gear. At this point I could almost feel the viewfinder of the submachine gun that one of them was training on the middle of my forehead. He kept it trained on me until I passed in front of him and moved out of his line of fire. Only then did he lower his weapon. Yes, that would have been worth watching: an accidental shooting on the anniversary of the Gdansk Agreements, in front of the shipyard, right at the foot of the monument. But that time I was on my own. I didn't want to have to go through the same ordeal again—and I didn't want anyone who might be accompanying me to go through it either.

I had caught a cold and was running a temperature. After much deliberation about the best way to celebrate the anniversary, I suggested that Danuta go in my place this time and leave flowers in my name. This would be a good follow-up to her success in Oslo. I prepared the text of my December speech (in which I traditionally summed up our activities and presented a sort of program for the future) and this time circulated it earlier than usual.

In the course of subsequent meetings and conversations I was severely criticized for this December 1983 maneuver. It will suffice to give a short transcript of one of those meetings that took place immediately after the anniversary. This reaction of those present was typical:

"You have, several times, agreed to meet us publicly in front of the monument: in November, in December, and then again in May. But when we get there we find out either that you are unwell, or that you have been forbidden to come. Don't you think that in the future it would be better to arrange our meetings in a more responsible manner?"

"Bravo! But do you think that I would be more efficient behind bars?

"Sometimes when you're trying to do something worthwhile you have to conceal your intentions. This doesn't mean I was trying to hide anything on December 16. You know that I was stopped thirteen times between Czestochowa and Lodz. I really did have a cold. I really was ill. But in a way that meant I was lucky, because how could I have repeated the August 1983 fiasco, when everyone else had to stay behind, and I had to go alone with my bouquet of flowers? I couldn't go through that again. The only solution was for my wife to go in my place. Everyone was surprised to see her, because I'd promised to be there even if I had to crawl! I sent my wife in my place. I did what I had to do, and still managed not to get shot. What would we have gained by that? Nothing. Would you have preferred to see me humiliated again, forced to abandon you again? Have you been watching me closely? I have a job to do. But I'm not going to shout from the rooftops or always act to the satisfaction of each and every individual in the group. Given my responsibilities, this just isn't possible. What would it have looked like if Walesa had been beaten back with truncheons, and if we'd all joined in the fight? What would I have done then—taken flight or joined the fight? And how was I supposed to do that? If there's someone among you who's burning with envy, whom you also favor, let him take charge. I think I'm making progress, but as you can see, I've got problems. I can't always ask you everything I should do before I do it, nor can I tell you everything I've done. And that's the way it's got to be."

Since early 1984, the movement has tended to concentrate its activity in four strategic areas, with less emphasis on day-to-day tactics. The first is an increased role in self-government for all citizens. The second, a reevaluation of the organization and overall management of the independent trade unions, and, here, our chief concern is to resolve questions about pluralism within the movement, and to decide whether, at times, local autonomy, both for region and for type of work, would be preferable to a central authority. You'll see that we have to do what is necessary to encourage participation of workers at all levels. And, if we're really talking about pluralism, it would seem to me that we should even acknowledge the existence of the authority's own trade union. The third area, workers' self-management at the workplace, boils down to the workers' participation in decision-making activity where worker productivity and broad economic considerations are concerned. And the fourth category has to do with reforming the legal system.

In schools outside of Warsaw, students rioted when authorities removed crosses from the schools, and an important issue was raised. We must understand that it is not simply a question of separation of church and state: in Poland, it is more a question of the government's denial of religious rights. And, during the early months of 1984, there was considerable unrest when food prices rose again. And price increases tend to upset all elements of society. One positive move by the government was the proposal of an amnesty, which, it appeared, would release some six hundred political prisoners sometime in the summer of 1984. Among these were "the Eleven," leaders who had been held since December 13, 1981, including Michnik, Kuron, and Modzelewski. Several of these prisoners rejected the idea of amnesty as they would do again in 1986, and participated in hunger strikes demanding trials so as to meet their accusers.

Just about the time that word of this amnesty began to trickle down to us, Bogdan Lis was arrested. He was operating underground at the time, with Borusewicz, the chief representative of the Gdansk region in Solidarity's underground wing. According to my information, he had been arrested at the side of a lake where he'd been taking a few days' rest. It seems he had a "friend" keen on money and foreign travel. So, we had a traitor in our midst, whom we identified but couldn't expose—he would only be replaced by another unknown infiltrator—so we had to go about excluding the "traitor" from meetings and misinforming him without arousing suspicion.

The worst of it was that Bogdan had been imprisoned under the absurd charge of "high treason." The trial was imminent and it threatened to set a dangerous precedent. I immediately took a public position on the matter in statements and interviews for the underground press:

> They are going to say that we worked for foreign spy networks—to which I say: You are an honest Pole and faithful to your ideals, faithful to August 1980, and the closest of my associates. You are loyal, sensible, and brave. I'm deeply indebted to you for all the work you have done and, for the time being only, I'll try to find someone of your caliber to replace you. We'll carry on fighting.

This sad affair cast a shadow over the amnesty when it was first announced and finally proclaimed by the authorities. The initial internment sentences of 1981 had already been commuted to prison sentences. The authority's official explanation was that the amnesty had been made possible in the aftermath of the District Council elections. In reality they didn't want to risk trials in which the detained activists could become public accusers of the regime. Despite the numerous and frequently insidious pressures that had been brought to bear on them and despite the threat of exile, the Eleven had shown themselves to be inflexible. They didn't wish to be treated like political prisoners, even though they had every right to be. They decided it would constitute a form of special treatment and so rejected the temptations that were offered to them in the form of more or less disguised acts of allegiance to the government. What they demanded was a trial, the right to answer their accusers. To this end the Eleven had taken part in a hunger strike.

As their legal situation deteriorated, I stepped up my dialogue with the episcopate. Before the scheduled meeting between Cardinal Glemp and Jaruzelski, I let it be known that the two issues on which I stood firm were trade union pluralism and the release of political prisoners, but not at the price of their exile.

For his part, Jaruzelski wanted to contain any possible boycott of the District Council elections and so he had begun attacking a number of politically active clergy, among them Father Jankowski of Gdansk and Father Jerzy Popieluszko of Warsaw.

Given the situation at the time of the elections, I announced that I would join the boycott. In a letter addressed to the president of the state electoral commission, which was cosigned by forty activists, we criticized the way in which elections were held, saying that it didn't allow the District Council candidates to present themselves democratically. Thus the people were denied self-government. As had been customary in Poland, since the close of the Second World War, the electoral committee had once more put their favorite candidates at the top of the list of approved candidates. This meant that the results of this so-called ballot were fixed. To this charge we added some words of protest against the various forms of repression practiced by the authorities in election procedures.

According to official announcements, the results of this election revealed that twenty-five percent of the eligible voters had failed to come forth to put their ballots into the box. In other words, more than *six million* Poles had categorically refused to give their support to the government. According to our calculations, there were about ten million of us at the time, maybe even more. This voluntary abstention came about despite the web of repression in which our countrymen were entangled. Despite intimidation, there were still enough of us who had managed to overcome our fears. You must realize that everyone is expected to vote in our country; there are reprisals—in the allocations for housing, for example— against those who don't. Our country was changing: people were beginning to reject the idea of a double standard. They were beginning to shy away from double talk. More and more people wanted to be able to express themselves openly. For me it was an extremely important sign—a sign that no one could misinterpret.

Despite the election boycott, most of the Solidarity activists were released in the summer. It wasn't clear what was going to happen once they were back on their feet. Would they go off and form their own group, outside our movement? I can't say I wasn't worried that this might happen.

But here they came, one by one, to pay their respects during the August commemorations. First, Adam Michnik. Then, Jacek Kuron. Then came Andrzej Slowik, who was responsible for the Lodz region, along with Kropiwnicki, Jan Rulewski, Andrzej Rozplochowski, Marian Jurczyk, representing other regional constituencies. In some of these meetings we took up the finer points of unfinished arguments from December 1981. Though years of hardship and suffering stood in between, we were able to develop a new perspective and were in a better position to appreciate ideas that had been confirmed by the test of time.

Father Jerzy

> My Country,
> so many times swamped in blood,
> how deep your wound is today,
> and how endless your suffering.
> How many times have you sought freedom,
> how many times been strangled by the hangman;
> but then it was always by the hand of a foreigner,
> while today, brothers are killing brothers. . . .

It's a poignant song, a sad song: far from bringing us easy consolation it blends, as we sing it, with our sad memories of Father Jerzy, murdered by the authorities. This is the song we are singing as 1984 draws to a close. This is the song that rises to our lips in response to the abduction and martyrdom of the friend of Solidarity, this young priest from the church of St. Stanislaw Kostka of Zoliborz in Warsaw.

It was in October 1984 that Father Popieluszko walked into the center of our lives. Our movement, like any other, had plenty of faults, but he was the one who would hold us all together.

Perhaps a life had to be sacrificed in order to uncover new hidden mechanisms of evil, and in order to bring out the desire for good, for openness and trust. This is what the Polish Primate said at Father Jerzy's grave. But his death revealed something else, too: the fundamental and indestructible links that exist between our people and the activist church. In Jerzy Popieluszko we had a witness who could not have been more worthy of his faith, who had challenged those of us who were not sure if it was worth fighting for the right to lead an independent life, for the right to express ourselves freely, for the right to keep faith with August 1980, with its agreements with Solidarity, with the hope that we'd been cherishing.

It seemed that any action would inevitably be rewarded with brutal interrogations, searches, the persecution of one's family and imprisonment. The situation was hopeless. It was a breeding ground for martyrs. And yet here was Father Jerzy who had been murdered, but who still lived on as a victor. "Solidarity lives, because you gave your life for us!" I proclaimed at his grave.

Things happened as follows: On Friday, October 19, 1984, in the evening papers, a news item appeared that broke with usual journalistic form. It was about a Warsaw priest who was missing—a search was under way. On Saturday the 20th, I left for the capital to meet with our advisers and receive confirmation of the meeting planned with the Temporary Coordinating Committee. On Sunday, I returned to Gdansk. On Monday morning, I reported to work as usual at six in the morning. Toward two in the afternoon, some service cars parked in front of the third entrance, which I usually went through on my way home, and waited there. Given the heightened atmosphere of tension since Father Jerzy's abduction, it was unlikely that I'd be vanishing into thin air. The security officials stayed planted in front of the shipyard with their eyes fixed on Bogdan Olszewski and Henio, who had come to pick me up as usual. But whenever I was due to make a contact with the TKK, I played my cards differently. Two o'clock came and went. Then it was twenty past the hour, half past . . . at ten to three, the alarm went off. But I was already well on my way.

This meeting with the representatives of the underground TKK took place very near Gdansk and resulted in the following joint declaration:

Poland has been deeply shaken by the abduction of Father Jerzy Popieluszko. The most devoted of its worker priests has been taken from it. His courageous fight for the dignity of workers has conferred on him an unquestioned moral authority and brought him immense reserves of sympathy from millions of Poles.

This abduction is not an isolated incident. On the day after December 13, 1981, there were a number of similar incidents in which the victims were partisans of Solidarity. To the list of those murdered during martial law, to the list of the victims of repressive measures taken by the so-called defenders of law and order during the strikes and peaceful demonstrations in churches, we add today the name of a man of the cloth who has been kidnapped by "unidentified criminals." Here is proof that, from now on, terror and blackmail are to become an integral part of the methods of political repression practiced against the citizens of Poland.

In a country where the legal system is a mockery, where the forces of law and order serve the interests of the government in power and elude the control of the people, such an incident is liable to bring with it unpredictable consequences.

Once again, it turns out that the violations of the August 1980 Agreements have set a dangerous precedent for the use of violence as a means of resolving social problems.

Signed: President of NSZZ Solidarity, Lech Walesa
       Temporary Coordinating Committee of NSZZ Solidarity
       B. Borusewicz (Gdansk)
       Z. Bujak (Masovia)
       R. Szumiejko (Member of the National Commission) and representatives of the Cracow and Katowice regions.

After my meetings with the representatives of the TKK, followed by an evening of prayers in the Zoliborz church, I went home to Gdansk and, feeling very emotional, I rang up Konrad Maruszczyk. Then I invited several friends over and told them what was happening. We all hoped and prayed that Father Popieluszko was still alive, but we feared the worst. We also wondered if those "at the top" weren't perhaps hatching some obscure plot. Vigils were organized, with texts for meditation based on verse and extracts from Father Jerzy's sermons in every city of the country. If so many millions of people went down on their knees, we felt, surely, we couldn't fail to get results.

The next day, the church of St. Brigid filled up with one wave of people after another, one prayer group after another. Some people came straight from the shipyard after work. Night had fallen when Father Jankowski, standing in front of the altar, turned toward the congregation and said: "There is one among you who shares your ideas and who wishes to express the things you feel. His heart will translate the language of your hearts. Consider his words carefully."

Though I went there often enough, it was the first time I had stood up to speak in the parish church of the Gdansk shipyard.

As you know, I'm not in the habit of using the pulpit to further our cause or share my thoughts. But this time the situation is so serious and events are so critical that I have decided to make an exception. I know what you expect of me, and I, for my part, would like to know what I can expect of you. I have no intention of lingering on the subject of what has happened to Father Popieluszko—each of us has his own fears and suspicions on that score.

We are going to continue to meet in the church of St. Brigid and St. Nicholas day after day in order to try to find an answer to our questions. Someone has decided to play a nasty trick on us. They have tried to engineer a reaction from the activists and from the entire population—myself included. That much was certain. We never wanted to seize power, nor are we about to become involved in internal struggles in attempts to monopolize it. We should be concentrating our attention on how they were trying to make use of us in this affair. Those who abducted Father Popieluszko wanted to create a panic, they wanted to promote unrest in order to turn us into cannon fodder. We must be aware of this and not let ourselves be manipulated; this awareness will be our strength.

We must not allow ourselves to be dragged into a new battle that someone or other is trying to provoke now that it's become apparent that martial law has resolved nothing. Someone is banking on a revolution, banking on seeing us all following one another like sheep. We'll give him his revolution, but not in the way he hopes. We've chosen evolutionary change, we've chosen nonviolence. We're not going to play the government's game.

Either we show our strength by going to the foot of the monument in memory of the fallen—laying ourselves wide open to assault—or we disarm them by showing our strength in our places of work, and to show that we are strong when we are on our knees at prayer. This is how we'll bring about a peaceful solution. That's why, while I'm fully aware of what you're going through, I ask you again not to allow yourselves to be provoked during the week ahead. After that, we'll see. We must find a Christian solution that avoids violence, because violence is too high a price to pay. We must not let ourselves be manipulated!

After the communiqué announcing that Father Jerzy Popieluszko's body had finally been found, we expected the funeral to take place the following Saturday. That Saturday was a workday, so that anyone wishing to attend had to ask for leave. Before leaving to spend All Saint's Day at my family's grave in Sobowo, I asked for a delegation from St. Brigid to go to Warsaw, fully intending to accompany the delegation myself.

The parish of St. Brigid's was in a state of siege. Father Jankowski had been receiving threatening phone calls and letters warning him that it wouldn't be long before he shared Father Popieluszko's fate. He had to inform the Gdansk district attorney and then undergo interrogations, and in the end was forced to seek protection from the security forces, even to lock the gate to the churchyard and the presbytery and suspend the religious visiting hours he had recently reinstated. I was worried about him: he was a symbol of a certain attitude toward freedom in the eyes of the militia and the security forces, as he was in ours.

I, too, was in danger. The country was in an ugly mood. I consoled myself with the old saying: "I'll live well until I die." To those who warned me against going out alone in the evening, I replied: "As martyrs, we'll be a force to be reckoned with, don't you think? We'll then have victory in no time. And if we go out in fours, they'll simply abduct all four of us."

On Friday, November 2, after work, all of us who were to attend Father Jerzy's funeral gathered together in the courtyard of the presbytery. That very morning, an officer from the Gdansk security forces had come to tell Father Jankowski that the officer had been put in charge of the delegation's security during the journey. Our procession consisted of, in front, the blue Mercedes belonging to the Diocese followed by two taxis, and Father Jankowski and I in the second car. A car with secret police in it followed us like a shadow. Two other special cars formed the tail of the procession. We set out in a thick fog.

Halfway there, during a brief stop, a driver coming from the opposite direction happened to mention that there was a roadblock just outside Mlawa. It seemed that the militia were stopping and checking all cars bound for Warsaw, and creating a long traffic jam. As it turned out, we were able to make our journey without once being stopped and checked. The behavior of the secret police, on the other hand, was ominous. With their holsters open and their hands thrust inside their jackets, they seemed to confirm the promise made by the head of the detachment, Captain Rozanski, when he said that they would use their weapons against any strangers who approached us unexpectedly.

In Warsaw, at the episcopal secretariat on Wronia Street, Father Alojzy Orszulik, director of the press office, greeted me with the words: "I heartily congratulate you on your last speech."

"I hope that doesn't mean I'm not good for anything in Warsaw!" I suggested that it was just the beginning.

Bronislaw Geremek and Tadeusz Mazowiecki arrived soon afterwards. Right up until the last moment, it still wasn't certain whether or not I would speak. We spent the rest of the day making preparations and calling meetings.

The next morning, Krzysztof Sliwinski had organized a visit to the Indian Embassy, which was in deep mourning after the tragic death of Indira Gandhi. We signed the register of condolences. Reflecting on all such tragedies that were being played out throughout the world, we remarked on their similarity.

At ten o'clock, we were driven to a spot not far from the church of St. Stanislaw. We made the rest of the journey on foot. The crowd in front of us was immense, but the people of Warsaw were quick to recognize us and the crowd opened to let us through. People were sobbing, women called out to me: "My son!"

The arrival of the Solidarity delegation transformed the sad gathering at the church of St. Stanislaw from a simple funeral into an enormous demonstration whose mood was a combination of hope and despair.

There were delegations from all over the country, representing large business concerns, foundries, mines, shipyards, and cultural associations. They seemed surprised to discover that the funeral would be held in Father Jerzy's own parish. The people of Warsaw, on the other hand, clearly approved of the decision not to bury Father Jerzy in Powazki, the largest cemetery in the city, but near his own church, surrounded by his own parishioners. Thanks to the cult of which he has since become the object, his grave in the center of the Warsaw neighborhood of Zoliborz is a continuing reminder in the heart of the capital of the presence of this priest and the ideas he stood for.

Everywhere you looked there were Solidarity flags, streamers bearing the same inscription, and signs bearing the names of cities. On the fence surrounding the church you could read the full account of the odious crime that had been committed against Jerzy Popieluszko.

There are some people who have such strength that even when they leave this world, they leave behind a part of themselves, a precious gift to the rest of humanity. Father Jerzy was such a man: his death had gathered us together, had resolved arguments and differences of opinion, caused an island to appear on the troubled ocean that was known as martial law. That island was authentic Poland. The former parish priest of the church of St. Stanislaw had said so himself in his moving sermons: "I see before me all of Poland. The true Poland that believes in God. A Poland that aspires to freedom and sovereignty."

They were lofty words that expressed exactly the vision revealed to us that day. When they asked me in Warsaw a year later what I thought was the significance of Father Jerzy's death, I could repeat word for word what I had said then: in dying he had set us a task for the present, for the days to come, and for the distant future. This tragedy had already borne fruit, for there were many—and

I was referring particularly to the young—who finally understood that Christian morality and Polish traditions were so deeply imbedded in our national identity that it was impossible to imagine a future without them. If we wanted to build a better future, we had to look for our inspiration to the teachings of Christ.

Before the ceremony began, I met the full contingent from the trade unions in the presbytery. I was waiting for the principal organizer of the funeral, Cardinal Glemp, to invite me to speak.

When he arrived at the church, the Primate asked me to make my speech in the name of Solidarity. I took my place in front of the microphone, but when I saw the size of the crowd in the streets, in the squares, and even on the rooftops, I made a sudden decision to change my speech by improvising a new introduction and a new conclusion:

> Fate has decreed that I be the one to express our words of farewell to Father Jerzy Popieluszko. His sacrifice sets a task for the present as well as for the future.
>
> We trusted in his teaching implicitly and we know what he expects of us now. He expects us to carry on his work. As Christians, today we must show what it means to be Christian.
>
> To the list of all those who have given their lives for Poland, to the names that are inscribed on the monuments of Warsaw, Poznan, the Baltic coast, and Silesian mines, we add today the name of this Warsaw chaplain and worker priest.
>
> Father Jerzy was the victim of violence and hatred which he answered with peace and love. As we stand over the grave of our brother, let us take an oath never to forget his death. Let us always preserve the memory of Father Jerzy, and let us always remember his teachings. [Cries of "We promise!" followed!] The entire life of this good and courageous man, this extraordinary priest, pastor, and leader of the national cause, bears witness to the unity of church and nation. From August 1980 until the present moment, from the foundries of Warsaw and Gdansk, and the holy places of Bytom, Jasna Gora, and Bydgoszcz, Father Jerzy showed himself to be a faithful friend to Solidarity by preaching the word of Jesus and the teachings of St. Peter without once interrupting his prayers for his country.

306

Poland, which has priests like him and a people so faithful, and so unified, will never perish.

As we say good-bye to you, oh servant of God, we promise you that we shall never submit to repression. [Applause, cries of "We promise!"] We promise to remain unified in our efforts to serve our country, to answer lies with truth, to answer evil with virtue. [Applause.] We say good-bye to you with dignity, and in the hope of peace and social justice for our country. Solidarity lives on, because you have given your life for us. [Cries of "Solidarity!"]

Standing beside Father Popieluszko's aged parents, at the foot of the grave that was to shelter his body, I felt the crowd swell with confidence; I felt their faith in moral values strengthen, their faith in the necessity of realizing these values in society. The more this conviction spread, the stronger would be our defense against evil, against the pitfalls of chaos and despair.

Conclusion

My story ends with a death, the death of Father Popieluszko. At the news of this tragedy, all Poland came to a standstill, dumbstruck, overcome by horror and grief. But we also asked ourselves: after this, what next?

The theoreticians believe that if we've reached a political impasse and can find no political means of responding to the conditions that prevail, then we must admit defeat and accept that the events of the last forty years have bowed our heads and broken our backs forever. Experience has taught me that when political methods fail, there are others that may work. In fact, it's precisely because, in our situation, political action was not an option, that I refused to sit around doing nothing, waiting for that option to appear.

There's not one among us who wouldn't like to see sweeping reforms and all those in government replaced who have shown themselves to be either incompetent or corrupt. If our leaders come to realize that repressive methods are bad methods, if they could only accept that our claims are justified, or if, not even acknowledging this, they resolve to make amends, and set about the task of improving the economy, making the law worthy of the name again, reinstating essential civil liberties, then Solidarity's prayers would be answered. If nothing is done to satisfy the basic needs and aspirations of our people, then, rather than resign themselves to inaction, they will fight, and, whether it's in a day or whether it's in ten years, Solidarity will be born again.

I can envisage two quite separate scenarios, as I write these words in 1987: if government measures are too slow or too superficial and our country continues to stagnate, then there will be an outburst of legitimate protest along the lines of August 1980 and earlier. This time, however, we shall have learned from experience, and draw some useful lessons from action we have taken in the past. If, on the other hand, the government continues the line of action it began with the release of political prisoners, if it decides to initiate a process of democratization and to recognize the legitimate rights of workers to seek protection from the church, then in the long term our hopes may be answered and the August Agreements fulfilled.

In both cases, it's not private or group interests that count, but the fulfillment of our ideals: either through the expedient of legitimate and spontaneous protest or through the government's decision to promote change. It's clear that in the second instance, certain people will find themselves out of the action—beginning with myself. But neither I nor my associates have such personal stakes in the game. The only thing that has ever mattered is our cause and the realization of our ideals. And as for the monument in our memory, it will have to wait for a century or two anyway.

What is certain is that we can't turn the clock back. Progress may be slowed down but never reversed. When tape recorders began to be imported into Poland from the West, the first thing the authorities did was to pass a regulation banning the unauthorized possession of tapes. Their circulation was checked, but not stopped, and today it's no longer an issue. More recently, the same thing happened with videos. Free expression, whether underground books or videotapes, cannot be silenced.

Sooner or later the authorities will have to agree to reforms. They should be using their imagination right now to devise new solutions for the future, but once again they're too busy playing musical chairs. It's one of the tragedies of our time that, while the general IQ of our population rises, that of the government in power stagnates.

From time immemorial men of goodwill have referred back to the natural order of things, a natural order in which they play an integral part. In the world of ideas we have created nothing new. The world evolves according to a system of communicating vessels: there are periods of imbalance that lead to wars, but before long the levels are equalized and people are free to move around again as they wish. Eventually all the world's citizens will have unrestricted passports, or maybe there won't even be a need for passports. They'll be able to choose their nationality and decide where they want to travel and to live. That's already happening in the West, and will come to pass in the Third World, where national differences will eventually blur. It's what we expect to happen here.

I'm an idealist, in the sense that I would like to see us move toward an ideal that I believe in. But I know how each of us has his own set of standards, formed by childhood, school, living conditions, and experiences in adult life. Though private standards differ they must also share common points of reference. We're never going to go back to the time when men fought with daggers and swords and went to war to settle personal disputes. Already the young people of every nation are coming to resemble each other more and more, and are slowly becoming strangers to chauvinism and racism.

Organizing a set of basic personal values to which one can refer is a long and difficult process: it took me years and is today still incomplete. I know who I am and what I stand for. Now I am able to devote my time and energy to other problems.

This kind of spiritual equilibrium doesn't exempt one from fear. Fear takes many forms: there's fear in the face of suffering, fear of not having enough time, fear of not being able to explain oneself, fear of not doing well enough, fear of death. How is one to cope? I once knew a priest who was putting money to one side so that he would be able to afford a nurse when he was no longer able to care for himself. "You saved your millions for nothing," I told him. "If you're struck down by some terrible disease, no one will come to care for you despite your money. But if you've been kind and generous when you were in good health, many will help you for nothing."

A life devoted to the exchange of ideas doesn't mean freedom from loneliness. Most of my tasks involve group effort, and Danuta has always stood by and supported me in my work. I am almost always in the company of others, but that doesn't prevent me from feeling almost always alone.

I sometimes feel as if I belong to a past age, the age which is evoked in our national anthem, "Poland has not perished." The conditions in which this anthem saw the light of day are much the same as those we live under today, and the same can be said of the hopes and values it expresses: courage, defiance, pride. But there will come a time, which I won't live to see, when narrow Polish problems have been brushed aside, replaced by harmony and peace over our entire planet, and I expect that our children or our children's children will then be able to sing another, more positive song. Until that time we have work to do.

Gdansk
March 1987

Index

313

315

National Commission of Solidarity, 174, 186–89
  "Big Three" meeting and, 196
  Bydgoszcz affair and, 187–89
  extremists within Solidarity and, 197–99
  martial law and, 205, 219, 226
  separate building for, 200
Nazis, 8–9, 25–26, 261
Negotiations
  Gdansk protest of 1970 and, 67
  Gdansk strike of 1980 and, 119–21, 130–31, 133–38
  Jaruzelski and, 184–85, 187
  martial law and, 223, 227
  Solidarity and, 181
  Szczecin strike of 1970 and, 73–74
  Walesa's imprisonment during martial law and, 221
Newspapers. See also *Coastal Worker*; *Voice of the Coast*
  banned papers and, 254
  Gdansk protest of 1970 and, 82
  Gdansk strike of 1980 and, 120
  Lech Walesa and, 263
Nobel Prize
  for literature, 146, 292
  Walesa's, 12–13, 112, 166, 282–94
Nonviolence, 285, 287, 292
Northern shipyard, 45, 71
NSZZ Solidarity. See *Solidarnosc*
Nuclear accident at Chernobyl, 268
Nuclear arms, 2

Obodowski, Jerzy, 169
Ochab, Edward, 84
Office of Security. See UB
Olszewski, Jan
  Bydgoszcz affair and, 188
  Solidarity and, 153–54, 157
  Warsaw union meeting of 1983 and, 272
Olszowski, Stefan, 194–95
"Operation Smokescreen," 257–60
Operation "Walls," martial law and, 206
ORMO Voluntary Reserve of Citizen's Militia, 48n, 53. See also Militia
Orszulik, Father Alojzy, 220–22, 225–27, 304
Otwock villa, 216–18, 220
Overtime at Gdansk shipyards, 82–83

Paczeks (Walesa's neighbors), 283–84
Paris Commune shipyard, 45
  firings at (1970), 75–76
  strike of 1970 and, 81–82
Patriotic Union of Grunwald, 182
Pawlowski, Kazimierz, 19–20

Pay raises
  Gdansk strike of 1980 and, 118–19, 121, 125
  "twenty-one demands" of MKS and, 132
Pension benefits, 132
"People Alone Have the Power, The" (Danuta Walesa's radio interviews), 230–36
Persen (Swedish correspondent), 292
Piasecki, Bronislaw
  "Big Three" meeting and, 197
  "Lenin shipyard" story, 54–55
  student protests of 1968 and, 53
Piast mine, 225
Piecework production, 44–45, 60
Piecko (Gdansk shipyard manager), 86
Pienkowska, Alina, 110–12
Pienkowski, Jerzy, 62, 179–80
Pietruszka, Bogdan, 146
Pilsudski, Marshal Jozef, 8, 18–20, 184, 192
Plock, 176, 228
Plonska, Maryla, 103
Poland. See also specific topics
  Constitution of, 7, 93–94, 131, 142
  districts of, 142n
  economic sanctions against, 225, 264–65
  economy of, 88–89, 93–94, 132, 161, 168, 171, 195, 225, 264–65, 289
  future of, 150–51, 308–11
  history of (brief chronology), 7–13
  new era in, 1–2
  Popieluszko's murder and, 305–8
  post–World War I progress in, 24
  religion and, 306
  social revolution in, 59, 146, 152
  Soviet Union and. See Soviet Union
  tripartite system for, 194
  Yalta conference and, 2–3
  youth of, 97, 253
"Poland has not perished" (anthem), 311
Police. See also Militia; SB (Security police); UB (Office of Security)
  description of, 48n
  martial law and, 205, 209
  Wujek mine incident and, 217
Polish Journalists Association, 254, 256
Polish Press Agency, 284
Polish-Soviet War of 1919–1920, 8, 18–19
Polish Teachers Union, 271
Politburo of Polish Communist Party, 105
  Gdansk protest of 1970 and, 60
  Gdansk strike of 1980 and, 129–30
  Rakowski and, 182
Political prisoners, 296–99

320